ALFRED WIENER AND THE MAKING
OF THE HOLOCAUST LIBRARY

Parkes-Wiener Series on Jewish Studies
SERIES EDITORS: DAVID CESARANI AND TONY KUSHNER

The field of Jewish Studies is one of the youngest, but fastest growing and most exciting areas of scholarship in the academic world today. Named after James Parkes and Alfred Wiener and recognising the co-operative relationship between the Parkes Centre at the University of Southampton and the Wiener Library in London, this series aims to publish new research in the field and student materials for use in the seminar room, and to re-issue classic studies which are currently out of print.

The selection of publications will reflect the international character and diversity of Jewish Studies; it will range over Jewish history from Abraham to modern Zionism, and Jewish culture from Moses to post-modernism. The series will also reflect the multi-disciplinary approach inherent to Jewish Studies and at the cutting edge of contemporary scholarship, and will provide an outlet for innovative work on the interface between Judaism and ethnicity, popular culture, gender, class, space and memory.

ALFRED WIENER

and the
Making of the Holocaust Library

BEN BARKOW

VALLENTINE MITCHELL
LONDON • PORTLAND, OR

Published in 1997 in Great Britain by
VALLENTINE MITCHELL & CO. LTD
Newbury House, 900 Eastern Avenue
London IG2 7HH

and in the United States of America by
VALLENTINE MITCHELL
c/o ISBS, 5804 N.E. Hassalo Street
Portland, Oregon 97213-3644

British Library Cataloguing in Publication Data

Barkow, Ben, 1956–
    Alfred Wiener and the making of the Holocaust Library. –
    1. Wiener, Alfred   2. Wiener Library – History   3. Jewish
    libraries – Great Britain   4. Holocaust, Jewish (1939–1945) –
    Library resources   5. Civil rights workers – Germany –
    Biography   6. Jews – Germany – Biography
    I. Title
    026.9'405318"092

    ISBN 0-85303-329-3 cloth
    ISBN 0-85303-328-5 paper

Library of Congress Cataloging-in-Publication Data

Barkow, Ben, 1956–
    Alfred Wiener and the making of the Holocaust Library / Ben
Barkow
        p.   cm.
    Includes bibliographical references and index.
        ISBN 0-815303-329-3 (cloth). — ISBN 0-85303-328-5 (pbk.)
        1. Wiener, Alfred, 1865–1964.   2. Jews—Germany—Biography.
    3. Refugees, Jewish—England—London—Biography.   4. Wiener Library–
    –History.   5. Jews—Germany—History—1933–1945—Library resources–
    –England—London.   6. Holocaust, Jewish (1939–1945)—Library
    resources—England—London.   I. Title.
    DS135.G5W54   1997
    026'.940318'092—dc21
    [B]   96-49266
                                                                      CIP

Typeset by Regent Typesetting, London
Printed by
Bookcraft (Bath) Ltd, Midsomer Norton, Avon

To the memory of Dr Kurt Zielenziger,
Bernhard Krieg and Dr Margarethe Wiener

Contents

List of illustrations

between pages 108 and 109

1. Alfred Wiener and his father
2. Alfred Wiener with comrades-in-arms during World War I
3. Jan van Eijkstraat, Amsterdam
4. Members of the JCIO staff in Amsterdam
5. David Cohen attending a Joodse Raad meeting
6. The Wiener Library at 19 Manchester Square
7. Louis Bondy
8. C.C. Aronsfeld and Eva Reichmann
9. Members of the staff on the balcony of Manchester Square
10. Susanne and Werner Rosenstock, Ilse Wolff, Alfred Wiener, Eva and Hans Reichmann
11. Leonard Montefiore
12. Alan Montefiore, Walter Laqueur and Tony Wells
13. HRH the Duke of Edinburgh with Lewis Golden
14. David Cesarani, Christa Wichmann and Ellen Schmidt

Preface

THE WIENER LIBRARY is the world's oldest institution founded specifically for the collection and dissemination of information about Nazi
Germany and its attack on European Jewry. If 'Nazi Germany and its attack
on European Jewry' seems a clumsy way of saying 'the Holocaust', it is nevertheless a historical necessity. At the time of the Wannsee Conference in
January 1942 – where the details of the Final Solution were worked out –
the Wiener Library had already been in existence for almost a decade, piling
up the evidence, sending out the warnings. Unlike most of the world's
Holocaust memorial institutions, which have been founded to commemorate a
catastrophe located irrevocably in that 'other country' of the past, the Library
alone was functioning at the time to document the unfolding catastrophe as
contemporary history.

This fact alone makes it a unique phenomenon in Jewish life. And yet
the Wiener Library does not enjoy the sort of financial and political support
lavished upon a host of other research centres and museums from Israel to
America. It has never been recognised as having unparalleled merit. And while
a Holocaust museum for London is debated, the Wiener Library is perceived,
by most of those involved in the discussion, as peripheral to such a venture.
Why?

Some of the answers will emerge in the pages that follow. A key issue is
surely the Library's roots in the Germany of the Weimar Republic. In the late
nineteenth century and throughout the lifetime of the Republic, Germany's
Jews looked on the communities from Eastern Europe with little short of
disdain. They saw themselves as the Jewish elite, by virtue of living in the most
advanced, cultured and civilised country on earth. Those from the East, the
Ostjuden, were at best second-class citizens, at worst social outcasts. So it is
understandable that after the War the Jews of Israel and the United States (the
majority originating from the East) enjoyed to a certain extent the boot being
on the other foot. There may even have been something like an unspoken
assumption that Germany's Jews had somehow 'brought it on themselves'
through identifying with their host nation so closely, and making such efforts

to integrate and bring about what is now termed a multicultural society. Against this sort of background the Library found the going tough and this has, to a certain extent, remained the case.

The Library's relatively secure financial position today has been achieved through the heroic struggle of a group of dedicated people combining generosity, perception and business acumen. Its reputation has been enhanced by the high-profile role adopted by its director, David Cesarani. The challenge for the second half of the 1990s is to gain recognition for the Library as occupying a place at the heart of the network of organisations set up to honour Holocaust victims and study the social, economic and cultural processes that brought about this defining moment in human history.

This book combines the story of a man's life and the history of the institution he founded and led for 31 years, approximately half its existence.

The man, Alfred Wiener, was a naturalised British citizen who had arrived here in 1939 and opened the doors of his Library as the Second World War broke out. He had come from Berlin via Amsterdam and had a long and impressive record of working for the rights and civil liberties of Germany's Jewish community and against Nazism.

In most things, Wiener valued discretion. Many people have described him as secretive and the evidence bears this out. Towards the end of his life he went so far as to mark envelopes containing receipts for his expenses 'Top Secret'. After he retired from full-time work at the Library he attempted to write his memoirs, but failed. By the time he had pared down his recollections to those he was willing to share with the public, there just wasn't anything meaningful left to say. The consequence of this reticence is that his life story is difficult to piece together. Many facts are necessarily left out in the pages that follow.

And yet the biographical aspect of this book is essential if one is to understand the formation and development of the institution he gave his name to. The life and the library are inseparable.

What was he like? In appearance he was of medium height (5ft 7in), with closely cropped hair but balding (even as a 20-year-old student). He dressed with all the formal dignity of the age and commensurate with his status. His face was kindly and shrewd, though hardly handsome. It is apparent even from photographs that he was a charismatic figure. The eye drifts past other figures, fixes on him, and stays there. He was a natural diplomat. Talking to people, persuading them, winning them over – all this was second nature to him. He had an easy, relaxed manner, a ready wit, a fund of entertaining stories, plenty of endearing eccentricities and an excellent memory. What went on behind the façade was anybody's guess.

Wiener was a clever and very determined person. He was always a man with an agenda, and he generally reckoned that keeping it to himself improved his chances of getting his way. Furthermore, he was every inch the authoritarian. While most people who met him were charmed and liked him, some were more cautious about him. In the office he never encouraged informality or familiarity among his staff. He could be a bully: when subordinates were called to his office they were not invited to sit down, even if they were female or elderly.

This rather cold aspect of his personality was combined with a serious and high moral purpose and an ever-present willingness to help. He was impressively loyal. If someone he barely knew in the 1920s wrote to him in the 1950s asking for help or wanting merely to renew the acquaintance, his responses were warm and generous. He did not spare himself in his efforts on others' behalf.

He was not physically a brave man. It cannot be ignored that he spent the Second World War in the United States while his family and friends were trapped in Europe. Yet he had seen military service in the First World War and knew what it was like. How that experience affected him can only be guessed at and it is not for someone without such experience to judge him. And what he lacked in physical courage he made up for in moral bravery.

Wiener was a flawed, imperfect human being. His failings are plainly visible. But this describes only what he had in common with other people. Most of us have not created anything so remarkable as the Wiener Library. Alfred Wiener did.

WHAT GOES ON AT THE WIENER LIBRARY?

Clearly the rise of Holocaust and genocide studies as a subject of academic interest, with its own departments in universities and specialist journals and in which careers and reputations can be made, has affected the scope and nature of the Library's work. Put in a nutshell, 20 years ago the Wiener Library's subject matter was poorly supported and unfashionable. Today it attracts major funding and has an aura of respectability and even glamour about it. Lavishly appointed museums of the Holocaust exist in many countries and more are planned every year.

The net result is that some of the work formerly done at the Library is now done more successfully elsewhere. Consequently the Library has reviewed and altered some of its priorities. During the 1960s it enlarged its focus to address all issues falling under the heading of contemporary history. In particular it paid close attention to issues arising out of the Cold War and the Middle East conflict. With the appointment of David Cesarani, initially as director of studies, then as successor to Walter Laqueur, closer links with university departments have been built up, and an outreach programme launched involving regular visits by the director to schools (and regular visits to the Library by school parties). The dramatic political changes in East Europe have led to a narrowing of the Library's collecting policy: it is now more focused on its core subject of Nazi Germany, the Holocaust and the lives of the Jewish communities that were destroyed.

Staffing levels at the Library are far lower in the 1990s than they were in the 1950s, 60s or 70s. At times in the last decade staff shortages have been so acute that the day-to-day running of the Library has been affected. Gradually, as the financial squeeze has eased, it has been possible to alleviate this slightly. In early 1995, the Library consisted of the Director; his secretary; a librarian; a deputy librarian; a cataloguer; a person to run the photo-archive, manage the periodicals, and maintain the computers; a part-timer to look after Appeal matters, and a receptionist.

In a typical day the Wiener Library will receive between five and 20 visitors. Some, if they are old hands, need little looking after; others, especially school pupils and undergraduates, require a considerable amount of help and attention. Elderly visitors have often come in search of information about the fate of lost loved ones. The discovery of a familiar name in one of the Holocaust memorial volumes has on occasion led to sad and emotional scenes in the reading room.

In addition to visitors, each day brings endless phone enquiries – some will involve the staff in lengthy periods of research – and letters. Newspapers, magazines, television and radio companies and publishers make frequent and demanding use of the photo archive.

That is the public face of the Library. Behind the scenes, the staff grapple with space shortages for the books and other collections (a happy problem, this, for a librarian), cataloguing backlogs, maintaining the video collection (to tape or not to tape), preserving the document collection, filing, stacking, shelving.

The Wiener Library boasts one human resource other libraries have to manage without: a team of highly skilled and incredibly devoted people who give their time and labour for nothing. Among the activities carried out by the volunteers, the one that visitors to the Library would probably miss the most, is the maintenance of the Press Archives. This is run entirely by the volunteers: it would be quite impossible to keep this service going if people with the language skills and intelligence to read German and French newspapers and cut out all the items of interest to the Library had to be paid commercial rates. Similarly, the small exhibitions staged in the Library's foyer are assembled and presented by a volunteer. Other tasks carried out on a voluntary basis include cataloguing original documents and compiling summaries of programmes held on video. Any person making full use of the Wiener Library will rapidly find himself owing a debt of thanks to these unobtrusive heroes and heroines. Their importance to the Library was formally recognised some years ago when one of their number, Martin Goldenberg, was co-opted onto the Executive Committee.

Acknowledgements

———❦———

U NTIL YOU WRITE a book, you don't know what being grateful means. First and foremost I want to thank Alfred Wiener's family. Professor Ludwik and Mirjam Finkelstein have welcomed me into their home and spoken openly and frankly about Wiener; they have read the manuscript and commented most helpfully and have provided many of the splendid photographs of Wiener. That Mrs Ruth Klemens was less closely involved was due chiefly to her living in the United States. Neverthless, she and her husband were attentive and added many interesting and important facts.

People who have worked at the Library were open and forthcoming. Mr C.C. Aronsfeld was very generous with his time and spared no effort in reading the manuscript and suggesting improvements. Miss Marion Bieber was no less generous and steered me towards a much sounder understanding of events during the 'Laqueur era'. Mrs Ilse Wolff, Mr David Kessler, Lord Beloff, Mr Lewis Golden, Miss Joan Stiebel – all contributed those unique personal insights that often reveal the true character of a time or event.

The contribution made by Professor Walter Laqueur is beyond calculation: he commissioned the study in the first place never flinched when I plagued him with questions large and small, and focused on reading the manuscript during a particularly busy and difficult period. His own paper on the Library's history, published in 1983 in a special issue of the Wiener Library Bulletin, was the starting point of this study. It is amazing how often I returned to it in the course of my work. I happily acknowledge my debt to him.

His successor, David Cesarani, supported the project wholeheartedly, gave the manuscript a thorough going over and offered valuable suggestions for the final section.

Mrs Christa Wichmann's knowledge of the library she headed for 25 years is unparalleled. She knew where I could lay my hands on papers that hadn't seen the light of day for decades and infallibly answered all my questions either directly or by pointing me to the right book, paper or person.

Tony Wells generously handed over to me the papers and other materials he had assembled in preparing an extensive piece on the Library's history which appeared in the *Wiener Library Newsletter* some years ago.

My colleagues and comrades Gaby Popp, Liz Boggis, Rosemarie Nief, Margot Trask, Stefan Gellner, David Irwin, Anne and Tom Beale, Julie Woodland, Anne Goodwin, Christine Patel and Amy Thomas have made the Library a wonderfully supportive and friendly place in which to work. All the volunteers have been interested and helpful, particularly Ralph and Sophie Bergman, Ludwig and Anna Spiro, Erna Nelki, Gerry Sigler and Martin Goldenberg.

Lutz Becker and Tony Kushner read the manuscript with a great deal of care and attention and made fundamental suggestions for helping me get the form and structure of the book right.

On a personal note I would like to express my thanks to Lyn – whose surname was Penfold when I started the book and Barkow by the time I finished – for our life together, Dorothy Hamilton for her help and Tina Honeywood for her enduring friendship.

Finally, Mr Ernst Fraenkel was forbearing and generous, even when he couldn't altogether conceal his impatience with a project that was taking too long.

Personal Note

—◦◦◦—

IN THE COURSE of writing this book several people have expressed curiosity about what motivated me to research the subject. A little personal history may serve to explain my concern with the Library and its subject matter.

I was born in Germany and grew up largely in Britain. My parents were children in 1933 and teenagers in 1945. My father's family was Berlin Protestant, interested in business, uninterested in the fate of the Jews. My father, as a lifelong Socialist, despaired of his parents' attitude and never really forgave them.

My mother's family lived in Breslau. My grandmother was Protestant, my grandfather was too, his father having converted from Judaism when he married. Under the Nazis my grandfather was classified as a *Mischling* of the first degree. In his career as a school teacher he experienced little difficulty: he was forbidden to teach German but carried on teaching Latin (and, privately, Greek). Eventually he was inducted into forced labour in one of *Organisation Todt*'s facilities in Silesia. He survived.

He had three sisters. All were more religiously inclined than he. One converted in youth to Roman Catholicism and has lived out her life as a nun. She was in no particular danger until the Bishop of Freiburg asked her to undertake work with baptised Jews and she extended her activities to helping non-baptised Jews as well. Arrested by the Gestapo, she was sent to Ravensbrück. She too survived. The other two sisters converted to Judaism and emigrated to Palestine together in 1928. In 1936 the older of the two made a fatal decision to return to Germany for a visit, where she compounded her error by falling in love with and marrying a Jewish man. For a time the two lived underground with false papers. When they were arrested he managed to swallow the poison they carried. She was prevented from following suit. She was deported to Theresienstadt, and from there to Auschwitz, where she was killed. The Nazis, with their demented love of nomenclature, had classified her as a *Geltungsjüdin* – one who though not a Jew, is to be counted as one. The younger of the emigrés never returned to Germany. My mother as a schoolgirl was made to feel an outsider in her own country and endured a number of bad experiences at the hands of those more powerful and callous than she.

I grew up in a home where family friends were Jewish and non-Jewish in about equal measure. It was never much of an issue. A bond that mattered more was a German background and a hatred of the Nazis and everything they stood for.

In families such as mine the past throws long psychological and emotional shadows. For us the Third Reich and the War are, in a very striking way, unfinished business. Rage, guilt, shame, sorrow and disgust vie with one another – it is almost impossible to know what to feel. Working at the Wiener Library has given me, if not resolution, at least the opportunity to think about such things and be with others engaged in the same struggle – with a sense of community I have not known elsewhere. Studying its history has helped me understand what being German can mean. Above all it has brought home to me the catastrophic mistake the German people made when they decided they would be better off without their Jewish compatriots.

PART ONE

Alfred Wiener

CHAPTER ONE

Early Life and Influences

A LFRED WIENER was born on 16 March 1885, in Potsdam, the most important Prussian garrison town, where the Kaiser had his summer residence. Potsdam was the very embodiment of Prussian militarism. For Wiener, this fact was of enormous importance. He identified with the place of his birth, and its prevailing ethos, to a remarkable degree. The alleged Prussian virtues of orderliness, reliability, punctuality and sense of duty were all ones he aspired to and lived by. It seems as if, for Wiener, no wrong could come out of Potsdam. After the Second World War, he happily attended class reunions and dismissed as absurd the idea that there might be Nazis among his former classmates. For him it was inconceivable that students from the Potsdam Gymnasium – imbued with the 'Spirit of Potsdam' – could have been associated with the forces that had driven him into exile and his family to the brink of destruction.

This abiding loyalty to his birthplace seems to have been made up of two elements. Eva Reichmann, both a colleague and friend, has written that for Wiener 'his real home, in the emotional sense of the German word Heimat, was Germany, or more exactly, German Jewry.'[1] Being a German Jew meant, as far as Wiener was concerned, giving equal weight to each of those terms.

At the same time there is something strange in this loyalty, difficult to understand even in retrospect. An appeal to a 'spirit' of Potsdam, or Prussia, or Germany belongs to the realm of national mystique. In the same way as it is inaccurate to speak of a characteristic Jewish mentality, it is not certain whether there ever was a specific Prussian mentality. In any case, there is an element of clinging for a sense of self to a system of values which did not (and probably could not) live up to Wiener's imagination and hope. That he continued to stand by these ideals and in some way even tried to embody them, can only be understood by an effort of historical empathy. The world he grew up in was very different from that after 1933.

From the age of three until 1896, when he was 11, Wiener's family lived in Bentschen, a small market town near the city of Poznan, on the Polish border.

Bentschen had a population of 3,400, of whom around four per cent were Jewish. The precise reasons for the move are unclear, but family ties were involved. His mother, born Amalia Rosenberg, was born in the nearby village of Strese and her sister's family lived in Bentschen. The Pick family of Bentschen were relatives, and Wiener remained in contact with his cousin Herbert Pick until the outbreak of the Second World War, when Herbert helped Wiener secure loans for the Jewish Central Information Office.

According to Wiener himself, the Jewish community of Bentschen was not especially pious (fromm), nor of high social rank. The town had no Jewish physician or lawyer; but two inns, two hardware shops and a clothes shop were under Jewish proprietorship. Daily life revolved around market days on Tuesdays and Fridays. For the largely Polish population of the neighbouring towns and villages, the time after church on Sundays was put aside for trading and dealing.

Relationships between German, Polish and Jewish communities were generally good. Wiener's father was a member of the Polish (therefore Catholic) choral society, and also a leading member of the German (and Protestant) *Stammtisch* (an informal group meeting regularly at the inn). Not that this kind of mixing was the rule – perhaps his father was as gregarious as Wiener himself would be. More generally, the communities rubbed along cordially and for the most part respected the distances between them.

It can be inferred that the Wieners were to be found near the top of Bentschen's modest social ladder. His father Carl was a businessman, running a haberdashery. His uncle, David Deutsch (whose shop was next door to Carl's) made regular trips to Frankfurt/Oder (a centre for trade in agricultural and industrial goods) to attend the trade fairs. While the common expectation was that Bentschen boys went into apprenticeships and trade, Wiener leaves no doubt that he was always destined for better things.[2]

A short report of Bentschen, which Wiener wrote for the Wiener Library's eyewitness accounts archive, contains several vivid vignettes of Bentschen life:

> The community had a beautiful synagogue, which my blessed father helped restore and dedicate during the time I lived there. Bentschen always had a Jewish teacher, cantor and kosher butcher. I recall the names Hirschovitz, Jospe and Freudenberg. The first two also gave religious instruction and taught Hebrew. This was generally unsatisfactory as is known from old reports.
>
> The community members mostly ran clothes shops, haberdasheries, shops for cheap jewellery, grocers shops and such like. Others had restaurants with bars, usually with a farm; others again, though only a few, dealt in cereal and grain, and also usually had a farm as well. Bornsteins, one of the few hotels

in Bentschen, was under Jewish proprietorship, and connected with an iron-mongers; there was also a second ironmongers (Krause). There were also rag-and-bone men, hawkers (buyers of skins, furs and such like). The community cared for a few elderly and sick women.

The inner Jewish life was distinguished by the fact that the so-called modern part of the community hardly ever visited the synagogue apart from high days and holy days. The orthodox part of the community was by far the smaller. On the other hand, in my day all the Jewish businesses were closed on Saturdays, whether the owners were orthodox or not. Usually one went on Saturday afternoons to the riverside inns on the Obra. There was also a sort of Jewish social club, which staged a ball once or twice a year.[3]

One further fact about Bentschen is significant. Among the Jewish families settled there was that of Ludwig Hollaender, who was later to be Wiener's boss at the Centralverein (CV). It is not known how well Wiener knew Hollaender as a boy, but the connection must have been known to them both when Wiener joined the CV.

From 1896 when the family moved back to Potsdam, Alfred attended the Evangelische Victoria-Gymnasium. He left the Victoria-Gymnasium in 1903 and began theological studies at the Lehranstalt (Hochschule) für die Wissen-schaft des Judentums in Berlin. This institution was founded by Abraham Geiger, the radical reformer. He had originally intended it to be purely for the scholarly and critical (wissenschaftliche) study of Judaism, although it quite rapidly developed into a seminary for rabbis and religious teachers. Among the teachers were leading academics and writers of the day, including Heymann Steinthal and Sigmund Maybaum. After Wiener had left Ismar Elbogen and Leo Baeck also taught there.

At the Hochschule Wiener learned to take an academic, scholarly approach to Judaic studies which was to stay with him for life. Aside from Talmudic and Biblical studies, he had the opportunity to read history, archaeology, philosophy and philology.

Wiener attended the Hochschule for several semesters before deciding that, as a matter of conscience, he could not continue his plan of becoming a rabbi. Among his teachers, Abraham Yahuda exerted a particularly strong influence on him, and may have been decisive in steering him away from a life of religious leadership. Wiener remained in contact with Yahuda, and it is likely that the two were able to renew their friendship during the war, when both were in the United States. It is known that Yahuda visited the Wiener family in Golders Green on occasion after the war.

Wiener continued at the Hochschule, but also enrolled at the University of Berlin in Oriental languages, history and philosophy. One fellow student,

Rabbi Neufeld, described him as a serious and high-minded young man, 'a good comrade, a fair, formal opponent with whom one could conduct a quiet and serious discussion'.

Among the other people Wiener met at this time was the son of Ephraim Cohn-Reiss, the director of the schools programme in Palestine which had been set up by the Hilfsverein der deutschen Juden (Mutual Aid Organisation of German Jews). This may have provided an early contact with Paul Nathan, the director of the Hilfsverein.

In 1907 after a bout of influenza, Wiener took his physician's advice to spend the winter in Italy, but was encouraged by Yahuda to travel on to Egypt. Yahuda had a brother there who worked as a dealer in books and manuscripts. Wiener could act as his assistant, and see what so far he had only read about.

Setting out in October, he passed through Bavaria and Austria (dutifully noting the beauties of nature as he went). In Trieste he stayed with Rabbi Brettholz and travelled by ship from there to Cairo in the company of a penniless Jewish boy from eastern Europe, who was hoping to make his fortune in Palestine.

It is not known in detail what Wiener did in the Middle East. Certainly he travelled as widely as he could, taking in Palestine and Syria, and acquiring a good knowledge of local affairs and generally falling in love with Arabic culture. In Cairo he became acquainted with Paul Kahle, the orientalist and Old Testament scholar. Kahle helped him out of some financial difficulty by sending him pupils to learn German. In this way, Wiener eked out a living while pursuing his studies. It is characteristic of him that he remained in touch with Kahle until close to the end of both their lives. He returned to Germany in 1909.

Surprisingly, Wiener's Middle East experiences did not make a Zionist of him. The explanation lies in his attitude towards his homeland, which has already been touched on, and his nationalism in general. He simply could not see how a national identity could be 'manufactured' by declaring a piece of territory the Jewish homeland. He staunchly believed that for a German Jew to embrace Zionism was fundamentally to damage his spirituality:

> . . . we must remain both Germans and Jews, in our hearts and our will, because we cannot be anything else. If we tear ourselves loose from our German People, both our Germanness and our Jewishness will be destroyed.[4]

On his return from the Middle East, Wiener went to Heidelberg, where he continued to study until 1911, writing his doctoral thesis on a narrow branch of Arabic literature, *Die Farag b'ad as Sidda Literatur*, with which he graduated in 1913. In the meantime, he showed ambitions to become a lecturer, giving his first public talk (with slides) in January 1910, on *Volksleben im Lande der Bibel* (Everyday Life in the Land of the Bible).

With his studies complete, the 28-year-old orientalist was thrown for the first time into the uncertain world of work. The realities of life now caught up with him quickly. He was faced with the task of reconciling considerable ambition with the fact that the easiest routes to success (through law or medicine) were the ones he had denied himself. Perhaps he had come to doubt his academic devotion, or perhaps his political awareness was growing. Whatever the case, when the opportunity arose to work for Paul Nathan as his private secretary, he grasped it firmly. Wiener relished the opportunity to work with such an eminent and clever man. It was also true that he needed some solid professional experience for his *curriculum vitae*.

The years Wiener spent with Paul Nathan, from 1911 until 1914, gave him a clear sense of what he wanted to do. Nathan was widely regarded as the leader of non-Zionist German Jewry. He and Wiener broadly agreed that abandoning German identity was no answer to the Jewish 'question'. Nathan had been editor of the Berlin liberal periodical *Die Nation* until 1903, after which his political aspirations seemed to lose some of their strength until he became co-founder of the Hilfsverein. The aim of this organisation was to improve social conditions and boost the political clout of the Jewish communities of eastern Europe and the Middle East. Nathan became particularly involved with educational issues. Through the Hilfsverein he encouraged the setting up of schools in which modern instruction was to lay the foundation for the increasing economic and political emancipation of Jewish communities in Romania, Turkey, Galicia and Palestine. Nathan was especially interested in Palestine, which he visited four times, establishing no less than 28 schools there, ranging from kindergartens to the Polytechnic (Technicum) in Haifa.

Nathan was also very active in defending Jewish libel victims. He was closely involved in the defence of Salomon Schwarz, a Hungarian butcher accused of committing 'ritual murder' in 1892, and wrote an account of the trial, which focused on the polemics and propaganda of the anti-Semites. Later he was involved in the defence of the Russian Menahem Mendel Beilis, similarly accused. In this, as in the earlier case, Nathan studied the propaganda methods used by the anti-Semites, and was later able to alert Wiener to the importance of collecting, studying and analysing propaganda as a means of countering its message.[5]

In the course of their educational work, Nathan and Wiener came under fire from Zionists on account of their advocacy of German as the language of tuition in some of their schools. This was a controversy which raged only within the German Jewish community. In schools established by the French Alliance, there was no question about the probity of teaching in French, and, similarly, in English-established schools teaching was in English. Nevertheless, Nathan's view that German should be the teaching language in some of the advanced schools as well as in the Technicum earned him considerable enmity in some quarters. On a visit to Jerusalem in 1913 he was jeered at in the streets, and even pelted with stones, according to Wiener.

Wiener remarked that Nathan was 'not a straightforward personality. One seldom saw him cheerful. He could never really laugh properly at all.' He was an able and enthusiastic talker, yet had few close personal friends. Wiener considered himself one of the few people who got to know him well. His summing up was that Nathan was a man 'whom life had never given the opportunity fully to develop his potential.'[6]

In the autumn of 1914 Wiener left Nathan and took over the editorship of the *Hamburger Israelitisches Familienblatt*, the newspaper of the Hamburg Jewish community, and one of the leading Jewish-interest papers on the national scene. It was later transferred to Berlin, where it took on considerable educational and political significance in the 1920s. Wiener was not there for long. He received his call-up papers for military service in April 1915 and this particularly formative phase of his career came to an end.

Wiener didn't have the slightest hesitation or reservation about doing his patriotic duty. He was proud to serve the fatherland and would always continue to be so. He received his basic training, then joined the foot artillery and saw action on both the Western and Eastern fronts. He took part in the Turkish campaign in 1916, at which time he worked as a translator. He also took part in the battles of Romani, Katia and Bir-el Abd.

In December 1916 he was transferred to the educational unit (Lehrkommando) of the heavy artillery. After suffering bouts of dysentery which brought him near to death, he was put in charge of producing an army newspaper, *Yildirim*, which based him first in Jerusalem and later in Damascus. Somewhere along the line he struck up a friendship with General Kress von Kressenstein and kept up a correspondence with him which was only terminated in the 1930s, at Wiener's insistence, in case it posed a danger to the General. In addition to his editorial duties, Wiener is known to have produced articles and brochures on cultural and historical topics which were aimed at educating the soldiery.[7]

Wiener was a dutiful and deeply patriotic soldier, and was awarded the iron cross (2nd class) and the iron crescent (given to those who saw service in the Near East). Yet he appears not to have been ambitious for promotion, and this is reflected in his limited progress up the military hierarchy. His decorations were clearly prized items. They were kept by his family when they were sent to Westerbork and later to Belsen. They were finally lost in 1945 when his daughter Ruth threw them into the Atlantic shortly before she and her sisters landed in New York. They apparently feared that German military honours would create difficulties with the immigration authorities. Dr Wiener was to some extent upset at their loss.

The German defeat was of course an epoch-making event. The settlement which the allies imposed sowed the seeds of catastrophe across Europe. Wiener probably did not realise it at the time, but the nation which had shaped him and to which he remained loyal was irrevocably altered. In a sense his exile began the moment he returned to Germany and discovered that nothing was the same. The abdication of the Kaiser probably shocked him. Republican politics and culture can hardly have been to his liking (although of course he acknowledged the cultural achievements of the Republic later, once they were established as an orthodoxy). The instability, the extreme volatility of the period must surely have distressed him and the vicious fantasy of a Jewish-inspired 'stab-in-the-back' dismayed him.

It is one of the ironies of twentieth-century history that the Weimar Republic – which, as Peter Gay has remarked, was born in defeat, lived in turmoil, and ended in disaster – embodied the 'final' emancipation of the Jews in Germany. For the best part of ten years it was possible for a German Jew to feel he had full and equal rights with any Gentile, and that he was more deeply integrated into society than ever before. While Jewish nationalists disputed the reality of this, others, including Ludwig Hollaender and Wiener, did not. They felt that a historic moment had arrived in which Germany's Jews could lead the rest of the German people to a better future because the German experience of Versailles echoed the Jewish experience. Opponents of Weimar democracy and Jewish emancipation made their views plain in the use of phrases such as the 'Jewish Republic'.

To understand Wiener's career in the 1920s and early 1930s it is necessary to bear in mind the conditions and thinking that characterised Republican life, and the varying attitudes towards the Jews among different groupings. Among Protestants anti-Semitism was fairly common, taking the form of what has been called 'moderate Judeophobia'. A more extreme attitude dominated one small Protestant group: the 'German Christians' sought to deny Christ's Jewishness and worked actively for Nazi victory.

The Roman Catholic Church, while no stranger to anti-Semitism, was opposed to right-wing extremism, which it denounced as un-Christian and was generally more supportive of the Jews – perhaps because German Catholics knew what being a persecuted minority could be like.

In the academic world anti-Semitism of the extreme kind characterised much of the student body. Among the professors, however, things were less clear. Radical Jew-hatred characterised some academics, while in certain places faculties were described as being wholly free from anti-Semitism.

Among the political parties, the Communists were vehemently opposed to Weimar democracy and freely appealed to the myth of capitalism as a predominantly Jewish creation. Communists tried to appeal to those of the extreme right with cries such as:

SA and SS! You have shot enough workers. When will you hang the first Jew?[8]

The other major left-wing party, the Social Democrats, was solidly behind republican democracy and saw anti-Semitism as an element in efforts to undermine the Republic. The weakness in this stance was that it partly blinded its supporters to the true nature of extreme right-wing anti-Semitism – which was never just a weapon in the fight against the Republic.

The Roman Catholic Centre Party was the second largest republican party – it opposed anti-Semitism as tending to encourage religious persecution of all kinds.

The German Democratic Party professed itself to be liberal and opposed to anti-Semitism, yet compromised itself in its efforts to win over elements from the right-wing parties. The other important home of the middle-class vote, the German People's Party, officially rejected anti-Semitism but was not a vocal opponent and in general refused to recognise the scale of the threat posed by the Jew-hating right-wing extremists.

The CV naturally formed allegiances with the pro-republican parties which stood against anti-Semitism. In particular, it formed a successful partnership with the Social Democratic Party and its paramilitary wing, the Reichsbanner Schwarz-Rot-Gold. Wiener never revealed which party got his vote during the Weimar years. It is safe to assume that no party exactly represented his point of view but that on balance he would have found the Social Democrats the lesser of the range of evils on offer at the ballot.

The specific content of the anti-Semitic slanders was anathema to Wiener. The anti-Semitic claim that Jews were incapable of loyalty to the nation and were essentially 'international' in character seemed to him to strike at the very heart of German Jewish identity. The allegation of Jewish alignment with communism offended Wiener very deeply as well.

Eventually Wiener found a job – thanks to an introduction arranged by Nathan – with Germany's largest Jewish civil rights group, the Centralverein deutscher Staatsbürger jüdischen Glaubens. The name of this most conservative of Jewish organisations neatly encapsulates its fundamental political outlook: the Central Union for German Citizens of Jewish Faith. Initially hired as the syndikus (a sort of secretary) of the Greater Berlin chapter of the organisation, Wiener rose fairly rapidly to become deputy syndikus of the national organisation and finally full syndikus, a position of some importance in the German-Jewish community. He remained in this powerful position until his departure from Germany in 1933.

The Centralverein (CV) was the leading non-Zionist Jewish organisation in Germany. Its Director at this time was Ludwig Hollaender who, as already mentioned, had grown up in Bentschen. The CV had been founded in 1893 by a group of people, one of whom was probably Hollaender's father. Certainly young Hollaender read the pamphlet written anonymously by Raphael Loewenstein and entitled *Schutzjuden oder Staatsbürger?* (Protected Jews or Citizens?), in which the formulation 'German citizens of Jewish faith' appeared for the first time. In one of his few autobiographical remarks on record, Hollaender states that he attended all the meetings preceding the setting-up of the CV when he was a schoolboy. It seems safe to assume that he continued to attend the meetings of the young organisation. Alfred Hirschberg has described how Hollaender met all the leading Jewish figures of the day, including Hugo Preuss who later framed the constitution of the Weimar Republic. After completing his law studies in Munich, Hollaender was invited in 1907 to join the CV as syndikus. It was felt that his combination of intellectual rigour, legal training and the ability to speak persuasively in public fitted him well for the job.

In a speech he gave soon after joining he made it plain that he wanted to democratise the CV and improve its organisational efficiency 'Organisation is everything,' he declared like the Prussian he was. He proposed to take the fight to the anti-Semites, and pursue a more aggressive line in asserting Jewish civil rights. He was also instrumental in shaping the CV's policy in regard to Jewish nationalism, arguing forcibly that no Zionist need leave the CV on account of its basic position about the indissolubility of the German and the Jewish in the German Jew.

The year before the outbreak of the First World War Hollaender had suffered a heart attack, which made him unfit for military service. Instead, he rallied others with speeches of such nationalistic fervour that they are quite startling to a modern reader:

> Loyalty is the root of our religion, as our religion is the root of our loyalty. Providence has willed it that we are Jews. The commandment to every man of honour is: Rally round the flag! Round a flag which has been held aloft for 3,000 years, a flag which has remained immaculate. There is blood enough on it, but it is our own!

And he concluded, 'Deutschland, Deutschland über alles!'[9]

Some of Hollaender's remarks throw an interesting light on the mentality of the right-wing German Jewish community of that period. In 1925 when the city of Cologne was celebrating 1,000 years of the German Rhine he wrote:

> We Jews belong to this national German state without feeling the need to abandon anything of our historical character, especially our religious character . . . The Centralverein was founded to bring to final fulfilment our legal emancipation and to bring about our true emancipation. And so we take part in these millennium celebrations in true love of our Fatherland and our religion, to faith and homeland.[10]

In this statement perhaps the most striking feature is the resonance of the word 'final', which reverberated so ominously through the dominant scientific and political rhetoric of these years. Finality, it seems, was on everyone's agenda. Again:

> It is not by chance that we belong to the German people. It is a historical fact which, after all the experiences which the Jews have lived through on German soil over the centuries, has become a condition of our very existence and a matter of our most profound happiness.[11]

It is easy to see why Wiener joined the CV: these views were very close to his own, and one suspects that Hollaender may have served as something of a role model and intellectual hero for Wiener. Hollaender was appointed director of the CV in 1921, when he was 44 years of age. The president of the CV was Julius Brodnitz, and the two men worked in close collaboration, formulating policy and agreeing strategy. Internally Hollaender constantly sought the views of his co-workers, even those in low-status positions and gave everybody a chance to air his opinions. Hollaender was a courageous man. He is on record as having publicly denounced Hitler as a traitor. He also accused a high-ranking military officer of slander after a survey suggested that the Jewish community as a whole had not done its duty during the war.

One of Hollaender's important achievements was the setting up in 1920 of a publishing house associated with the CV. Originally called the Gabriel-Riesser Verlag, it later became the Philo Verlag. The aim of this venture was to issue materials on what Hollaender saw as a 'science of the Jews' to complement the 'science of Judaism'. Hollaender aimed at nothing less than 'a comprehensive programme of enlightenment, based on the knowledge of the human mind and of society.' He wanted to elaborate Eugen Fuchs's notion of 'a scientific examination of the psychology of the masses and research into the repeated phenomena of mass suggestion, in brief, sociological, psychological and psychoanalytical research'. Through this approach the irrational nature of anti-

Semitism would be exposed, and understanding between Jew and Gentile would be promoted. With the benefit of hindsight this is clearly a programme rooted in nineteenth-century rationalism and it is tempting to dismiss it as inappropriate in the context of the 1920s. Nevertheless, it was a valid proposition at the time when there was still some reason to hope that a majority of German people might be willing to listen to reasoned argument. [12]

One of the other prime movers behind the Philo Verlag was Paul Nathan. Hollaender and Nathan were confident that rational investigation and argument, combined with effective mass communication (a sort of politically correct counter-propaganda) would undermine the popular appeal of anti-Semitic propaganda. Wiener shared this belief and was encouraged in his view that people would reject the Nazi programme once they saw the destructive principles it was based on.

In addition to its publishing ventures, the CV also issued a newspaper, the *CV Zeitung*, which achieved a circulation of 55,000. Wiener contributed regular articles to it. Various periodicals were also issued by the CV including *Der Morgen*.

By the late 1920s, the CV had become the largest organisation representing the Jewish interest in Germany, with a membership of around 70,000. This was to a large extent Hollaender's achievement: he was determined that the CV should accommodate all shades of opinion. He was adept at holding people together, even if, as Leo Baeck put it, the CV's unity seemed balanced on a pinhead. The CV was formed of 21 regional branches and 555 local groups 'organised to varying degrees'.

The Putsch led by Hitler in Munich in November 1923 was of course a miserable failure. Many may have been led to complacency by this humiliating defeat. The Republic had easily withstood the attempt to overthrow it. But Hitler's trial for high treason made him famous throughout and beyond Germany. His short and far from humiliating imprisonment gave him the authority of a political martyr. The crushing of the Putsch was not the end of Hitler, but rather the beginning.

By 1924, after Hitler's release from Landsberg, Hollaender began to perceive what was happening. He saw the conflict between republicans and Nazis as one between the order and civilisation associated with the Germany of Goethe and a new irrational and chaotic tendency in which Schadenfreude seemed to have been elevated to a political principle. 'Drums are beating for *coups d'état*, for civil war, for pogroms,' he wrote.[13] From this time on, the CV's efforts became increasingly focused on the battle against the Nazis.

Wiener's work at the CV was of two main kinds. He was active as a propagandist, both in print and as a public speaker and was one of the organisation's leading political thinkers, helping Hollaender formulate policy and overseeing its implementation. The main focus of his work was of course domestic, but he maintained a keen interest in Palestine, which he visited and wrote about during this period.

Wiener attacked his work with great energy and enthusiasm. A co-worker, Kurt Alexander, who joined in May 1919 and remained until 1921, recalled the wry amusement with which he and Wiener were regarded by Hollaender, who admonished them one day: 'Meine Herren, arbeiten Sie nicht so intensiv, sonst könnte der Antisemitismus vorzeitig zuende gehen!' ('Gentlemen, don't work so hard, or anti-Semitism might come to an end prematurely!').[14]

Something of Wiener's commitment comes across in a pamphlet he published in 1919, entitled *Vor Pogromen?* (Before Pogroms?). In 15 densely-written pages he surveyed the publications of various anti-Semitic groups and tried to expose how they were linked to each other. He tried to turn their rhetorical strategies against them, accusing anti-Semitic street gangs of being involved in intricate conspiracies backed by powerful interests. He warned that current activities in the press and in the streets were preliminary to organised violence against the Jews. Paramilitary groups for carrying out pogroms were being assembled. Those sections of society at the rough end of the economic process were being whipped up into an anti-Jewish frenzy. Already such efforts were bearing fruit, as violence erupted more and more frequently on the streets of Berlin and other great cities.

The pamphlet ends with an appeal to ordinary Germans to look coolly and rationally at the anti-Semitic message. They would recognise its irrationality and the absurdity of attacks which accused the Jews of being capitalists and Bolsheviks at the same time, of having begun the war, of having dragged it out needlessly, of having stabbed the fatherland in the back to end it prematurely, and finally, for good measure, of having initiated the Russian Revolution.[15] Wiener concluded:

> Everyone must be prepared to fight pogrom-anti-Semitism, if they don't want to see the blood of citizens on the pavements, or for history to report to our descendants of bestial murders and violence. Anti-Semitic hatred is the precursor of anarchy.[16]

How successful Wiener's attempt at counter-propaganda was, is open to question. Adopting the methods of one's enemies is a questionable strategy, and what shows through is that Wiener lacked talent in this field. At points in the pamphlet he appears to be merely substituting his own conspiracy-theories for those of the fascists.

The most effective parts of the pamphlet are the direct quotations from anti-Semitic publications, horrifying in their violence and fanaticism:

We will shortly free ourselves, totally and without mercy, from these alien bloodsuckers, the Jews.[17]

Massacres of Jews must take place so that they, the prophets and murderers of God, feel in their own persons that the Mosaic prophecies are true.[18]

Among Wiener's activities in his early years at the CV was public speaking. Although not much is known about these lectures, a handful of invitations preserved at the Wiener Library gives some indication of the frequency of these events and the topics covered, while the published text of a lecture given at Dessau in January 1924 gives a glimpse of how Wiener structured his presentations:

18 March 1919, addressing the Potsdam chapter of the CV, subject: *Im Kampfe mit den Antisemiten.*

16 September 1919, the Berlin-Schöneberg chapter, subject: *Die antisemitische Hochflut.*

23 November 1919, the Hamburg-Altona chapter, subject: *Die antisemitische Hochflut.*

24 February 1920, the Berlin-Osten chapter, subject: *Was will der Antisemitismus?*

17 March 1920, the Berlin-Nordwest chapter, subject: *Was will der Antisemitismus?*

26 April 1920, the Berlin-Nordwest chapter, subject: *Was will der Antisemitismus?*

27 April 1920 the Berlin-Neuköln chapter, subject: *Was will der Antisemitismus?*

And so on. Wiener enjoyed public speaking and also enjoyed getting out and about meeting people. This lecturing work was part of the nuts-and-bolts routine of trying to build a consensus against the anti-Semitic right and he undoubtedly saw great value in it.

The lecture he gave in Dessau was entitled 'Das deutsche Judentum in politischer, wirtschaftlicher und kultureller Hinsicht' (German Jewry in political, economic and cultural perspectives). The published version takes as its motto a quotation from Gabriel Riesser which underlines Wiener's own position and that of the CV:

Who challenges my claim to my fatherland challenges my right to my own thoughts, my feelings, to the language I speak, to the air I breathe. For that reason I will defend myself against him – as I would against a murderer.[19]

Comparing the persecution of the Jews in modern Germany with that suffered by the early Christians and by Roman Catholics in the 1870s, Wiener argued that such accusations were as old as time itself, and had been levelled – slander for slander – against every national, cultural or ethnic group that ever had enemies. He then examines the question of the 'Jewish spirit' as it is defined by those of the 'völkisch' movement and others of the anti-Semitic right. Adherents of the 'völkisch' viewpoint defined the essence of 'German-ness' using a strange and almost untranslatable formulation originating with Richard Wagner:

Being German means doing a thing for its own sake.[20]

A logical implication of this is that being other than German (for instance, Jewish) means being motivated by the crude desire for gain and being incapable of the lofty spirituality of the Germans. Wiener teases out the spurious affinities proposed by the 'völkisch' party: Jews are materialistic and acquisitive, Germans are idealistic and selfless; Germans are patriotic and nationalistic, Jews are loyal to no nation and uphold no patriotic principles.

Wiener attempted to refute the view that Jews are left-wing and unpatriotic. He argued that plenty of people in right-wing political groups are Jewish. Indeed it is a truism that the entire outlook of German conservatism was forged by Friedrich Stahl, a Jew who actively opposed Jewish emancipation and led the right-wing Evangelische Oberkirchenrat Party in the Prussian upper House. Wiener also challenged the anti-Semitic propaganda claims that Jews had failed to defend their fatherland during the war. Many extreme rightists argued that the statistics of the fallen showed that only a tiny percentage of Germany's Jews gave their lives and that this showed Jews to be unworthy of being German. Wiener cited the CV's statistics that up to November 1916 some 12,000 Jews had given their lives – 1,500 short of the 13,500 which would have made the Jewish sacrifice proportionately equal to that of German Gentiles. He pointed out that more Roman Catholics died than Protestants. It would be considered outrageous to propose that German Protestants had been less patriotic than German Catholics – how can it possibly be acceptable to lay such charges at the door of the Jewish community?

Wiener also took on the issue of alleged Jewish control of industry and finance and the fantasy of a Jewish 'world government', countering with docu-mented facts concerning the might and political clout of the Siemens and Stinnes industrial empires.

He concluded with a heartfelt statement concerning the true aspirations of Germany's Jews:

We German Jews do not want anti-Semites, nor do we want philo-Semites –
what we wish for is impartiality, fellow citizens who do not judge the
German Jews according to the prejudices of the newspapers, but according
to the work and achievements which correspond to reality.[21]

In other words, the German Jews claim precise parity with all their fellow
citizens and demand to be judged on their merits, not on the bigoted lies of
their enemies.

Wiener got married in 1921, to Dr Margarethe Saulmann, a woman ten
years his junior, and a formidable academic in her own right. Trained as an
economist, she was the treasurer of a society for female academics and later
analysed the Nazi economic programme two years before they came to power
in a publication called *Vom Nationalsozialistischen Wirtschaftsprogramm* (Of the
National Socialist Economic Programme).[22]

In 1922 the couple had their first child and only son, named after Wiener's
father Carl (who had died when Wiener was ten). The child died in 1928. In
1927 the couple had a daughter, Ruth Hannah, in 1930 a second daughter, Eva
Elise and in 1933 a third daughter, Mirjam Emma.

One of the disappointments Wiener faced in his work for the CV was the
failure of those on the political right to recognise the dangers of anti-Semitism.
Being rejected by those who he felt should have been his natural political allies
hurt him, and he felt the betrayal deeply when the patriotism and sacrifice of
so many Jews in the War was belittled.[23]

Besides his work at the CV, Wiener pursued various interests during this
period. Never one to lose contact with old acquaintances, he was a leading light
in the Reichsbund jüdischer Frontsoldaten (Imperial Association of Jewish ex-
Frontline Servicemen), and also in the Bund der Asienkämpfer (an association
for those who had served in Asia), of which he was the secretary. He also served
for several years as the president of the Jehuda Halevy Lodge of B'nai B'rith in
Berlin. Lodge activities would remain a particular interest throughout his life.
Above all, he continued his studies in orientalism, reading widely and attending meetings at all the leading German societies in the field. In particular he
was the secretary of the German Society for the Study of Islam.[24]

NOTES

1. Eva Reichmann, 'Alfred Wiener – the German Jew', *Wiener Library Bulletin*, Jan., Vol. XIX,
   1965, pp. 10–11.
2. Most of the information about Wiener's time in Bentschen comes from Alfred Wiener,
   *Bentschen vor 60 Jahren: aus dem Leben einer kleinen jüdischen Gemeinde, in Erinnerung an
   Ludwig Hollaender*, np, nd.

3. Die Gemeinde hatte eine schöne Synagoge, die mit Hilfe meines seligen Vaters in den Jahren, wo ich dort lebte, schön erneuert und feierlich eingeweiht wurde. Bentschen hatte stets einen jüdischen Lehrer, Kantor und Schächter. Ich erinnere mich an die Namen Hirschovitz, Jospe und Freudenberg. Die ersten beiden erteilten auch Religions und hebräischen Unterricht. Es ging dabei so unerfreulich zu, wie das ja aus alten Berichten und dergleichen bekannt ist.

   Die Gemeindemitglieder hatten meistens Garderobengeschäfte, Stoffgeschäfte, Putzgeschäfte, Kolonialwarenhandlungen und dergleichen mehr. Andere hatten eine Gastwirtschaft mit Ausschank, oft mit Ackerbaubetrieb, andere wenige wieder betrieben Getreidehandel, hatten auch meistens daneben noch Ackerwirtschaft. Eines der wenigen Hotels in Bentschen war Bornsteins Hotel, es war in jüdischem Besitz, verbunden mit einer Eisenwarenhandlung; auch eine zweite jüdische Eisenwarenhandlung (Krause) war im Ort. Auch Lumpenhändler, Hausierer (Aufkäufer von Häuten, Fellen und dergl. auf dem Lande) gab es. Für einige alte kranke Frauen sorgte die Gemeinde.

   Das innere jüdische Leben äusserte sich darin, dass der sogenannte moderne Teil der Gemeinde kaum das Gotteshaus ausser hohen Festtagen besuchte. Der orthodoxe Teil der Gemeinde war der weit kleinere. Dagegen waren zu meiner Zeit alle jüdischen Geschäfte am Sonnenabend geschlossen, ob die Inhaber orthodox waren oder nicht. Gewöhnlich ging man dann am Sonnenabend Nachmittag in die Gartenlokale an der Obra. Es bestand auch eine Art jüdischer geselliger Verein, der ein oder zweimal im Jahr einen Ball veranstaltete . . . Alfred Wiener, *Einige Mitteilungen über die jüdische Gemeinde und die Juden in Bentschen*, document PIa, No 455 in the Wiener Library's Eyewitness Account series.

4. . . . wir müssen vom Herzen und vom Willen aus Deutsche und Juden bleiben, weil wir nicht anders können. Reißen wir uns aus unserem deutschen Volke heraus, so geht unser Deutschtum und unser Judentum zugrunde. Alfred Wiener, *Kritische Reise durch Palästina* (Berlin: Philo Verlag, 1927), p. 118.

5. For Paul Nathan, see Ernst Feder, 'Paul Nathan, the Man and his Work', in *Leo Baeck Yearbook*, III, 1958, pp. 60–80.

6. From a fragment of Wiener's uncompleted memoirs, Wiener Archive, Wiener Library.

7. Information about Wiener's war record is taken from a typewritten *curriculum vitae*, Wiener Archive, Wiener Library. Additional information was provided by Professor Ludwik Finkelstein, Alfred Wiener's son-in-law. Sadly, none of the articles and brochures he produced at his time have survived.

8. Quoted in Donald Niewyk's survey, *The Jews in Weimar Germany* (Baton Rouge and London: Louisiana State University Press, 1980), p. 69. My summary of the Weimar political scene is based on this excellent book – which is marred only by an incorrect reference to Wiener as a 'Berlin Rabbi'.

9. Alfred Hirschberg, 'Ludwig Hollaender, Director of the CV', *Leo Baeck Yearbook*, VII, 1962, p. 45. This is an excellent source for Hollaender and the early history of the CV.

10. Alfred Hirschberg, 'Ludwig Hollaender', p. 49; the quotation originally appeared in the *CV Zeitung*.

11. Alfred Hirschberg, 'Ludwig Hollaender', pp. 49–50.

12. Alfred Hirschberg, 'Ludwig Hollaender', p. 57.

13. Quoted in Alfred Hirschberg, 'Ludwig Hollaender', p. 51.

14. Contained in a letter dated 12 Feb. 1955 written to Alfred Wiener on the occasion of his 70th birthday and bound in a volume entitled *Dr Alfred Wiener, Glückwünsche zum siebzigsten Geburtstag 16 März 1955*.

15. Alfred Wiener, *Vor Pogromen? Tatsachen für Nachdenkliche* (Berlin: 'Gabriel Riesser' Verlag, 1919). The Gabriel Riesser imprint was a forerunner of the Philo Verlag.

16. Zum Kampfe gegen den Pogromantisemitismus muß sich jeder bereit finden, der nicht will, daß Bürgerblut über die Pflaster rinnt, und daß die Zeitgeschichte bestialische Morde und Gewalttaten unsern Nachfahren überliefert. Die antisemitistische Hetze ist die Vorfrucht der

Anarchie. Alfred Wiener, *Vor Pogromen?*, p. 15.

17. Von diesen fremden Blutsäugern, den Juden, werden wir uns binnen kurzem befreien, restlos und erbarmungslos. Alfred Wiener, *Vor Pogromen?*, p. 10.

18. Judenmassakers müssen also sein, damit sie, die Propheten und Gottesmörder, am eigenen Leibe fühlen, daß die Mosaischen Prophezeihungen wahr sind. Alfred Wiener, *Vor Pogromen?*, p. 10.

19. Wer den Anspruch auf mein deutsches Vaterland bestreitet, der bestreitet mir das Recht auf meine Gedanken, meine Gefühle, auf die Sprache, die ich rede, auf die Luft, die ich atme. Darum muß ich mich gegen ihn wehren – wie gegen einen Mörder. Alfred Wiener, *Das deutsche Judentum in politischer, wirtschaftlicher und kultureller Hinsicht* (Berlin: Philo Verlag, nd.), half-title page.

20. Deutsch sein heißt eine Sache um ihrer selbst Willen tun. Alfred Wiener, *Das deutsche Judentum*, p. 11.

21. Wir deutsche Juden wünschen uns keine Antisemiten, wir wünschen uns auch keine Philosemiten, keine Judenfreunde – wir wünschen uns Justosemiten, Volksgenossen, die in ehrlicher Arbeit für Volk und Vaterland auch dem deutschen Juden nicht nach den Zeitungen und mit Vorurteilen, sondern lediglich nach den Leistungen, die der Wahrheit und der Wirklichkeit entsprechen, beurteilt. Alfred Wiener, *Das deutsche Judentum*, p. 26.

22. Margarethe Wiener,*Vom Nationalsozialistischen Wirtschaftsprogramm*, 2nd ed. (Berlin: Philo Verlag, 1931).

23. The Wiener Library still has an album containing photographs of dozens of memorials to the Jewish fallen, which Wiener used in making presentations.

24. Wiener's typewritten cv, see note 7.

CHAPTER TWO

Palestine and Controversy

I N THE SPRING of 1926 the CV sent Wiener on a 35-day study trip to Palestine, accompanied by his wife, to gather information about Jewish settlements and Arab–Jewish relations. After his return, he wrote up his findings in a book entitled *Kritische Reise durch Palästina*, which is undoubtedly his most important written work.

Wiener's angle of approach was determined pretty much by the CV position on Palestine:

> If the settlement of Palestine were nothing but a large welfare project, the CV would have nothing to say against it. But the settlement of Palestine is primarily the aim of Jewish nationalist politics. For this reason its support and furtherance is to be rejected.[1]

Wiener was not against Jews settling in Palestine, but opposed the creation of a Jewish national homeland. Most of all, he objected to the Zionists themselves, their fervour and their rejection of what he held most dear. He was offended at being labelled by them a 'leading anti-Zionist', feeling that they should regard him as neutral or at worst sceptical. He didn't much appreciate having his attention directed constantly to projects which showed the Zionist enterprise in a good light, while not being allowed to ferret out its many failures, or indeed the rich indigenous culture which interested him so much. He noted how the Zionists had provided themselves with the means of knowing precisely who was visiting Palestine at any given time: when Wiener got off the boat at Port Said and went to the railway station, he was addressed by name by the man running the Zionist information kiosk there.

On his first day in Jerusalem he was approached by Fritz Löwenstein, the head of the Zionist Information Bureau, who offered to conduct him personally on a free tour of the settlements, which was to last several days. Wiener declined. He seems to have felt that he was being got at by people determined to bombard visitors with propaganda and who manifested a callous disregard for the rights and culture of the Arabs whose land they were appropriating. In his book, Wiener described these things under the heading of 'General obstructions'.[2]

Kritische Reise examines the situation in Palestine at a time when the country and the movement to settle it were in crisis. To some extent, Wiener wanted the book to be an introduction to the subject and so it includes basic data on demographics, size and so on. In particular he illustrated strikingly the small size of the Mandate and the tiny amount of land settled by Jews (less than 1,000 sq km). This compared with 4,370 sq km settled in Russia and 5,960 sq km in Argentina. In terms of population, he calculated that in September 1926 there were some 158,000 Jews in Palestine as against 641,000 Muslims. The Jewish population had increased from around 11 per cent of the total in 1900 to around 18 per cent in 1926. From these statistics Wiener concluded that Palestine was not able to absorb the stream of Jewish migrants coming from eastern Europe, most of which was formerly taken up largely by the countries of North and South America.

After a brief (and mostly positive) survey of Baron Rothschild's PICA (Palestine Jewish Colonization Association), Wiener got down to brass tacks and reviewed the settlements and the achievements of the settlers.[3]

He began with the He-Halutz settlers. He-Halutz ('the Pioneer') was founded in Russia when Russian Jewry was in turmoil after the pogrom of 1881 and was dedicated to training settlers for life in Palestine. It had split in 1923, the 'official' part representing class warfare and a collective way of life, the 'unofficial' representing itself as a national Jewish workers' movement. Wiener scoffed at the youthful idealism of the Halutzim, pointing to the enormous sums of money apparently wasted in subsidising settlements which had no hope of achieving self-sufficiency. He argued that these people had turned Palestine into a socialistic experiment: here socialist ideals of co-operative living could be put into practice in the absence of any class war against capitalism. But such idealism comes at a price. By 1926 the position of many of the Halutzim had deteriorated to the point where they were forced to return to their countries of origin.

Wiener recognised the achievements of some of the co-operative undertakings, such as Solel Bone, the building concern set up by the General Federation of Labour (Histadrut), but could not resist quoting the Zionist fortnightly, *Mischer W'taasaa*, that Solel Bone had become a burden to the pioneer movement by constantly reorganising itself and constantly drawing on subsidies. In fact, Solel Bone went bankrupt in 1927, only being revived in 1935.

Wiener also questioned the viability of the K'vutza movement (the predecessor of the kibbutzim and the characteristic form of settlement established by the migrants of the Second Aliya – or wave of Jewish settlers in Palestine).

Some of the larger settlements were certainly successful, providing excellent care for their elderly and young, with their own schools and even their own dentists. But for the smaller groups, life was harsh. However Wiener's basic objection seemed to lie elsewhere, and he clearly regarded the communal life with suspicion:

> The income of the K'vutza is pooled. Salaries are not paid. Provisioning is communal. Everyone must, by turn and by ability, be sometimes farmer, sometimes kitchen help, sometimes coachman, sometimes administrator. There are wash-communes in these K'vutzot, that is, even personal hygiene is a shared property. Marriage in the religious sense, or according to civil prescription – which doesn't in any case exist in Palestine – is generally unknown. One simply finds oneself together. If children are born the parents must give them up to the [female] child-carers.[4]

Wiener confessed himself at a loss to understand how anyone could stand this way of life:

> How depressing it must be for any reasonably cultured person to live for years in such accommodation, which offers him nothing warm and heartfelt, and in such close companionship, which seldom allows him to be by himself. Concerning the moral aspects of the K'vutzot I do not feel myself to be qualified to judge.[5]

Reviewing the employment situation, Wiener is at his most gloomy. By the end of 1926 there were about 8,000 unemployed Jews in Palestine, and few who had work were engaged in activities they were trained for or interested in. Despite the slogan that no one goes hungry in Palestine, hunger and want were prevalent. Yet Wiener freely acknowledges the great generosity of the people, particularly the hard-pressed K'vutzot, most of whom were helping to support a group of unemployed wanderers. However he argued strongly against the K'vutza as an acceptable form of settlement – chiefly on the grounds of their cost and slap-dash organisation.

More to his liking was the Moshav, a type of settlement generally established on Jewish National Fund land by those who found the socialistic rigours of the K'vutza too much to bear. Their chief distinction lay in the acceptance among Moshavim of the concepts of private property, marriage and a measure of social inequality. In other respects they followed the lead of the K'vutzot.

An interesting omission of Wiener's is any discussion of the agricultural innovations introduced by these types of settlers. With hindsight, these inno-vations were the most important thing about them. While the First Aliya settlers farmed monocultures, either grapes for wine to be exported or grain for consumption at home, the K'vutza and Moshav reared mixed crops for home consumption. This freed them from two huge constraints: the vagaries of international markets and excessive vulnerability to drought.

What he did take up was the controversial issue of Arab labour. For most of the settlers of the First Aliya, there was no question about whether it was proper to use Arab labour. There was no alternative. For the Second Aliya settlers, however, it was a hotly disputed matter. For these settlers, it was of crucial importance that all settlements be built and run exclusively by Jews: only in this way would they establish their proper moral claim to the land. Wiener largely attributed the healthy financial condition of the older colonies to their use of cheap Arab labour, and the woeful dependence on subsidies from abroad which characterised the K'vutza on their high-minded insistence that only expensive Jewish labour be used. Wiener, with a sad avuncular air, wrote that he doesn't want to belittle the idealism of the K'vutzot, but that harsh realities must be faced. Not only is it financially unwise to avoid employing Arabs, it also fosters rather than reduces tension between the groups, and highlights a chauvinism which bodes ill for the future.

In reviewing Zionist efforts at improving relations with their Arab neighbours, Wiener found them wanting and was not slow to point to Jewish philistinism in denigrating Arabic culture as crude and peasant-based:

A people with such a rich history, a people whose countries are graced with the most beautiful memorials of unsurpassed architecture, decorated with splendid artifacts . . . such a people should not be ignored or treated with suspicion, rather, one should make every effort to live with them in friendship.[6]

Briefly surveying Tel Aviv (doomed: no one will want to live there) and the prospects for Hebrew Research Institutes (doomed: what respectable academic reads Hebrew?), Wiener reaches the question of propaganda. In a section entitled 'Disastrous Propaganda' he rehearses his argument. The effect of the constant Zionist propaganda effort is to render the real Palestine 'unknown', and to create exaggerated hopes and expectations, which inevitably lead to disappointment. His leading objections are its relentlessness, the fact that it puts – to his mind – worthier causes in the shade, and its success.

After a brief survey of other matters, Wiener concluded his *Reise*:

Who would be so presumptuous as to wish harm or collapse on the Jewish national work in Palestine? But as long as Zionism has the goal of gradually forming a future national state out of the homeland . . . as long as Zionism addresses the German Jew as though he were in banishment, in the distance, the Jewish German will have, by virtue of a sacred obligation, to reject the furtherance of building Palestine into a national homeland. For we must, in our hearts and minds, remain Germans and Jews, because we cannot be anything else. If we tear ourselves away from our German people, we will lose our Germanness and our Jewishness.[7]

An interesting parallel exists to Wiener's journey. In 1924 the Jewish novelist Alfred Döblin left Berlin and spent about two months travelling around Poland, investigating the lives of the Jewish communities and exploring what his own Jewishness meant to him. His trip resulted in a book called *Journey to Poland*.

In a sense the two men travelled in opposite directions: Döblin backwards in time to his family's origins and to ways of life largely abandoned by Germany's urban Jews; Wiener forwards to explore whether Palestine could become a viable homeland for the Jewish people. The two men returned to Germany unable – both physically and spiritually – to be at home anywhere else.

Wiener's book attracted a considerable amount of attention, numerous hostile reviews (notably in the Zionist *Jüdische Rundschau*) and sparked a controversy which smouldered for several years. It was sufficiently widely read to have gone through three reprints within a year and marked the highpoint of Wiener's profile as a public figure in Germany.

Chief among Wiener's detractors was Richard Lichtheim, a distinguished German Zionist leader who had edited the Zionist Organisation's journal *Die Welt* from 1911–13 and resigned from the Zionist Executive in 1923 over disaffection with Weizmann's policies. In 1925 he had joined the Zionist Revisionists, whose policy was to call for a return to Herzl's vision of Zionism and to influence British policy to pursue the aims and intentions of the Balfour Declaration.

Lichtheim dismissed Wiener's book as a 'failed experiment'. He was insistent that the purpose of any work on Palestine can only be to answer the questions whether or not the Jewish national aspiration is desirable, whether it is politically and socially feasible and by what means it should be achieved. Wiener had gone in search of a non-Zionist Jewish Palestine and failed to find it. What he has to offer is only criticism and hostility: 'Kein Plan, kein Programm – und nur Furcht vor dem Zionismus'. (No plan, no programme – and nothing but fear of Zionism):

The intention of this book is to keep German Jewry from collaborating in the Palestine effort and from sharing in the Keren Hayesod ('Foundation Fund', the financial arm of the Zionist Organisation) – Dr Wiener plainly stresses those decisions of the CV which relate to this. That is the final purpose of this book.[8]

Lichtheim's attack raises some valid points about Wiener's book, but is clearly political in intention. His main criticism is that Wiener does not follow an agenda which the Zionists would like to set for him. He dismisses Wiener's argument about the essential Germanness of German Jews and argues that Jews don't go to Palestine in order to be German but in order to be Jews.

In its small way, the controversy around Wiener's book reflects the larger debate around Zionism which rumbled fruitlessly on throughout the 1920s and early 1930s. Frequently there seems a wearing circularity to the arguments and counter arguments. Few in these recurring skirmishes fought cleanly, certainly not Lichtheim. By the same token, Wiener's claimed neutrality of outlook is hardly credible although it seems at times that he genuinely and naively believed in it.

While the controversy aroused by *Kritische Reise* was still current, Jewish–Arab relations plunged to a new low. In August 1929, after months of simmering trouble around the Western Wall, a riot broke out which eventually left 129 Jews, 90 Arabs and 2 Britons dead and around 800 people injured. Wiener noted that these were the sort of statistics one expects from a battlefield rather than a city in peacetime.

In the wake of the riot a boycott of Jewish businesses was launched, and fears grew of a general Arab uprising. Wiener argued that this flashpoint, a violent dispute over access to the Wall, was the greatest of all threats to Palestinian Jewry. He rushed into print with a 53-page booklet entitled *Juden und Araber in Palästina*, aimed at introducing calm and realistic discussion into the frantic atmosphere.

Wiener was critical above all of Jewish attitudes towards the Arabs, which he saw as the chief cause of the dispute. Zionist leaders from Herzl to Weizmann had been dismissive and cruel in their statements about the Arabs. Typical is a remark by Herzl that 'in our opinion they [the Arabs] will benefit most from it [the Jewish national home] because they will get work, commerce and culture in their poor barren land'. Wiener went on to argue that the Zionists seriously underestimated the quality of Arab political organisation, and the level of their intelligence about Zionist policy. Informed Arabs were well aware of the wording of the Balfour Declaration and it had not escaped them that the Zionists were active in lobbying against the second part of the Declaration, which guaranteed the religious and civil rights of non-Jews in Palestine. While the Declaration in its final form put the brakes on the immediate realisation of Herzl's dream of a *Judenstaat*, it naturally raised Zionist expectations that the national homeland was a realisable goal worth fighting for. So, could anyone wonder that among the Arab population tensions should be so high, and that any perceived infringement of their rights would draw a violent response?

Wiener argued that because a kind of primitive, vulgar nationalism is an almost necessary adjunct of Zionism, the danger is that the region will suffer a sort of Balkanisation:

> Because the nationalism of the majority . . . is always seeking an object at which to ignite itself, because the overwhelming sense of its own power gives it a tendency to claim for itself issues more or less closely related to it – the purely *religious* Wailing Wall has become a crucial *national* question – that is why an understanding between Jews and Arabs is so immensely difficult to bring about.[9]

In fact he doubted that it was even within the bounds of the possible.

Wiener's assessment of the Arabs was that they were outflanked by the Zionists in terms of propaganda skills, organisational ability, human resources and ability to mobilise international support. Arab nationalism was embryonic and ill-formed. Low literacy rates and an uncritical faith in their religious leaders made them bad players at politics and disposed them to being whipped up into violent frenzies by crude propaganda. Once roused to such violence they were difficult to soothe and impossible to cope with. So while Wiener argued that Zionists should immediately have recognised and respected Arab civil rights and pleaded for the Arabs to reciprocate, he did not believe either side capable of the needed compromise and was deeply pessimistic about the future.

NOTES

1. Wäre die Besiedlung von Palästina nichts weiter als ein grosses soziales Hilfswerk, so wäre vom Standpunkt des Centralvereins gegen die Förderung dieses Werkes nichts zu sagen. Die Besiedlung von Palästina ist aber in erster Linie das Ziel nationaljüdischer Politik. Ihre Förderung und Unterstützung ist daher abzulehnen. Quoted in Alfred Wiener, *Kritische Reise durch Palästina* (Berlin: Philo Verlag, 1927), p. 8. The statement originally appeared in the *CV Zeitung* in 1921.
2. Alfred Wiener, *Kritische Reise* , p. 15.
3. Alfred Wiener, *Kritische Reise* , Section III, pp. 43–109.
4. Die Einnahmen der Kwuzoth gehen in die gemeinsame Kasse. Löhne werden nicht gezahlt. Die Verpflegung ist gemeinschaftlich. Jeder muß der Reihe und der Eignung nach einmal Landarbeiter, einmal Küchengehilfe, einmal Kutscher, einmal Verwalter sein. Es gibt in diesen Kwuzoth Wäschekommunen, d. h. selbst die Leibwäsche ist gemeinsames Eigentum. Eine Eheschließung im religiösen Sinne oder nach staatsbürgerlicher Vorschrift, die in Palästina übrigens nicht besteht, kennt man im allgemeinen nicht. Man findet sich zusammen. Werden Kinder geboren, so müssen diese von den Eltern den Kindepflegerinnen ausgehändigt werden. Alfred Wiener, *Kritische Reise* , p. 50.

5. . . . Wie muß es einen kulturell einigermaßen anspruchsvollen Menschen bedrücken, Jahre lang in kümmerlicher Unterkunft, die ihm nichts Warmes und Herzliches bietet, und in steter enger Gemeinschaft, die es ihm selten erlaubt, mit sich allein zu sein, zu leben. Über die sittliche Seite der Kwuzoth ein Urteil abzugeben, halte ich mich nicht für befugt. Alfred Wiener, *Kritische Reise*, pp. 51–2.

6. Ein Volk, das eine so reiche Geschichte hat, ein Volk, dessen Länder noch heute mit den schönsten Denkmälern unvergänglicher Baukunst, glänzenden Kunsthandwerks geschmückt sind . . . dieses Volk sollte man nicht ignorieren oder gar verachten, sondern man sollte mit ihm möglichst in Freundschaft zu leben versuchen. Alfred Wiener, *Kritische Reise*, p. 79.

7. Wer wäre so vermessen, dem national-jüdischen Palästinawerk irgendwelche Schädigung oder einen Zusammenbruch zu wünschen! Solange aber der Zionismus sich das Ziel steckt, aus der Heimatstätte den künftigen jüdischen Nationalstaat allmählich zu formen . . . solange der Zionismus auch den deutschen Juden als im Galuth, als in der Verbannung, in der Fremde anspricht, wird der jüdische Deutsche, aus heiligem Zwang handelnd, es weit von sich weisen müssen, den nationalen Palästinaaufbau zu fördern. Denn wir müssen vom Herzen und vom Willen aus Deutsche und Juden bleiben, weil wir nicht anders können. Reißen wir uns aus unserem deutschen Volke heraus, so geht uns unser Deutschtum und unser Judentum zugrunde. Alfred Wiener, *Kritische Reise*, p. 117–18.

8. Das deutsche Judentum soll durch diese Schrift von der Mitarbeit an Palästina, von der Beteiligung am Keren Hajessod ferngehalten werden – Dr Wiener hebt die diesbezüglichen Beschlüsse des Central-Vereins deutlich hervor. Das ist die letzte Absicht dieser Schrift. Richard Lichtheim, *'Kritische Reise durch Palästina' (Eine Antwort an Dr Alfred Wiener, Syndikus des Zentralvereins)*, np (Zionistischen Vereinigung für Deutschland, nd.), p. 31.

9. Weil der Nationalismus der Menge . . . immer auf der Suche nach einem Objekt ist, an dem er sich entzünden kann, weil er aus überströmendem Kraftgefühl die Tendenz hat, sogar Gebiete die ihm mehr oder weniger benachbart sind, in seine Sphäre einzubeziehen – die religiöse Klagemauer wird zur nationalen Kernfrage – deshalb ist das Einvernehmen zwischen Juden und Arabern so unsäglich schwierig einzuleiten. Alfred Wiener, *Juden und Araber in Palästina* (Berlin: Philo Verlag, 1929), reprinted from Der Morgen, Vol 5, No. 5, p. 32.

CHAPTER THREE

Last Years in Germany

Wiener's pessimism about Palestine may have been added to by sad events in his personal life, his son Carl having died in 1928. Undoubtedly the political situation in Germany also coloured his outlook. Ever since Hitler's release from Landsberg prison in 1925, Wiener and the CV had monitored the progress of the Nazi party as it struggled to achieve power and went about building the unofficial state-within-the-state which served it so well after the Machtergreifung.

In the 1920s most people derided the Nazis and saw little danger in Hitler. Typical was the attitude of Otto Landsberg, one-time Minister of Justice and a leading figure in the Social Democrats (and himself a Jew), who is quoted as having said in 1928:

> Here in the Reichstag they are a little group of 12, and so have no political significance . . . it would be a mistake to take these people seriously politically.[1]

In a strictly parliamentary way, there may have been some truth in this. In the election in May 1928, the Nazis polled around 800,000 votes out of a total of 31 million. Yet party membership was growing: 27,000 in 1925; 72,000 in 1927; 178,000 in 1929.

After the catastrophic inflation of 1923, which fermented social unrest culminating in Hitler's Beer Hall Putsch, the relative economic prosperity of the mid- to late 1920s seemed to rule out the prospect of a Nazi take-over. Yet for Wiener and others at the CV, the alarming thing was the success of the Nazi propaganda campaign, which was focused on the industrial poor and on isolated rural communities. Among these socially alienated groups, the Nazis built up solid support – which translated into votes at election time.

After the collapse on Wall Street in October 1929, economic depression spread across the world. In Germany the depression hit early and hard, since the country had relied so heavily on US loans to stay afloat. This gave the Nazis the opportunity they had been waiting for. Their 'natural' constituency among the impoverished grew at a staggering rate as unemployment soared and the social security apparatus crumbled. In the election of September 1930 the Nazi share of the vote rose to 6.4 million, an almost eightfold increase on their 1928 vote. In the first round of the presidential elections of March 1932, Hitler gained 11.3 million votes; in the second round in April 13.4 million. After a spring of political back-stabbing, intrigue and ever-mounting violence in the streets, the Nazis won 230 seats in the Reichstag in the elections of 31 July 1932. This made them the largest party, but they lacked an absolute majority. Between them, the Nazis and Communists were in a position to make Parliamentary progress impossible. More political infighting followed throughout the summer. The chancellor, von Papen, proposed to use the crisis to reform the constitution of the Republic in such a way as to permit an authoritarian state to replace the republic. This was blocked by Schleicher and Hindenburg, and yet more elections were then scheduled for November to try to end the deadlock.

From the beginning of 1932 Wiener saw it as his priority to visit leading politicians, industrialists, businessmen, church leaders and others with influence, and put before them the evidence accumulated by the CV of what Nazi rule would mean. In this as in most of their activities, the CV was shadowing the Nazis rather than taking the initiative: at one meeting Wiener was told he was occupying a chair in which Hitler had sat not 24 hours earlier, similarly pleading his case.

A detailed record of two of these meetings has been preserved. On 14 July 1932 Wiener went to see Erwin Planck, secretary of state in the Reich Chancery and the son of the physicist Max Planck. Two days later, on 16 July, Wiener went into a meeting with a certain Herr von Steinau-Steinrück, a consultant to Wilhelm von Gayl, the extreme right-wing Minister of the Interior. These documents are worth quoting, because they demonstrate something of how Wiener went about his tasks, and because they plainly show that neither of the people he spoke to understood accurately what was taking shape in Germany, or at least that they were not prepared to discuss the matter seriously with the CV's representative. From the first:

> I took Dr Planck through the situation rapidly by showing him the materials. He said he fully understood our needs and anxieties, and condemned the agitation directed against us. He had never made a secret of his attitude. He had deliberately attended the Rathenau commemoration after taking office. The present Government had been formed precisely to prevent the threat of revolution. People had been fearing for the continuance of the State's instruments of power, these fears were now unnecessary. The

Government had the instruments of power firmly in hand and would energetically repulse any attempt to overthrow the Government, from whichever quarter it came. Without wishing to belittle its importance, he saw in the mounting agitation only electioneering. He repeatedly expressed his regret. He didn't think much of the idea of a pronouncement now, before the elections. It would only achieve the opposite of what was desired. I replied to this that I don't think much of declarations at this time in any case. Perhaps we could both consider if other means might not be better. I asked him whether an audience with the Chancellor himself might have something to recommend it. He, Planck, thought it would be more sensible to contact the Minister of the Interior. He would speak with him on the telephone and prepare the way. I said I knew Steinau as an old school-friend. He replied that I should also discuss the visit with him. Gayl was a thoroughly decent and open-minded individual, who fully understood our concerns.

I then asked him whether Hitler was aware of this agitation. Planck replied that he had spoken with Hitler many times recently. He (H.) condemned this agitation thoroughly. H. was a decent, idealistic person, if somewhat excitable. He would be speaking to him in the coming days and would pass the necesary information on to him. We agreed that he would pass on to Hitler the statements of the S.A. leader Jago from Neustadt and the latest incidents of desecrating cemeteries.[2]

Wiener can hardly have been encouraged by Planck's attitude, which was surely rooted either in cynicism or naivety. Two days after this meeting Wiener went in to the second meeting with Steinau-Steinrück:

I told him the following:
. . . it should be considered whether pressure could be exerted on the National Socialists to moderate their agitation. He replied that it would certainly be possible to discuss this with Hitler. How far his influence might reach he could not say. As far as Goebbels was concerned, who (as he put it) has complete power, matters were such that the Reichs Minister of the Interior had no influence on him. He [Goebbels] had been requested, through an intermediary, to present himself at the Ministry. He had reacted sullenly to this, and had not come. Two discussions had already taken place with Captain von Goering. He makes a thoroughly pleasant impression when he speaks. Nevertheless, on closer observation, one had the impression that he did not have his nerves under control, and that there was something indefinable within him. In addition, the political leaders of the National Socialists are political novices for whom politics is in most cases a toy. The Cabinet does not regard the National Socialists as different from any other group. But the National Socialists believe that they are Germany.[3]

In practical terms, this was even less useful than the earlier meeting. Between them, the two quotes offer a remarkable snapshot of the political stalemate of that period.

With power almost in their grasp, the Nazis allowed themselves to be out-manoeuvred and had to agree to yet more elections in November 1932. Their funds and energy depleted, they failed to maintain their momentum and lost 2 million votes and 34 seats. Yet they remained a powerful parliamentary presence, and with the SA – a paramilitary force of 400,000 – to back up their arguments with fists and clubs, they were unlikely to stay quiet for long.

In December 1932 Schleicher attempted to stabilise the situation by putting himself forward as chancellor. His plan was to form a broad coalition taking in the Social Democrats and even the left wing of the Nazi party, in an effort to divide the Nazis and keep Hitler from power. Eventually this scheme failed. Hitler's control of his party was strengthened after a showdown with the Strasser faction. Schleicher was now discredited in the eyes of Hindenburg, who turned once more to von Papen. Von Papen had developed the notion of a right-wing coalition with the Nazis. Hindenburg eventually gave this plan his support. He dreaded the constitutional violations proposed by Schleicher as an alternative, and he allowed himself to believe Hitler's assurance that he would uphold the constitution if he was appointed chancellor. The chancellorship would be Hitler's, von Papen as vice chancellor would keep him in order and a cabinet full of non-Nazis would maintain the status quo. On 30 January 1933 Hitler was sworn into office.[4]

For Wiener, Hitler's victory was nothing less than a catastrophe, politically, professionally and personally. It is reported that both Wiener and Ludwig Hollaender (whose health was in any case poor) suffered an emotional and physical collapse at this time. Hollaender emerged from his breakdown a spent force. He was never really active again and died three years later. When Wiener recovered, it was to the realisation that for him it was all over in Germany. He continued to go through the motions, but his thoughts were all with leaving as quickly as possible.

Once Hitler was in office, the CV soon became a target of Nazi attention. As early as March 1933 their offices were raided and printed materials taken away. Press reports were circulated that much of the material was 'illegal' (a phrase generally taken to mean communist), in an effort to discredit the organisation and alienate its support.

In the wake of the raid, Hermann Goering, then Prussian Minister of the Interior, summoned Wiener and the CV's president, Julius Brodnitz. The details of the meeting are not recorded, but Wiener and Brodnitz demanded and got permission to produce a press release refuting the allegation that the CV had been involved in 'illegalities'.

Through the spring and summer Wiener made his preparations to go into exile. Given his views about the indivisibility of the German and the Jew in a German Jew, the pain he felt at this decision must have been intense.

Events in Germany during the second half of 1933 confirmed that Wiener's decision to leave Germany was timely. About a month after the CV's Berlin offices were raided, the syndikus of the Hessen-Nassau organisation, Dr Martin Marx, was arrested, together with the former head of the Frankfurt political police, Ferdinand Mührdel, on charges of bribery and corruption. The accusation was that Marx had, between 1928 and 1933, bribed Mührdel to provide him with copies of official documents, had bought protection for Jews, and had generally hindered and interfered with the proper course of bureaucratic functioning.

Behind the charge lay Nazi outrage that Marx had successfully managed to have several Nazis removed from office on the grounds that their flagrant anti-Semitism rendered them unfit for public service. With Mührdel's help he had managed to protect the Jewish community from anti-Jewish excesses on a number of occasions. The two had become personal friends, exchanging birthday presents and so forth.

Marx was held in custody for five months before the case went to trial in October 1933. After ten days in court, during which the prosecutor argued that the CV was subversive and supported communist activities and Wiener's successor Alfred Hirschberg appeared for the defence, the case was dismissed. Marx and Mührdel were immediately rearrested and placed in 'protective custody' for a further two months with no charges brought against them. From the safety of Amsterdam, Wiener can only have followed these events in dismay.[5]

NOTES

1. 'Hier im Reichstag bilden sie [the Nazis] ein Grüppchen von 12 Abgeordneten, bedeuten also politisch nichts . . . es wäre falsch diese Leute politisch ernst zu nehmen.' Quoted in Hans Reichmann, 'Der drohende Sturm' in Hans Tramer (ed.), *In zwei Welten: Siegfried Moses zum Fünfundsiebzigsten Geburtstag* (Tel Aviv: Verlag Bitaon, 1966), p. 562.
2. Ich trug Herrn Dr Planck kurz die Lage unter Vorlage des entsprechenden Materials vor. Er sagte, er habe volles Verständnis für unsere Not und Sorgen und verurteile die gegen uns gerichtete Agitation durchaus. Er mache auch aus seiner Haltung nie ein Hehl. Er sei nach seinem Amtsantritt absichtlich zur Rathenau-Gedenkfeier gegangen. Die jetzige Regierung sei grade deshalb gebildet worden, um der drohenden Revolution vorzubeugen. Man habe auch für den Bestand der staatlichen Machtmittel gefürchtet, diese Befürchtungen seien jetzt nicht mehr vorhanden. Die Reichsregierung habe die Machtmittel fest in der Hand und werde jeden Versuch, von wo er komme, die Regierung gewaltsam zu stürzen, energisch abschlagen. Er sehe übrigens in der ansteigenden Agitation jetzt eine Wahlmache, ohne daß er damit ihre Bedeutung herabmindern wolle. Er sprach wiederholt sein Bedauern aus. Von

einem Pronunziamento der Reichsregierung jetzt vor den Wahlen halte er nichts. Man würde das Gegenteil erreichen. Ich erwiderte darauf, daß ich von Kundgebungen in dieser Zeit überhaupt wenig halte. Vielleicht überlegen wir beide, ob nicht andere Wege besser seien. Ich fragte, ob nicht eine Vorstellung beim Reichskanzler selbst empfehlenswert sei. Er, Planck, meint, es wäre zweckmässiger, baldigst den Herrn Reichsinnenminister aufzusuchen. Er würde mit dem telefonieren und den Weg vorbereiten. Ich sagte, daß ich den ihm bekannten Herrn von Steinau (persönlicher Referent des Reichsinnenministers) als Schulfreund gut kenne. Er erwiderte, ich solle auch mit ihm über den Besuch sprechen. Gayl sei ein hochanständiger, aufgeschlossener Mensch und Charakter, der für unsere Sorgen volles Verständnis habe.

Ich fragte Planck ferner, ob Hitler diese Hetze kenne. Planck sagte, er habe in letzter Zeit wiederholt mit Hitler gesprochen. Er (H.) missbilligt diese Hetze durchaus. H. sei ein anständiger, ideal gesinnter Mensch, wenn auch aufgeregt. Er spreche ihn in diesen Tagen und werde ihm die nötigen Mitteilungen machen. Wir verabredeten, daß Planck die Äusserungen des S.A.-Führers Jago in Neustadt (Hardt) und die letzte Auflage der Friedhofsschändungen zur Weitergabe an Hitler von uns übermittelt werde. Alfred Wiener, 'Unterredung mit Herrn Staatssekretär der Reichskanzlei Dr Planck am 14 Juli 1932 um 5 Uhr in der Reichskanzlei', Wiener Library document archive, item 796.

3. Ich sagte ihm folgendes:

Es wäre zu erwägen, ob nicht auf die nationalsozialistischen Führer ein Druck, die Agitation zu mässigen, ausgeübt werden könne. Er sagte darauf, daß sich mit Hitler wohl reden liesse. Wie weit sein Einfluß reiche, könne er nicht ermessen. Was Goebbels anginge, der, wie er sich wörtlich ausdrückte, unbeschränkte Vollmacht in Händen habe, so liegen die Dinge so, daß man auf ihn vom Reichsinnenminister aus keinen Einfluß besitze. Man habe ihn durch eine Mittelperson gebeten, einmal im Ministerium zu erscheinen. Er habe darauf sauer reagiert und sei nicht gekommen. Mit Hauptmann von Goering habe man schon zweimal verhandelt. Dieser mache, wenn er spreche, einen durchaus angenehmen Eindruck. Trotzdem habe man aber, wenn man genauer beobachte, den weiteren Eindruck, daß auch er seine Nerven nicht in der Hand habe, und daß irgend etwas Undefinierbares in ihm stecke. Im übrigen seien die Führer der Nationalsozialisten im allgemeinen politische Anfänger, für die die Politik in den allermeisten Fällen nur ein Spielzeug sei. . . Das Kabinett stehe nicht anders zu den Nationalsozialisten als zu jeder anderen Gruppe. Die Nationalsozialisten aber glaubten, sie seien Deutschland. Alfred Wiener, 'Unterredung mit dem persönlichen Referenten des Herrn Reichsinnenministers von Gayl, Herrn von Steinau-Steinrück am 16 Juli 1932, nachm. 4 Uhr im Reichsinnenministerium', Wiener Library document archive, item 796.

4. For a concise and neat account of Hitler's coming to power, see Joseph W. Bendersky, *A History of Nazi Germany* (Chicago: Nelson-Hall, 1985).

5. For details of this trial see the reports of the *Jewish Telegraphic Agency Bulletin* for Oct. 1933, pp. 12–24.

CHAPTER FOUR

Exile and After

Fʀᴏᴍ ᴛʜᴇ ᴛɪᴍᴇ Wiener left Germany, his career and the development of what came to be known as the Wiener Library were so closely intertwined as to be inseparable. I shall restrict myself here to sketching in the rather hazy picture of Wiener's life inasmuch as he had one away from his Library.

He was of course not alone in reaching his decision to leave Germany. 1933 saw the greatest wave of Jewish emigration from Germany prior to the period 1938–39. Up to 45,000 people fled and sought a new home elsewhere. Of these, one source compiled at the time indicates that 5,000 went to Holland, and that 4,000 of these were Jews. This figure compares with 25,000 who went to France (mostly Paris) and 3,000 who came to Britain.

It is accepted that many more wanted to leave, but opportunities to do so were limited. The most important of these limitations were the ability to transfer capital and the immigration restrictions imposed by receiving nations. Age, occupation and contacts all played a part as well. For Wiener, as a respected member of the middle classes and leader of Germany's Jewish community, the technicalities of the move probably involved few difficulties.

Wiener's choice of Holland as a place of refuge was an understandable one. Among the attractions of Holland were its physical proximity to Germany, the close cultural and linguistic links between the two countries (even without speaking Dutch, a German could reasonably expect to get by), and Dutch neutrality during the First World War – which meant that there was slightly less hostility to Germany and Germans than in, say, Belgium or France.

The first wave of emigration from Nazi Germany has been characterised as being 'tentative'. It wasn't a bad time to leave: there were comparatively few restrictions on the movement of Jewish capital and receiving countries took a more positive attitude than they were later able to do. It has also been noted that German Jews encountered fewer obstacles to immigration than other immigrants and could be generally assured of sympathy and help. Many felt that after the initial violence in Germany things seemed to be stabilising, even if they were less than ideal. This was particularly so after the events of summer 1934, when Hitler moved against the SA, and later merged the offices of the president and chancellor following the death of Hindenburg. The improvement in Germany's economic performance meant that Jewish businesses, like their Gentile counterparts, were more profitable than earlier.

The first wave on which Wiener exited his homeland, ended on 15 September 1935, with the enactment of the Nuremberg Laws in Germany. Germany's Jews were left in no doubt that they were to be excluded from citizenship. Emigration increased and was organised systematically by Jewish organisations, with some notion of clearing Germany of its Jews within a set time-frame. This effort collapsed after the Kristallnacht of November 1938, when it became 'evident that the German authorities would never consent to an orderly removal of the Jews, but would insist on getting rid of them in the shortest time possible, regardless of the suffering of the victims'.[1] Emigration rocketed: in the period 1933–37 around 140,000 people left; roughly the same number fled in just 1938 alone.

Back in 1933, of the total of 5,000 refugees in Holland, 3,000 were of German nationality. Among the rest were some so-called *Ostjuden* – Jews from eastern Europe. It seems a fair guess that the German Jews who chose Holland were, like Wiener, middle class and well-to-do. The fact that only around 500 of them were dependent for aid on the Comité voor Joodse Vluchtelingen (Committee for Jewish Refugees) confirms this impression. The rest had either the means or the contacts to make themselves self-supporting almost immediately.

Virtually no records have survived which give information concerning Wiener's private life during his years in Amsterdam. The probability is that he did not really have a private life. His activities relating to the establishment of the Jewish Central Information Office (JCIO) were all-consuming. He lived first in a hotel room which he shared with the JCIO. Later he took his family to a flat situated conveniently one floor below the JCIO.

He spent a good deal of time travelling – it is known that he visited Great Britain, Sweden, Poland and Czechoslovakia on JCIO business. He also made several trips to Switzerland in connection with the trials over the *Protocols of the Elders of Zion*. But for the most part, Wiener, ever secretive, almost disappears from view during the period 1934–39. His work was his life, his life his work.

His decision to move to London was determined by political developments: The Austrian Anschluss, the Kristallnacht, Germany's invasion of Czechoslovakia. He was paying regular and lengthy visits to London throughout 1938, preparing the ground for the removal of most of the books and other materials, looking for suitable premises, and establishing a network of contacts.

Once settled at Ford's Hotel, Manchester Street, approximately one minute's walking distance from the JCIO at 19 Manchester Square, his private life was rapidly overtaken by political events. The JCIO opened its doors on 1 September 1939. Initially the generally anticipated crisis did not materialise, it was the time of the so-called phoney war. But by November, David Cohen, the president of the JCIO in Amsterdam, was writing in alarm that Wiener should encourage his wife to leave Holland. Wiener wrote back:

> I have already asked my wife, in a letter a few days ago, to obtain at once Dutch identity papers. At the same time , I am not sure – this is for your own information – whether my wife actually wishes to come here with the children. However, I would urgently request you to see her and discuss matters with her. I have already written asking her to seek your advice, and I have just wired her enquiring whether I am to take steps tomorrow. . . to secure visas for her.
>
> Obviously I shall be unable to take any such steps if my wife be unwilling to leave the country, nothwithstanding the present situation. Possibly she has good reasons which I cannot from here fully realise.[2]

Despite his lack of success, he continued to try to persuade his wife to leave and to offer help in getting his colleagues out. In a telegraph he sent to Cohen shortly before the invasion, on 15 April 1940:

> Should you think necessary I could try on receipt of telegram of yours to obtain British entrance visas for Zielenziger Krieg Bettelheim Bielschowsky stop Feel obliged to make this communication in order to have done everything in connection with general situation stop All materials not absolutely needed in Amsterdam may as hitherto be sent to London.

In fact, as we shall see later, Wiener had made provision for both his family and his colleagues to come to London. Margarethe Wiener's decision not to leave Amsterdam was probably rooted in her wish to stay and support her sister and her family there. She and the Wieners' daughters, as well as Zielenziger, Bernhard Krieg (who had been in London but had to go back) and the other members of the Office were left stranded in Amsterdam. They were eventually taken to Westerbork before being deported to Bergen Belsen.

There is of course no question how deeply Wiener felt the separation from his family. In a letter written by A.R. Walmsley, formerly of the Electra House organisation, to Christa Wichmann in 1983 he recalled:

> I was visiting Dr Wiener very soon after the German invasion of the Low Countries – maybe it was just after the German bombing of Amsterdam.

Dr Wiener asked me to pardon his distress, because he had not been able to get any news about the fate of his wife and family who were of course virtually in the front line. He could not, I remember, keep the tears out of his eyes, but nevertheless he insisted on continuing to discuss whatever it was that I had come to see him about. . . I greatly admired his fortitude at that time . . .[3]

There are few recorded memories from which Wiener emerges so vividly as a human being.

Throughout the war, Wiener was in the employ of the British government. He was not exactly a civil servant; rather, various government departments, the BBC, the Ministry of Information, the Political Intelligence Department of the Foreign Office and others, paid monthly or quarterly grants to Wiener's Library in return for being kept supplied with information about developments in Germany.

Wiener's colleague, C.C. Aronsfeld, remembers Wiener suffering a second nervous collapse sometime after the outbreak of the war, which kept him inactive for some weeks, while he was nursed back to full strength by Eva Reichmann's sister, Elizabeth Jungmann, who would later become Lady Beerbohm, and who worked at the Library at this time. Thereafter, Aronsfeld recalls, Wiener very actively pursued a plan for going to America, both to secure new supply lines for material and because he found life in wartime London an intolerable strain.

The original plan was for him to stay there for a few months only and return once supply lines for the Library had been re-established. In the event, he was to stay there throughout the war. He worked for the British Political Warfare Mission in Washington, the British Information Services in New York, and for various US government departments.

Wiener was based first in furnished rooms in West End Avenue, later in the Century Hotel in Manhattan. On the whole, he does not seem to have liked New York much, but he enjoyed the work he was doing. In a report he wrote for his government employers he stated that, 'The American book market requires extensive inside knowledge as for instance the exact study of all new publications such as books, pamphlets, periodicals and newspapers. For this purpose it is essential to visit bookstores, read catalogues, study newspapers and to trace new publications etc.' It is safe to assume that for a man of Wiener's inclinations, such essential work didn't come as too much of a hardship.

After the War, and when he was back in London, Wiener wrote a reflective piece on the question of emigration to America for the Leo Baeck Lodge of B'nai B'rith. This short piece contains his impressions of the country:

The mighty size of this land, the variety of nature, of climate, unbearable humid heat, bitterly cold winter, tender Autumn days (Indian Summer), endless deserts, majestic mountains, unbounded plains are just as extra-ordinary as the riches of its natural world and its population of 130 million, constituted from every nation.[4]

Equally impressive for him was the speed and effectiveness of America's mobilisation after the attack on Pearl Harbour:

It is like a miracle, how speedily factories were brought into existence and to the peak of technical perfection for the mass production of aeroplanes, tanks, armaments, guns and the thousand necessities of the war. Just as speedily, in a land where conscription was unknown, an army of millions was assembled, comprising all services, which decisively influenced the course of the war.[5]

Yet while he was awed by the United States, by its riches and the energy of its people, he was far from overawed. He recognised quite clearly that in the land of opportunity, opportunity was not boundless and that American streets are no more paved with gold than any others:

Hard work awaits all those whose bank accounts cannot show a number of zeros behind the initial figure. The happy fact that since the start of the war there has been an astonishing demand, especially for educated manpower, which by and large is continuing, so that even older men and women can earn their bread, should not lead one into false ideas about the future.[6]

Similarly, he counsels Jewish migrants from Europe not to entertain unrealistic ideas about American attitudes towards Jews.[7]

Throughout the war years Wiener occupied a stateless and rootless position, deprived by the Nazis of German citizenship, yet lacking the qualifications for British or American nationality. Not only was this psychologically uncomfortable, it raised numerous practical problems and interfered with his work. By the summer of 1943 at the latest, he had decided to renounce any claim to German citizenship and to become a naturalised Briton. He set about the task with characteristic doggedness.

The first signs were not encouraging: the legal advisor to the British embassy in Washington informed him that five years' residence in the United Kingdom was the requirement, and if it was interrupted by more than six months' absence, the period prior to the absence would not count. This meant that when he eventually returned to Britain, he would have to serve the full five-year residence before getting his citizenship. The only hope for avoiding this was to argue that he had spent the years in America in the service of the Crown, which would mean that they could be counted as part of his residency. In July 1943 he turned to Stephen Heald in London for help and advice. Two years later in April 1945, after he had returned to London, he wrote to Walter Stewart Roberts of the Political Intelligence Department begging to submit proof that 'from 29 July 1940 to 15 March 1945 I was in the service of the Crown'. By the end of April 1945 he was able to write thanking Stewart 'for the steps you have so kindly taken to bring about a successful conclusion to my Application for Naturalisation.'[8]

Wiener's ambiguous position in America also roused the suspicions of the FBI. He himself was subjected to questioning and his colleague John F. Oppenheimer described how his wife was met at the home of her employer by FBI agents who took her 'to our home, questioned her intensively about our activities with Dr Wiener, searched my library and the piles of German newspapers which had accumulated . . . it took several months of explanations by Dr Wiener and myself until we were cleared.' Oppenheimer described Wiener as 'a man of unusual charm and knowledge. But the working of his mind and his actions have often been impenetrable and therefore open to questions.'[9]

The summer of 1943 found Wiener in Bermuda. This came about when a consignment of some 25,000 books and periodicals in German and other European languages were seized by the Imperial Censorship there. Wiener telegraphed his London contacts in May, alerting them to the prize, and in June Michael Balfour of the Politicial Intelligence Department wrote to Stephen Heald, director of the Reference Division at the Ministry of Information, that 'it would be the height of folly to neglect this possible source of information.' The same letter contains what was more or less a customary note of suspicion that Wiener might be taking advantage of the authorities for his own benefit: 'We think that the reservation in paragraph 4 of the telegram should be made very clear to Dr Wiener and that the length of his stay in Bermuda should be limited in advance.' Wiener also informed the British Political Warfare Mission in Washington about the haul and they too had an interest. In the event he spent just over a month there, from 21 August to 26 September, but sadly no record exists in the Wiener Library's archives which makes clear the precise nature of the material he secured for the authorities.[10]

By the beginning of 1945 Wiener knew he was returning to Britain. He was also informed that his wife and children had been released from Belsen and were on their way to Switzerland. By 30 January he had been informed by a family friend, Camilla Aronowska, that his wife had died shortly after crossing the border and had been buried at Kreuzlingen, near Lake Constance. Over the next few days he received numerous telegrams, some congratulating him on the release of his family, some informing him that the family was already safe in North Africa, still others commiserating on the loss of his wife. Margarethe Wiener in fact died of malnutrition and exhaustion within hours of regaining freedom. The children were handed over by the Swiss Red Cross to the US Army and hastily conveyed to Marseilles, from where they were to be sent to a UNRRA camp in Philipsville, Algeria. However, Wiener's energetic efforts on their behalf secured them places aboard a Swedish Red Cross ship, the *Gripsholm*, bound for New York. The fact that Wiener chose America may seem puzzling, given that he himself was on his way back to London. But in reality, he had little choice. Britain was still at war: he would have had difficulty securing visas for them, and there was in any case nowhere for the family to live in London. At least in America he had friends he trusted and could reassure himself that they would be safe and well cared for. He himself was forced to cancel his sailing in order to stay in America long enough to meet them. They arrived towards the end of February. During their first days on Ellis Island, Wiener was in daily correspondence with them (writing sometimes twice a day). They then moved into the Hotel Century in West 46th Street, where Wiener had been living. They stayed there for two weeks while they did their talking, then the girls went to live with foster families,[11] while Wiener's colleague and friend, John Oppenheimer, and his wife, were legally responsible for them. Wiener spent the remainder of March settling them into their temporary homes, then returned to London, where he arrived in April.

The girls spent two years living in America and remember it as a happy and secure time. They came to Britain in 1947, by which time Wiener had found a flat for the family in Bayswater, at 45 Queens Court, Queensway. There they rebuilt their family life and Wiener began to consider what was to be done.

In the event Wiener decided to continue the Wiener Library. While government support was largely withdrawn, the BBC continued to pay regular subventions, as did the Board of Deputies and various other bodies. Wiener was fortunate in enjoying a good professional relationship with Leonard Montefiore, an extremely wealthy man committed to a variety of Jewish and charitable causes. Montefiore gave considerable sums of money to keep the Library afloat and although it never became financially secure, it became, in Wiener's words, 'an annually-recurring miracle.'

Yet even as Wiener was working to secure the future of his Library, he had, realistically, to face the possibility that it might fail. With this in mind, he considered what else he might do. His choice fell on utilising his profound bibliographical knowledge: he would trade in second-hand and antiquarian books. He was in any case doing the rounds of the bookshops regularly on behalf of the Library and he had excellent contacts both in Europe and America to whom he might sell. In the 1940s and 50s he built up a respectable business, which he ran from home. It provided welcome additional income, and a sense of security that the Library had never given him. The presence in the house of mountainous quantities of books only occasionally drove his family to distraction.

In his private life, one of the most important developments in the immediate post-war period was that Wiener resumed contact with David Cohen, a contact that eventually built into a close personal friendship. In February 1946 Wiener went to Amsterdam. There was some business to sort out concerning the legalities of the JCIO and who owned the Wiener Library. Wiener was also concerned to try to recover some of the property he had lost in Holland. In addition, he wanted to lend Cohen his support during a time when he was being accused of collaborating with the Germans and of being a war criminal for his part in running the Joodse Raad. The two were in correspondence almost every week, and Cohen was kept closely informed about the formation of the new Board, and was eager to attend its first meeting as a guest.

In July 1946 Wiener sent him a copy of a book by Louis Bondy, who headed the London office of the Wiener Library through most of the war. Entitled *Racketeers of Hatred*, it was an exposé of Nazi propaganda, written using much of the Library's material.

One of the issues which brought Wiener and Cohen together was a bit of unfinished business from the Amsterdam days. The matter is set out in a letter Cohen wrote in August 1946 to Eduard Wallach in New York:

> When the office existed in Amsterdam we were always in financial need. Once this need was so great that we were obliged to address ourselves to the cousin of Dr Wiener, Mr Pick, who was, as you know, Director of the Egoro. He kindly gave us a loan on my guarantee. We repaid part of this loan but at last (sic) a sum of fl2400 ($1000) remained unpaid. Mr Pick then was obliged to ask for a guarantee in bonds and Mrs Wiener (Dr Wiener lived in London and it was already wartime) on my request signed a promise that the bonds Dr Wiener possessed at New York should be a guarantee for those fl2400. Of course Mr Pick did not act voluntarily but was obliged to do so because there was a control on his books from the side of the Government. It was always meant that this sum would not be charged to Dr Wiener but that we should ask Baron Goldschmidt Rothschild to quit this debt. Now as you know Mr Pick is dead and the new Director of the Egoro does not know what to do in this matter. Therefore I dare to ask you to discuss this matter with the Baron to explain the importance of the Office . . . and to send me a letter signed by him that he is ready to quit the debt.[12]

The squabbling over this debt rumbled on for some time, the Baron apparently proving intractable. In September Wallach wrote to Cohen:

The Baron feels that there is no reason for him to forfeit the amount of fl2400. If the Baron quits this claim for fl2400 against the Jewish Central Information Office, he would be required to remit to the Egoro Amsterdam, out of his own pocket, the equivalent in order that their books might be balanced and to make this payment good.[13]

Cohen replied rather crossly:

As a man I am ashamed to ask twice for the same thing. But as a Jew I should be ashamed to address myself to the Dutch Government which is now the manager of the Egoro in order to ask them to quit the debt, or to the new Board [of the Wiener Library] asking them to repay the sum and be obliged to tell them that Baron de Goldschmidt Rothschild refused to give from his own pocket the sum of about $1000 in order that a loan furnished by a Bank which administered his fortune to an office which had been constituted to combat national-socialism and its propaganda should be cancelled.[14]

Both Eduard Wallach and the Baron reiterated the impossibility of quitting the debt. The final outcome of this dispute is not recorded but the incident shows how, once the Nazi threat to Jewry had been defeated, Wiener had to struggle to maintain his Library and that many people seem to have regarded his work as an anachronism which no longer deserved support.

The Wiener family remained in their flat in Bayswater for several years, but eventually moved suburb-wards to Middleton Road in leafy Golders Green, where they occupied a comfortable and spacious house. Wiener himself was by now enjoying a much more settled and happy private life. He saw his daughters reach adulthood and establish themselves. In 1951 Ruth, the eldest, married and moved to Australia (she would eventually settle in the United States). A year later Eva married and moved to Israel. For a time this left Wiener and Mirjam, but in 1953 Wiener got married again, to Mrs Lotte Philips and this marriage brought him companionship and a level of domestic stability he had not known since Amsterdam.

Mirjam herself married in 1957. Her husband, Ludwik Finkelstein, became very close to Wiener in his last years. As a wedding present, Wiener let Finkelstein choose 300 books from his stock, stipulating only that he take a multi-volume biography of Bismarck because no library was complete without one.

By this time, the stock of Wiener's book business completely filled two rooms at home and was still expanding. Mirjam's decision to move out was to some extent hastened by the discovery that the stock had invaded the space under her bed and was taking over her own shelves. Most Saturdays Wiener would set off book buying, carrying a small briefcase. Returning home in a taxi, the family would heave a sigh of relief when he wasn't carrying large boxes. Inevitably, however, a second taxi would draw up groaning under the weight of the day's purchases.

During the 1950s Wiener began actively to make contacts in Germany, specifically among the various Christian denominations. He had always believed that establishing good relations between Jews and Christians was essential if Jews were to be on good terms with their neighbours. Now he felt that this was the best way to reach ordinary Germans, particularly the younger generation, and communicate to them the nature of the catastrophe that had befallen their country.

In an interview he gave to the *Wiener Library Bulletin* in 1958, Wiener spoke of this effort:

> We are making an effort to approach German youth in order to impress on them what we regard as the lesson of the past. Of course we can talk to them only if and when they want us to. The other day I addressed a group of German Protestants living in this country. In Germany itself our Director of Research, Dr Eva G. Reichmann, has occasionally spoken at conferences arranged by the Protestant Academies, bodies specifically founded for the purpose of exchanging opinions on current affairs . . . I have a feeling that German youth holds out a great promise. They do appear to appreciate their stake in a truly democratic Europe; they seem willing to learn the lesson of the past, and they have decided, once and for all, to wash their hands of the terror of totalitarian reaction. As a result of their shocking experience, young Germans fight shy of anything reeking of propaganda or suspected as the vested interest of a self-seeking faction. In these circumstances, there does seem to be a sporting chance of exerting a salutary influence.[15]

Such sentiments appear poignant to a modern reader: possibly there was justification for them in the late 1950s, or perhaps they evince a certain sentimentality on Wiener's part.

Eva Reichmann recalled these trips and what they might have meant to young German people:

> He knew very well that it was not the actual contents of his lectures that mattered. It was his personality, the personality of a German Jew, that defamed and ostracised human being that many of his listeners had never seen in the flesh. Dr Wiener's lively, impressive presence substituted the living reality for the phantom.

And what Wiener himself got out of them:

To him, these study groups and weekend conferences in Germany became a revelation. He radiated happiness when he told of them. . . In the youth that surrounded him, he felt himself reborn. In such hours of elation, it was as it had been before. He swept away awkward uncertainties and spoke again of the synthesis of German and Jewish ideals, in which he had believed in his youthful beginnings and which, in fact, he had never abandoned. That the dreams of his youth had come to life again, that they proved their power of spiritual reconstruction after an unheard-of devastation of mind and matter – that he felt to be their final triumph. No doubt ever penetrated into his conviction so jubilantly reasserted. Though the world which it had once reflected lay in ruins, shattered beyond resurrection, his life, the life of a German Jew, had come full circle.[16]

In 1955 Wiener celebrated his 70th birthday. This occasion was widely noted in the press, both German and Jewish, and to a certain extent the British national press as well. Wiener marked the occasion by visiting Germany, where he took part in the annual Brotherhood Week celebrations and gave some public lectures. He was honoured by the German government with the highest civilian decoration, the Grand Cross of the Order of Merit (Grosses Verdienstkreuz des Verdienstordens), awarded in London by the ambassador, Dr Schlange-Schöningen. The official declaration acknowledged his achievement in founding the Library and resisting Nazi oppression, but paid particular tribute to his readiness to reach out to a younger generation of Germans who were not directly involved in bringing about the Holocaust.

However the tribute that probably meant most to him came from another source. Writing in the *AJR Information*, Leo Baeck said:

All of us who fervently hope that the peculiar Jewish spirit which through centuries had steadily grown up within the Jewish community of Germany may survive and prove creative, feel greatly indebted to Dr Alfred Wiener. This spirit had its many battlefields, and to understand its character and power one must know what he was struggling for and fighting against. Books are witnesses of this spirit and these combats, and they must be given refuge and shelter.

Dr Alfred Wiener saw this clearly . . . By establishing the Library which rightly bears his name, he ensured their survival and took care of them . . . This library is, so to speak, an open-door library. Books are not only shelved but are made agencies and instruments. They are not idle books, but books that work. And Dr Wiener and the fine people who so devotedly and so unassumingly assist him, are always prepared to help the book and to help the reader, to bring the two together that they may meet one another.[17]

In the same number of the *AJR Information*, Eva Reichmann wrote, humorously yet shrewdly:

> A printed article does not seem the appropriate medium for expressing congratulations on Dr Alfred Wiener's 70th birthday, and neither does the English language. He himself is fond of his native German, which he miraculously succeeds in imposing on anybody to whom he happens to be talking, and he is a man of the spoken word rather than the written – unless of course, the written word occurs in sufficient profusion to acquire the status of a book: then it gains a fundamentally new meaning, rendering it eligible for inclusion in the Wiener Library. . .[18]

Aside from struggling with the Library's problems, Wiener tried to busy himself with writing his memoirs, but never really got anywhere with them (this was understandable, since he had the Library's continuing troubles on his mind and was in any case temperamentally disinclined to make personal revelations). It must have pained him somewhat that all his efforts and work had failed to secure the Library. Yet he was fortunate that he was almost entirely clear in his mind until the end and had enough challenges to keep busy and active.

Eventually on 4 February 1964 he died. His death certificate gives the cause as 'myocardial degeneration and aortic incompetence' – in other words, old age. Asked while on his death-bed what he was thinking about, he had replied tersely, 'the state'. Perhaps this was a fitting exit line for a man whose life was so taken up with contemplating politics, power and justice and who had struggled heroically to combat and mitigate the evils that flowed from Nazi Germany.

His passing was widely noted in the press. In *The Times* Aronsfeld honoured his old employer, noting how 'the innocence of his trust in human reason and in the power, almost the magic, of the printed word, contrasted oddly with the sure realism which guided his transactions. . . ' The *New York Times* pointed out that 'Although his whole institute was intended as an emphatic reminder of evil, Dr Wiener was foremost among those who tried to heal the wounds.' The *Jewish Chronicle* carried a large obituary by David Kessler (later the Chairman of the Library's Executive Committee), who wrote that:

> Alfred Wiener was an unusual man, who combined admirably the finest characteristics of the great German Jewish cultural tradition in which he had been nurtured and a profound love for the country in which he made his home as a refugee from the Nazis.[19]

In the German newspaper *Das Parlament* Eva Reichmann pointed out that by requesting that the psalms and prayers at his funeral be spoken in both Hebrew and German, Wiener remained true to his deepest beliefs. She went on to praise his never-faltering faith in the 'other Germany', the Germany of literature, music, philosophy.

The course of Wiener's life had passed through perhaps the most turbulent and horrific period in human history. What characterised him above all else was his ability and willingness to adapt in creative and positive ways to the massive dislocations of the age. While not losing sight of his frailties and failings, it is remarkable that he never gave up and took an easier route. With his position and connections he could have left Europe permanently in 1940 and rebuilt his life after the war. Or he could have let the Library go under and enjoyed the quiet prosperity of an antiquarian book dealer. Yet he clung to his vision of the Library as a unique and worthwhile institution and never failed to find ways and means of keeping it going. He had indeed been a master in the art of the possible.

NOTES

1. Arieh Tartakower and Kurt Grossmann, *The Jewish Refugee* (New York: Institute of Jewish Affairs of the American Jewish Congress and World Jewish Congress, 1944), p. 30.
2. Letter from Alfred Wiener to David Cohen, 12.11.1939, Wiener Archive, Wiener Library.
3. Letter from A.R. Walmsley to Christa Wichmann, dated 25.4.1983, Wiener Archive, Wiener Library.
4. Die gewaltige Grösse dieses Landes, die Verschiedenheit der Natur, des Klimas, unerträgliche feuchte Hitze, bitter kalter Winter, liebliche Herbsttage (Indian Summer), endlose Wüste, majestätische Felsengebirge, unbegrenzte Ebenen sind ebenso einzigartig wie die Bodenschätze, der Naturreichtum und die sich aus aller Herren Länder zusammensetzende Bevölkerung von 130 Millionen. Alfred Wiener, 'Der Einwanderer kommt nach Amerika', in F. Goldschmidt (ed.), *B'nai B'rith, Leo Baeck (London) Lodge No. 1593, Die ersten drei Jahre*, nd., np.
5. Einem Wunder gleicht es, in welcher Geschwindigkeit Fabriken, um Flugzeuge, Tanks, Geschütze, Gewehre und 1000 Erfordernisse des Krieges herzustellen, aus dem Boden gestampft und auf der Spitze technischer Volkommenheit und notwendiger Massenherstellung gebracht wurden. Nicht minder schnell stand in dem Lande, das keine Dienstpflicht kannte, ein Heer von Millionen in allen Waffengattungen auf den Beinen, dessen Leistungen den Kriegsablauf entscheidend beeinflussten. Alfred Wiener, 'Der Einwanderer kommt nach Amerika', in F. Goldschmidt (ed.), *B'nai B'rith, Leo Baeck (London) Lodge No. 1593, Die ersten drei Jahre*, nd., np.
6. Harte Arbeit erwartet einen jeden, dessen Bankkonto nicht einige Nullen hinter der ersten Zahl aufweist. Die erfreuliche Tatsache, dass seit Kriegsbeginn ein ungeheures Bedürfnis, insbesondere nach geschulten Arbeitskräften besteht, das bisher im Grossen und Ganzen anhält, sodass auch ältere Männer und Frauen ihr Brot verdienen können, darf über die Zukunft nicht hinwegtäuschen. Alfred Wiener, 'Der Einwanderer kommt nach Amerika', in F. Goldschmidt (ed.), *B'nai B'rith, Leo Baeck (London) Lodge No. 1593, Die ersten drei Jahre*, nd., np.

7. Alfred Wiener, 'Der Einwanderer kommt nach Amerika', in F. Goldschmidt (ed.), *B'nai B'rith, Leo Baeck (London) Lodge No. 1593, Die ersten drei Jahre*, nd., np.

8. Letter from Alfred Wiener to Walter Stewart Roberts, dated 28.4.1945, Foreign Office papers kept at the Public Record Office (FO 898/34/3).

9. Letter from John F. Oppenheimer to Walter Laqueur, dated 22.11.1983, Wiener Archive, Wiener Library.

10. Letter from Michael Balfour to Stephen Heald, dated 5.6.1943, Foreign Office papers kept at the Public Record Office (FO898/34/3).

11. One of these families was that of the Quaker pediatrician, Richard Day, who took in many refugees from Nazi Germany. Gitta Sereny, in her *Albert Speer, his Battle with Truth*, reveals that Speer's daughter Hilde also lived with the family, after her father was imprisoned. In an interview with one of Richard Day's children, Kate, Sereny records Kate's memories of 'the Wiener girls' who were fresh out of Belsen 'where their mother died' and who were 'very traumatised'. But Sereny did not apparently realise that these were Alfred Wiener's daughters. Kate's assertion that Mrs Wiener died in Belsen is mistaken.

12. Letter from David Cohen to Eduard Wallach, 29.8.1946, Wiener Archive, Wiener Library.

13. Letter from Eduard Wallach to David Cohen, 4.9.1946, Wiener Archive, Wiener Library.

14. Letter from David Cohen to Eduard Wallach, 10.9.1946, Wiener Archive, Wiener Library.

15. 'Work and Aims of the Wiener Library', *Wiener Library Bulletin*, Vol. XII, No. 3–4, 1958, p. 4.

16. Eva Reichmann, 'Alfred Wiener – the German Jew', *Wiener Library Bulletin*, Vol. XIX, 1965, p. 10–11.

17. Leo Baeck, 'The Man and His Work', *AJR Information*, March 1955.

18. Eva G. Reichmann, 'The Founder of the Wiener Library', *AJR Information*, March 1955.

19. David Kessler, obituary, *Jewish Chronicle*, 7.2.1964,

PART TWO

The Wiener Library

CHAPTER FIVE

The Germ of an Idea

IN DECEMBER 1925, in the week of the official publication of *Mein Kampf*, Wiener had written an article for the *CV Zeitung* in which he set out what he saw as the dangers facing Germany. He identified three major political tendencies. A central core of conservative parties of varying hues, sharing a commitment to preserve the Republic, was flanked at either extreme by the communists and Nazis, each dedicated to overthrowing the state. Wiener was in no doubt where the greater danger lay: the communists may have been abhorrent and wrong, but their policies rested on a rational set of views which could be countered by argument. The Nazi threat lay precisely in its appeal to the irrational. Wiener wrote that:

> We, the CV, are standing on guard. We know how to counter the enemy. For every one of their speakers we must have two, for every one of their leaflets, we must have ten. We must explain how things stand wherever this is necessary, in the Parties and in the Governments.

And he indicated what was at stake:

> We must explain to the German citizen the danger which may be brewing up behind the curtain of winter fog. We must say to him – and this is holy truth – fight the völkisch movement, not for the sake of Jewry but for the sake of the Fatherland, which will, under a Wulle or Hitler, sink into a sea of blood and tears, into the abyss.[1]

To combat this, the CV – in collaboration with the republican paramilitary organisation, Reichsbanner-Schwarz-Rot-Gold, which was allied to the Social Democrats – decided to launch a sustained counter-propaganda effort. These two organisations were pretty much alone in understanding the magnitude of the threat posed by the relentless campaigning of the Nazis. Yet even they were unable to formulate clear and coherent policies of opposition.

After the election of May 1928, the CV decided to commission an investigation into what lay behind the Nazi success in certain electoral areas, especially in Franconia, where one in 12 voters supported them – a proportion far in excess of the national average.

Walter Gyssling, a journalist and political activist who was a member of the Reichsbanner and who later ran the archive at the CV's Büro Wilhelmstraße, undertook the investigation. Gyssling had been born in 1903 in Munich, the son of an engineer father and an opera singer mother. As a student he had been active in left-wing republican student organisations. With his family's wealth consumed by the inflation, he abandoned his studies and became a journalist. In June 1928 he left Bavaria and went to Berlin, where he worked for the Verein zur Abwehr des Antisemitismus (Association to Resist Anti-Semitism) briefly before being taken up by the CV. He was recognised there as a leading expert on the Nazis, particularly on the psychology of Nazi propaganda.

In his study Gyssling reported that Nazi support was strongest among the lowest social classes, those in poverty or with good reason to fear poverty – such as the middle classes who had lost their savings in the 1923 inflation. The mass of the industrial workforce was relatively immune to Nazi appeal because they were not currently experiencing hardship. Gyssling travelled across the country in July and August 1928, gathering information and deepening the CV's understanding of the enemy. He concluded that the Nazi movement was a political force quite without precedent in German politics and counselled against using accepted standards in judging them.[2]

Within the CV there was a marked reluctance to accept the conclusions of Gyssling's shrewd report. In particular, Hollaender was concerned that the organisation should not just focus on the Nazis. When, in the autumn of 1928, Wiener presented a report to the executive committee of the CV on the signs of increased Nazi activity in rural districts, he was told bluntly that he was reading too much into isolated events. Wiener believed strongly that voting patterns revealed the rural poor to be especially vulnerable to Nazi propaganda. Amid a general boom the countryside was experiencing hard times and Wiener feared that the Nazis could build a power base there. By the following spring, the *CV Zeitung* was reporting a strong Nazi upswing in local elections.

It was as a response to the campaign led by Goebbels against Bernhard Weiss, the Jewish deputy chief of Police in Berlin, and against Jewish-owned department stores, that a special office was established in Berlin's Wilhelm-straße. The Büro Wilhelmstraße was not officially a department of the CV, but was very closely linked to the organisation. It was a semi-clandestine outfit, which received funding from numerous sources, many of which would not have been happy donating money to the CV directly on account of its hostility to Zionism. Its nominal head was the socially acceptable Max Brunzlow, a former police officer and member of the German Democratic Party. The CV's man in the Büro was Hans Reichmann, a lifelong friend of Wiener's. Gyssling was put in charge of accumulating an archive of Nazi propaganda, which formed the basis of the Büro's work.

The location of the Büro was significant. Wilhelmstrasse was in the heart of Berlin's Regierungsviertel, where government offices and embassies were concentrated. The offices of Ebert and Hindenburg were at number 73, with ministries clustered around. Round one corner was the Hotel Kaiserhof, where Hitler and the Nazis had their Berlin headquarters. Round another was the Brandenburg Gate and the Reichstag. It was the perfect place to locate an office whose purpose was to gather news and rumour, information and gossip.

The propaganda materials produced by the Büro were not intended to betray their specifically Jewish origins, although it was generally assumed that most anti-Nazi materials came from Jewish sources, or those in sympathy with the Jewish community. In content the leaflets and posters were reactive – countering Nazi claims and refuting misinformation. One election leaflet declared: 'Die Nazis sind unser Unglück!', parodying a famous Nazi slogan.

The Büro's materials were distributed nationally through the Reichsbanner. In the run-up to the September 1930 election, leaflets, posters and brochures were produced by the million. From this time on, other political groups were also targeted with Büro material during elections.

The Büro also produced a loose-leaf part-work, entitled *Anti-Nazi*. Compiled by Gyssling, it consisted of biographical sketches of Nazi personalities and summaries of their ideological positions and policy stances. It was modelled on an earlier CV publication (a Reichmann compilation) called *Anti-Anti*. This covered the wider field of anti-Semitism in general. *Anti-Nazi* carried the imprint of the Deutsche Volksgemeinschaftsdienst, a fictitious organisation used as a cover. Several other imaginary organisations were invented to conceal the work of the Büro, including the Ausschuss für Volks-aufklärung and the Bund Deutscher Aufbau. The materials generated by the Büro were also used as the basis of an exhibition set up at various meetings and press conferences in Berlin and throughout Germany.

The Büro also produced a fortnightly, later weekly, satirical paper called *Alarm*. This was intended to counter the Nazi paper *Der Angriff*, while not sinking to the extraordinary depths of Streicher's *Stürmer*. It was the brain-child of Alfred Schweriner, formerly Wiener's deputy, and was edited by him. It was regarded with a certain amount of suspicion and distaste within the CV as being too tinged with the gutter, yet it was recognised as being successful as a way of reaching a large working-class readership.[3]

Alfred Wiener was not directly involved in the daily work of the Büro, but he was fully aware of its existence and activities, and one of the shapers of its strategy and goals. He clearly recognised the importance of collecting every scrap of information available about the Nazis, but he did not share whole-heartedly Walter Gyssling's aggressive attitude on the question of propaganda. Wiener was committed to combating the appeal of Nazi irrationality with a programme of enlightenment, which took as its lodestone the power of rational argument and investigation. He could not have given unalloyed approval to a counter-propaganda campaign which did not shy away from violence, both physical and verbal, appeals to esoteric symbols, numerology and pseudo-mythical accounts of reality – all of which were advocated by Gyssling and his psychologist mentors. To Wiener this smacked of merely substituting one lot of vile mumbo-jumbo for another.

Gyssling's skill and achievements as an archivist, on the other hand, must have been enormously impressive to Wiener. Within the few short years of the Büro's existence, he amassed over 200,000 items, the bulk of them from authentic Nazi publications. Gyssling recalled in 1962 how he collected his material, and this memoir is worth quoting at length – because it throws a remarkable light on the practice followed by Wiener once his Jewish Central Information Office was established in Amsterdam:

> The daily surveillance of the press yielded most. The Büro Wilhemstrasse subscribed to all National Socialist papers. Since the number of these was increasing constantly from 1929–1933, and since many National Socialist weeklies were transformed into dailies, this resulted in a considerable quantity of work each day. Besides the NSDAP papers, the major Berlin dailies of all hues, from the extreme right-wing *Deutsche Zeitung* and the *Deutsche Tageszeitung* to the *Rote Fahne* of the KPD were kept under surveillance for items about the National Socialist movement and everything connected with it. In addition the major provincial papers like the *Frank-furter Zeitung* and the *Dortmunder Generalanzeiger* were surveyed. When local elections occurred in the Länder, subscriptions for local papers were taken out for the duration of the campaign. National Socialist periodicals were also monitored, and those of the movements related to National Socialism. Single issues of general press material containing important items relating to the NSDAP were frequently sent by local CV groups, or by provincial correspondents, or were collected by the archivist or other CV members during their travels. In this way there was practically no publication relating to the NSDAP that was not to be found in the archive. Naturally a rapidly accumulated library was also available, containing the entire National Socialist literature, as well as non-partisan *völkisch* literature, such as the books of Möller van den Bruck, as well as a sizeable collection of anti-Nazi books and pamphlets. Everything was incorporated into the biographical and subject archives by means of copying important quotations

and cross-referencing them. Above all, there were numerous provocative or significant quotations from Hitler's *Mein Kampf* uncovered by the Büro Wilhelmstrasse, and in the course of this careful analysis, many points were discovered which had been previously overlooked and never made use of in anti-National Socialist propaganda.[4]

These working methods were almost identical to those of the Jewish Central Information Office.

When Wiener left Germany in 1933 to go to Holland, he took with him the knowledge of how a bureau, of the sort organised and run by Gyssling, could be set up. He knew what sort of materials it should and could contain, where and how to get them and how to organise them. Lastly, he had his own ideas – rather different from Gyssling's – about the use to which they might be put. Conceptually at least, the Wiener Library had its origin not in Amsterdam in the mid-1930s, but in Berlin in the late 1920s.

The Büro itself continued to function until the Nazi seizure of power. At the end of February 1933 it was moved from Berlin to Bavaria, where it was destroyed during the war. Walter Gyssling left Germany in 1933 and settled in Switzerland (he had some claim to Swiss citizenship); he was active as a journalist until his death in 1980.

What Wiener lacked, once he was in Amsterdam, was the money and organisational backing to make the new bureau a reality. But he had a wide range of contacts from the CV and these included Professor David Cohen, the Professor of Ancient History at the University of Amsterdam and a leading member of Amsterdam's Jewish community.

Wiener first approached Cohen in August of 1933. Cohen wrote later that he knew Wiener through his work for German refugees coming to Holland, and because the two were in agreement as to the threat posed by Hitler, not just for Jews but for the world at large. According to Cohen, Wiener came to him with the proposal to found an organisation to fight Nazi propaganda, not exclusively in Holland (where this was already being done by the Press Department of the Comité), but internationally. They agreed that Cohen would serve as president and Wiener as director, a division which left Wiener in charge of all day-to-day matters and permitted Cohen to lend his prestige and influence to the venture, while not distracting him too much from his profession and existing extramural commitments.

David Cohen was a Zionist from youth and became one of Holland's leading advocates of the idea of a Jewish national homeland (although, curiously, he never made any attempt to go and live in Palestine or Israel after the war, when life in Holland became very trying for him). He was born in 1883 in the provincial town of Deventer. He was the oldest of six children. His father having died when he was 16, Cohen is reported to 'have felt paternally attached (to his siblings) throughout their lives'. He attended the 1907 Zionist Congress at The Hague and subsequently formed the Zionist Students' Organisation as well as Holland's first Zionist youth groups. Cohen was a superb student who studied classics at the University of Leyden. He was appointed to the Chair at Amsterdam in 1926. Between that date and the Nazi seizure of power, he earned an international reputation as a scholar and as an inspired public speaker. His position among the city's Jewish elite was secure.[5]

Cohen was very quick to grasp what Hitler's coming to power would mean to Holland's – and specifically Amsterdam's – Jewish community. In March 1933 he got together with Abraham Asscher and three others to form the Comité voor Bijzondere Joodse Belangen (Committee for Special Jewish Interests). The committee was created to unify the response of the various elements of the Jewish community to the refugee problem. Cohen served as its honorary secretary for the seven years of its existence. His duties involved fund-raising, representing the relief effort to a government which was very reluctant to allow refugees in, attending international meetings about refugee relief, countering Nazi anti-Semitic and anti-refugee propaganda and arranging entry permits for refugees where this was possible. According to his student, Henriette Boas, these activities took up 'hours each day'.

The Comité voor Joodse Vluchtelingen arose out of the committee created to take care of the day-to-day running of refugee work. This committee's work was based on three principles: firstly, that refugees should not become a drain on public funds; secondly, anyone settling permanently in Holland should bring jobs and business into the country; lastly, that its work should make use of other Jewish organisations as much as necessary in support of its first two principles. The committee shaped this approach in response to governmental hostility and fear of the consequences of allowing a large refugee population to build up. For one thing, the government was extremely anxious not to antagonise its powerful and volatile neighbour. For another, it feared that a large Jewish refugee population would awaken anti-Semitism at home and generate an upsurge in extreme right-wing and fascist political activity. Refugees should not be encouraged to regard Holland as a permanent place of settlement, but only as a passing-through point on the way to somewhere else.

Post-war, Cohen's reputation suffered gravely from his role in the Nazi-appointed Joodse Raad. But his decision before the war to work from within the system, to accept the government's attitude and try to maximise the good that could be done within the limitations it imposed, also attracted criticism. Many felt that he should have used all the means available to pressure and persuade the government to review its policy and open the doors to refugees.

At the end of October 1933 Cohen was in London to attend a conference organised by the Joint Foreign Committee of the Anglo-Jewish Association and the Board of Deputies of British Jews, the focus of which was how the international community of Jewish organisations might co-operate to organise and finance help to the swelling stream of refugees.

The conference was convened by Neville Laski and Leonard Montefiore, the presidents, respectively, of the Board of Deputies and AJA. It took place in Woburn House from 29 October to 1 November 1933. In attendance were 100 delegates, representing 44 Jewish groups from across Europe and the United States. At the conference, Cohen argued for the setting up of an intelligence-gathering office, which could supply information about Nazi thinking, ideology and propaganda. The conference accepted this, and the third of its published resolutions was:

> It is recommended that a Central Bureau shall be set up to collect information with respect to Nazi propaganda and to disseminate information thereon to existing organisations.[6]

In London this led to the establishment of a press office at Woburn House, which issued compilations of British and German press statements. In Amsterdam it led to the creation of what would become the Wiener Library, by providing Alfred Wiener with the backing he needed to get his project of a Büro Wilhelmstrasse-style information office off the ground.

That Cohen's brief from the conference so neatly coincided with Wiener's aims, suggests that there was some behind-the-scenes manoeuvring to persuade the conference to back the proposal for an information bureau. Wiener had arrived in Amsterdam in August and had probably busied himself in the months before the London conference lobbying individuals and organisations to build up interest in his project. In particular, it is certain that he built up his relationship with Leonard Montefiore, the president of the Anglo-Jewish Association, a relationship that would be vital to the Wiener Library for decades. Wiener perhaps also assembled the beginnings of his collection (while the matter remains in doubt, there is some speculation that Wiener may have taken part of the Büro Wihelmstrasse's collection with him, and that these formed the original core of the Wiener Library's holdings). In any case, when Cohen went to London he had a fully worked-out proposal in his pocket and could be fairly sure that support for it would be forthcoming.

Cohen wrote that the organisation's name, the Jewish Central Information Office, was chosen partly to reflect Wiener's 'wissenschaftlich' approach to his subject, but chiefly 'because we didn't want to make the organisation known immediately as a form of anti-Nazism, out of consideration for the Jews of Germany.'[7]

Cohen wrote that the office began its work on 1 February 1934, and that this should be taken as the foundation date of the JCIO and of the Wiener Library.

To establish the Office on a firm legal footing, a foundation was set up under Dutch law, called Het Centraal Joodse Informatiebureau; this was done through the good offices of a notary, Samuel Teixeira de Mattos. This foundation came into existence on 30 April 1935. Cohen quotes extracts from the documentation which define the aims of the foundation:

> The Foundation aims to distribute information on all matters which relate to the Jewish problem, in particular to Jewish organisations throughout the whole world, and upon request also to non-Jewish organisations, private individuals and in general to everyone for whom, in the judgement of the Board, it is desirable in the furtherance of its stated aim. The Foundation wishes in this way to serve the general interest; it has not been established to further the particular interest of private persons. The Foundation does not seek any financial advantages, it only aims to act informatively with regard to the Jewish problem for the various Jewish organisations and for the world.[8]

This politically neutral-sounding set of aims was later brought into rather sharper focus, as seen in a notarised document from 1939 – when the Office was moving to London :

> The aims of the office are: 1. To collect anti-Semitic materials, namely Nazi propaganda, as well as materials from other sources from the whole world and to convey these to Jewish organisations and other centres in order to combat them. 2. To disseminate information serving as enlightenment in regard to Judaism and as means of combating anti-Semitic tendencies. 3. To collect publications concerned with the Jewish problem and to spread them. In connection with these works, the Institute must treat all questions regarding the spiritual aims of National Socialism.

Wiener was rather charmingly described in this document as 'a first class expert in all questions regarding the Jewish problem', owing 'to his studies, his books and to his year-long (sic) activity . . . He enjoys utmost consideration also beyond Amsterdam and London.'[9]

If the Office was to be at all effective, it was necessary that it not be identified with any faction within the Jewish world: Zionists and non-Zionists must have equal confidence in its product. Consequently Wiener and Cohen attended the 19th Zionist Congress in Lucerne, Switzerland, which ran from 20 August until 4 September 1935. For Wiener, the polemicist against Zionism, it may have been a slightly uncomfortable experience, but the purpose of the visit was to get the JCIO recognised by the various organisations represented at the Congress, and to persuade individuals to co-operate in forming a JCIO board. It is unknown who was approached on this question, but Cohen recalls that Dr Marcus Ehrenpreis of Stockholm was present at the Congress, and that he later approached Wiener with the suggestion that the JCIO prepare a special prayer for the victims of persecution in Germany, which should be distributed to rabbinates of various European countries with the request that it be read out at synagogues on Yom Kippur, the Day of Atonement. Wiener and Cohen agreed to this and a brochure containing the prayer was printed in Amsterdam and duly sent out.

From early 1934 the JCIO acquired a secretary, Elisabeth Leda, who eventually married Louis Wolfgang Bondy, a linguist and journalist who was recruited in 1938. She went with him to London in 1939, but became seriously ill and died in the early stages of the war.

Wiener's *modus operandi* in building up the JCIO has been described to me by C.C. Aronsfeld, his assistant for many years. Wiener wrote to Jewish organisations around the world and also visited them in person, using his considerable diplomatic skills to persuade them of the need to take the JCIO's materials and, where possible, to make subventions in support of its work.

Despite meagre financial resources, the JCIO swung into action rapidly, and by the summer of 1934 had begun issuing a stream of publications detailing various aspects of the unfolding drama in Germany. On 6 July 1934 it published the first issue of a periodical entitled *Reports of the Jewish Central Information Office*. The *Reports* appeared at irregular intervals, sometimes only in German, sometimes in English and French as well.

The first issue appeared only in a German edition. It carried an editorial outlining the intentions of the publishers. An English translation of this manifesto appeared in the first English edition a few months later:

> The Jewish Central Information Office, with its headquarters in Amsterdam, concerns itself neither with politics in general nor with Jewish politics in particular. Nor does it support one form of the state more than another. Its sole function is to collect and disseminate information as to the situation of the Jews in the whole world, but primarily in Germany.
>
> The material handled by this Information Office speaks for itself; its own explanations are limited to the minimum necessary.
>
> It is in no sense the aim of the Jewish Central Information Office to compete with the Intelligence Service or Correspondents of the newspapers. Its thoroughly sifted materials will be drawn from less important though characteristic sources bearing a certain official or party-official stamp.
>
> No true estimate of the position of the Jews in Germany can be formed by

anyone who reads solely the leading and best known German newspapers. The real situation is more faithfully mirrored in the provincial press, in the technical journals and periodicals, as also in books, brochures and pamphlets. The Jewish Central Information Office keeps a vigilant eye on all of these.

In essence the JCIO Reports were summaries of items, ranging from newsclippings to books and pamphlets, as well as exhibition brochures, posters, fly sheets and press releases which the Office collected. Each article carried a number and a system of codes to show in what form the Office's client organisations could be supplied with the items reproduced.

Item number 1 was taken from the Nazi monthly, *Aufklärungs- und Redner-Informationsmaterial der Reichspropagandaleitung* – which had a circulation of 200,000 – and concerns the 'scientific' evidence backing Nazi claims that Jewish populations are 'volksfremde Schmarotzer' (alien parasites), and details the success of the Nazi movement in alerting the international community to the dangers it faces from Jews. The item contains a promise to continue the fight against the Jews without compromise, even should this lead to 'difficulties' ('den einmal begonnenen Kampf kompromisslos weiterzuführen, selbst wenn einstweilen dadurch Schwierigkeiten entstehen').

Among the other topics covered in the first issue were Julius Streicher's notorious 'Ritualmordnummer' of *Der Stürmer*, speeches by Goebbels, Gauleiter Wilhelm Kube and Wilhelm Frick, a report about an exhibition in Berlin called *Deutsches Volk, Deutsche Arbeit* (which portrayed Jewish writers as having 'poisoned' German culture) and several more items.

In addition to compiling and translating the items for the *Reports*, the JCIO issued special in-depth surveys of particular topics. The series was entitled *Records of Contemporary History* and the first-planned was intended to cover Nazi and anti-Semitic literature published since the Nazis came to power. For unknown reasons this never appeared. The first *Record* to appear was entitled *Der Kirchenstreit in Deutschland: Bibel und Rasse* (The Church Conflict in Germany: Bible and Race).

The JCIO also produced a large number of mimeographed reports on various topics, which it distributed to Jewish organisations abroad. A report written later in London makes the claim that during the Amsterdam years the JCIO produced 1,200 of them.

Around the end of 1934 the Office was visited by Neville Laski, president of the Board of Deputies. Laski wrote what was evidently a fairly critical account of the Office's achievements during its first year. In particular, he suggested that its work was too much slanted towards German-interest questions and was failing to provide material of interest or relevance to Jewish communities in other countries. Laski wrote:

If it is permitted to continue it must be adequately financed and if it continues on a basis of adequate finance it ought not to deal entirely with the German aspect of the Jewish question, but with the Jewish question generally. It ought to be possible to establish contact with Jewish organisations in different countries and educate them into sending information to and seeking information from, a central source which shall be wholly authoritative and immediately ready to furnish information much in the same sort of way as the research bureau of a political party.

David Cohen drafted a counter-memo to this, taking up and answering many of Laski's criticisms. At the crux of the matter lay the question of finance. Cohen wrote:

The decision in London in the year 1933 to found an information office has been taken unanimously by the great number of organisations being present. However, only some of the organisations who took this decision proved to be prepared, up to the present, to place the necessary funds at our disposal.

Cohen acknowledged that 'The achievements of the Amsterdam Bureau are . . . quite ready for development' but insisted that nothing was possible as long as the Jewish world at large failed to stump up sufficient money. He concluded that:

This development will not only depend on it what the direction and collaborators of the I.O. are able to do, but for an important part also from the circumstance, what will be made of this valuable instrument by the leading Jewish organisations and private personalities from all countries.[10]

Cohen and Wiener were also quite happy to admit that they needed an English-speaking journalist on the staff. Lack of money meant that they couldn't hire one for another three years.

A typewritten history of the JCIO compiled by Cohen, reveals that he and Wiener held regular unofficial meetings with representatives of the various organisations that supported the JCIO and subscribed to its materials. While Cohen's and Wiener's positions were never questioned, Cohen notes the fact that disagreements arose concerning how the Office went about its work. In particular, the Jewish Colonisation Organisation (ICA) took issue with the JCIO's policy of only disseminating information rather than going on the attack with propaganda of its own. The ICA wanted the Office to become active in publishing material in South America, where it had material interests, and where Nazi propaganda was being successfully disseminated. Wiener and Cohen refused to go along with this line of thought, arguing that they simply did not have the means to generate Goebbels-style propaganda. In what Cohen describes as an 'almost tragic' meeting, the representatives of the ICA board announced that their organisation would have to withdraw its funding. For the JCIO this was a serious matter, because the ICA had up to that point been its largest single donor. It was widely expected that the Office would have to close. However, Wiener had been very active in pursuing sources of funding and had succeeded in creating a support-base which was wide enough to allow for one or two supporters to withdraw without making the work of the Office impossible. At the time of the crisis, the Office was getting support from organisations in Holland, France, Britain, the United States, South America, Sweden, Austria, Palestine, South Africa, Switzerland, Serbia, Poland, Belgium, Luxembourg and Canada. Later it added supporters from Norway, Egypt, New Zealand, Hungary and Denmark. In its first year support came mostly from private individuals (11 organisations subscribed and 40 individuals), but by 1938 some 48 organisations were subscribing and only 36 individuals.

The JCIO also supplied a certain amount of its materials directly to government departments in various countries. Cohen states that he personally, as a citizen of a neutral country, undertook the work of sending these materials out. As head of the Comité, he had regular access to people in the Dutch and British governments. The Office's supporters in other countries also sent materials to their government contacts. While this served to extend support for the work of the Office, there is no evidence that it succeeded in influencing the policy of any European government.

One of the chief characteristics of the JCIO was its secretiveness. This is understandable. Its position in Holland was uncertain: the government tolerated it but was not prepared to incur German displeasure or compromise its neutrality by allowing the exiles excessive freedom. There was also the ongoing danger that the Nazis would take action on their own account to stem the flow of incriminating information to the outside world.

The discretion paid off. The Nazis never moved against the JCIO, even during the occupation of Holland. According to David Cohen, incriminating JCIO correspondence could have been found in any of the capital cities the Germans occupied, yet never was. Even when Cohen's flat was searched in 1940, none of the documentation relating to the Office was discovered.[11]

A drawback of the office's semi-clandestine status was that it made it extremely difficult to attract or appeal for funding. The continuation of the work depended on what Cohen and Wiener could raise through personal contacts. It is a tribute to their initiative and doggedness that the Office survived and that by the time war broke out it numbered 58 major Jewish organisations among its 'clientele'.

The Office began life in a hotel room in Sarphatistraat (no. 18) but, as the workload and staff grew, was moved into a salubrious suburb in the south of the city, to a first-floor flat at no. 14 Jan van Eijkstraat. There was no nameplate on the door to indicate what went on there. The flat below, on the ground floor, was home to the Wiener family.

In a letter written to Stephen Heald (one of Wiener's bosses in the British government during the war), which was undated but probably written in late 1939 or early 1940, Wiener gives some details about how the Institute was financed. He estimated that by 1939 the annual budget was around £6,000, and that this sum was raised in the following way: Holland £2,500; UK £600; US £600; South America £600; France £500; South Africa £400; Switzerland £300; Scandinavia £300; Balkan countries £50; Belgium and Luxembourg £30; Others £100.

NOTES

1. Wir, der Central Verein, stehen auf der Wacht. Wir wissen dem Feinde zu begegnen. Auf einen Redner müssen wir zwei setzen; auf ein Flugblatt müssen wir zehn setzen. Wir müssen überall, wo es not tut, bei den Parteien, bei den Regierungen, sagen, wie die Dinge stehen. Wir müssen unsere deutschen Volksgenossen aufklären über die Gefahren, die hinter dem Nebelvorhang des Winters vielleicht heraufziehen. Wir müssen ihm sagen – und das ist heilige Wahrheit – nicht um des Judentums willen Kampf und Abwehr der völkischen Bewegung, sondern um des deutschen Vaterlandes willen, das unter der Herrschaft eines Wulle, eines Hitler in ein Meer von Blut und Tränen, in den Abgrund sinken würde. Alfred Wiener, 'Der Winter', *Centralverein Zeitung*, Dec. 1925, Vol. IV, No. 49, pp 765–6. Reinhold Wulle was an extreme right-wing politician and founder member of the Deutsch Völkische Freiheitspartei, which was allied to the Nazi Party in the late 1920s. He disapproved of Hitler's 'immoral' political practices.
2. Walter Gyssling, *Propaganda gegen die NSDAP in den Jahren 1929–1933*, unpublished manuscript, dated Oct. 1962. I am very grateful to Dr Arnold Paucker of the Leo Baeck Institute, London, for making this manuscript available to the Wiener Library. For a survey of the CV's defensive actions see his excellent *Der jüdische Abwehrkampf* (Hamburg: Leibniz Verlag, 1969).
3. For Büro Wilhelmstrasse etc. see Hans Reichmann, 'Der drohende Sturm' in Hans Tramer (ed.), *In zwei Welten: Siegfried Moses zum Fünfundsiebzigsten Geburtstag* (Tel Aviv: Verlag Bitaon 1966), pp. 556–77; Arnold Paucker, *Der jüdische Abwehrkampf* (see note 25); and Donald Niewyk, *Socialist, Anti-Semite and Jew* (Baton Rouge: Louisiana State University Press, 1971).
4. Das meiste lieferte die tägliche Kontrolle der Presse. Das 'Büro Wilhelmstrasse' war auf alle Nationalsozialistischen Zeitungen abonniert. Da deren Zahl von 1929–1933 ständig anwuchs und viele nationalsozialistische Wochenblätter im Laufe dieser Jahre in Tageszeitungen umgewandelt wurden, ergab sich daraus allein ein recht bedeutender täglicher Arbeitsfall. Neben der NSDAP-Presse wurden die wichtigsten grossen Berliner Tageszeitungen aller Richtungen von den rechtsextremen Blättern wie der 'Deutschen Zeitung' und der 'Deutschen Tageszeitung' bis zur 'Roten Fahne' der KPD laufend auf Mitteilungen über die nationalsozialistische Bewegung und alles, was mit ihr zusammenhing, kontrolliert, daneben auch einige grosse Provinzzeitungen wie die 'Frankfurter Zeitung' und der 'Dortmunder

Generalanzeiger'. Wenn in einzelnen Ländern Landtagswahlkämpfe stattfanden, wurden für die Zeit ihrer Dauer auch führende Zeitungen des jeweiligen Landes gehalten und gelesen. Ebenso kontrollierte das Büro Wilhelmstrasse laufend alle nationalsozialistischen Zeitschriften und diejenigen der dem Nationalsozialismus verwandten Bewegungen. Einzelstücke anderer Presseerzeugnisse mit wichtigen Artikeln oder Nachrichten bezüglich der NSDAP wurden oft von den Ortsgruppen des CV und von direkten Korrespondenten in der Provinz eingesandt oder beschafft, auch vom Archivar und von Angestellten des CV von ihren Reisen in die Provinz mitgebracht, so dass es kaum eine wesentliche die NSDAP betreffende Publikation gab, die sich nicht im Archiv fand. Natürlich war auch eine im Lauf der Jahre rasch anwachsende Bibliothek vorhanden, die das gesamte nationalsozialistische Schrifttum, aber auch nicht parteigebundene sogenannte völkische Literatur wie etwa die Werke Möller van den Bruck umfasste und dazu eine stattliche Anzahl antinationalsozialistischer Bücher und Broschüren. Sie alle waren ebenfalls durch Herausschreiben wichtiger Zitate und mittels Hinweiszetteln in das Gesamtsystem des Sach- und Personalarchivs eingeordnet. So wurden im Büro Wilhelmstrasse vor allem zahlreiche provokatorische oder sonst bedeutsame Zitate aus Hitlers *Mein Kampf* herausgeschrieben und bei dieser sorgsamen Analyse des Werkes wurden viele Stellen gefunden, die bis dahin kaum beachtet und niemals in der antinationalsozialistischen Propaganda ausgenützt worden waren. Walter Gyssling, *Propaganda gegen die NSDAP in den Jahren 1929–1933*, unpaginated.

5. H. Boas, 'Professor David Cohen Remembered', *Wiener Library Bulletin*, Vol. XXI, No. 4, 1967, pp. 5–7.

6. *Conference for the Relief of German Jewry, Reports and Resolutions* (London: Joint Foreign Committee, 1933).

7. 'weil wir mit Rücksicht auf die deutschen Juden die Organisation nicht von vornherein als eine Art contra-Nazismus bekanntgeben wollten'. From an unpublished document by David Cohen, *Geschichte des Central Jewish Information Office in Amsterdam*, July 1959, Wiener Archive, Wiener Library.

8. Die Stiftung hat den Zweck, Informationen zu erteilen in allen Angelegenheiten, die sich auf das jüdische Problem beziehen, und zwar an jüdische Organisationen in der ganzen Welt, und auf Anfrage auch an nicht-jüdischen Organisationen, Privatpersonen und im allgemeinen an Alle, für die dies laut Urteil des Vorstandes wünschenswert erscheint zur Erreichung des gesetzten Zweckes. Die Stiftung will auf diese Weise dem allgemeinen Interesse dienen; sie ist nicht gegründet im Hinblick auf das besondere Interesse von Privatpersonen. Die Stiftung bezweckt keine finanziellen Vorteile, sie will nur durch ihre Arbeit informativ wirken im Hinblick auf das jüdische Problem für die verschiedenen jüdischen Organisationen und für die Welt. David Cohen, *Geschichte des Central Jewish Information Office*.

9. Draft document, undated but presumed from c. 1939, Wiener Archive, Wiener Library.

10. Undated, presumably draft, memorandum by David Cohen entitled *Tasks and Aims of the Jewish Central Information Office*, Wiener Archive, Wiener Library.

11. 'The Early Days of the Wiener Library', *Wiener Library Bulletin*, Vol. 10, No. 1–2, 1956, p. 16.

CHAPTER SIX

Protocols, Frankfurter Trial, Kristallnacht

ASIDE FROM ITS routine work, the JCIO paid special attention to three major events which took place during these years. The first was the trial in Switzerland of the publishers of an edition of the *Protocols of the Learned Elders of Zion*. The *Protocols* is among the most notorious anti-Semitic slanders of the twentieth century. It was written in Paris in the 1890s by an unknown writer working for the Russian secret police. In form it was a plagiarism of a book by a French writer, Maurice Joly, entitled *Dialogue aux Enfers entre Machiavel et Montesquieu*, which had been published in the 1860s. The *Protocols* purports to contain the protocols of a conference of Jewish leaders from around the world, in which a global conspiracy is revealed, the aim of which is to exploit democratic freedom to enslave or destroy the Gentiles.

The *Protocols* was widely circulated and read in the wake of the First World War, especially in Germany – which was fertile ground for those offering up scapegoats. The Nazi party was quick to exploit the *Protocols* for its own purposes. The book was distributed in the German-speaking world through the Welt-Dienst organisation, based in Erfurt. Welt-Dienst was the brain-child of a retired colonel, Ulrich Fleischhauer. Fleischhauer had been an active anti-Semite most of his life, and had founded the U. Bodung publishing house in 1919. He was a follower of Theodor Fritsch (the editor of one of the most widely circulated editions of the book) and had been a friend of Dietrich Eckart, the writer of *Bolshevism from Moses to Lenin*, who had been closely associated with Hitler in Munich. Fleischhauer had written to Hitler in 1933 offering support and help. He set up a fortnightly periodical, also called *Welt-Dienst*, initially published in three languages, but eventually translated into as many as 18. The organisation also held international congresses, and published a notorious six-volume encyclopedia of anti-Semitica called *Sigilla Veri*. In the pre-war years the Welt-Dienst organisation was one among many private outfits that agitated against the Jewish community. For a time it was subsidised by the Ministry of Propaganda and later by the foreign policy office of the Nazi Party. It led a precarious and shady existence on the periphery of Nazi political life, and was eventually dispensed with, when all such activities were brought under central control.[1]

The JCIO drew attention to the *Welt-Dienst* periodical in the second issue of its *Reports*. A quotation from *Welt-Dienst* makes clear how closely it echoed the *Protocols*:

. . . only a few recognise even now after the splendid victory achieved by Hitler over the infamous Jewish-Bolshevik gentry, so effectively unmasked in the 'Protocols of the Elders of Zion', that the frightful disclosures there made are being strikingly confirmed day by day by the revolutionary and subversive tactics observable in Russia, Mexico and Spain, whose aim is the extermination of the Christian creed and of Christians also.[2]

The Welt-Dienst organisation had close links to the distributors of the *Protocols* in Switzerland. In June 1933 the Swiss fascist organisation, the National Front, distributed copies of the *Protocols* at a meeting in the Berne casino. The League of National Socialist Eidgenossen also distributed anti-Semitic literature at the meeting. The Jewish Community of Berne and the League of Swiss Jewish Communities jointly brought a criminal charge against the League of Swiss National Socialists and 'persons unknown'. The charge alleged that the *Protocols* constituted a falsification and was apt to give 'grave offence', and that other publications caused grave offence and were indecent. At the suggestion of the counsel for one of the plaintiffs, the Berne court decided to call together a committee of experts to advise about the authenticity of the *Protocols*. It nominated its own expert and required each of the other parties to nominate an expert too. A year later in October 1934 the defendants had failed to find their expert. Since the prosecuting side had an array of experts which included Chaim Weizmann, the defence felt itself to be at a disadvantage and requested an adjournment. The trial finally got under way in April 1935.

In the interim, Ulrich von Roll, a member of the National Front, contacted the German Nazi Party directly to appeal for help. The response was to put them in touch with the Welt-Dienst organisation and Fleischhauer. Documentation now housed at the Wiener Library in Tel Aviv makes it clear that Welt-Dienst was supplying more than expertise, and was channelling money from the Nazis to the defence. Eventually, Fleischhauer himself appeared as the expert witness, with a posse of White Russian anti-Semites to back him up and a written opinion comprising some 400 pages of invective. He acknowledged that the *Protocols* was plagiarised from Maurice Joly's *Dialogue aux*

Enfers, published in 1864, but argued that Joly himself was a Jew, and that his book in fact contained the Jewish conspiracy for world domination only in code.

When the trial ended, the court found that the *Protocols* was a plagiarism and were indecent. An appeal was lodged and heard two years later. This confirmed that the *Protocols* was a forgery, but found that it was not indecent – a decision which was exploited by the fascists.

The JCIO was actively involved in supplying the prosecution with materials. Wiener had early developed an interest in the *Protocols*, and the Office was in possession of a comprehensive collection of materials concerning the forgery and its history. Wiener also attended the trials for a time, being accompanied, according to Cohen, by Marcus Ehrenpreis, a witness for the plaintiffs. Wiener wrote an account of the final session of the trial, including a detailed and almost verbatim record of the judgment.[3]

It is possible that it was at this time that Wiener first met James Parkes, another bibliophile and fledgling librarian. Parkes was living in Geneva and involved in projects aiming to improve Jewish–Christian relations. He took a lively interest in the trial and had in his library a rare copy of the *Dialogues aux Enfers*. The Swiss Nazis visited him regularly, posing as students. They later made an attempt on his life and tried to steal the book. Later, when they were both in Britain, Wiener and Parkes corresponded regularly and developed an acquaintance bordering on friendship. In the late 1950s when the Wiener Library and the Parkes Library were both struggling, a plan was evolved to merge them.

The *JCIO Reports* continued throughout the rest of 1934, but stopped with issue No 8, April 1935. It was felt that this form of communication was too time-consuming and expensive and was not achieving its aims. From this time on the Office concentrated on collecting and issuing reports on particular topics.

After the first year or so the publications of the JCIO settled into three basic categories. Firstly there were press releases. These were entitled *Presse-materialien* and were originally intended to be a weekly issue, but in fact were issued irregularly. Secondly, there were a variety of ongoing series of reports on particular topics (issued in English, German and sometimes in French), such as *The Position of the Jews in Germany*. Finally there were special reports on specific issues such as *Bolshevism and Jewry: American Refutations of National Socialist Claims*, and *The Situation in South Africa*.

One of the special topics on which a report was compiled was the economic boycott organised against Jewish businesses – the first nationwide campaign against Jewry organised by the Nazis after the seizure of power. This report was an edited version of issue 5–6 of the *JCIO Reports*. It examined the organisation of the boycott, highlighting the fact that it was called for and implemented not by the German government but solely by the Nazi Party. Among the things brought out is the minutely detailed nature of the planning and information-gathering behind the boycott and the strategy underlying the whole enterprise. The Nazis ostensible justification for the boycott was that it was in retaliation for the campaign of 'Greuelpropaganda' (atrocity propaganda) being propagated by 'world Jewry' against Germany. The Nazi Party administration issued a proclamation on 29 March 1933 stating:

> Now that *the internal enemies of the nation* have been rendered innocuous by the people itself, things are happening which we long expected. The Communist and Marxist criminals and their *Jewish intellectual inciters* who fled to foreign countries. . . are now developing from there an unscrupulous, treasonable campaign of incitement against the German people in general. Now that the lying has been made impossible for them inside Germany they start the same activities which they spread against Germany at the beginning of the war from the capital cities of the former Entente against the young national uprising. *Lies and defamations of atrocious perversity are let loose on the German people.* [4]

The boycott was initially intended to go on indefinitely, but was later restricted to one day in recognition of the damage it would cause to the German economy. It was timed to begin simultaneously in every city, town and village in Germany at 10.00 am on Saturday 1 April. Its astonishing organisational success reflects how the Nazi strategy of building a state within the state had paid off. The boycott was only possible because Nazi presence in all German towns was so well established.

The boycott signalled the beginning of a systematic national movement to expropriate Jewish property and persecute the Jewish population. In this way it served to legitimate the isolated instances of theft and brutality which the Nazis had previously designated 'Einzelaktionen'.

Also in the course of 1934 the JCIO issued *Der Kirchenstreit in Deutschland (Bibel und Rasse) (The Church Conflict in Germany (Bible and Race))*, written by Wiener and edited by Kurt Baschwitz. This reviewed the controversies raging in Germany about the correct way of interpreting the Bible, the developments in the Evangelical Church, the German *Volks* Church and the Christian opposition to the Nazis. In addition it contained a 42-page bibliography covering racial theory and religion. It was issued without any imprint details because, as Wiener explained in an appendix to his essay in the Wiener Library volume edited by Max Beloff, *On the Track of Tyranny*, the Dutch government would not have tolerated such an attack on its powerful eastern neighbour – especially coming from an organisation made up of victims of that neighbour.

The second of the major events which was of particular concern to the JCIO was the trial of David Frankfurter, a young disaffected Jewish medical student who assassinated Wilhelm Gustloff, the leader of the German Nazis in Switzerland. Gustloff had been one of the behind-the-scenes players in the distribution of the *Protocols*. The assassination took place in February 1936, and the trial followed that December. Although the Nazis did their best to make Gustloff into a martyr and use the occasion of his death for further anti-Semitic attacks, timing was against them: preparations for the 1936 Olympics in Berlin were in full swing and any violent excesses would have marred this major propaganda effort. So the Nazi response to the assassination was outraged but muted.

The JCIO took the opportunity presented by the assassination to compile a publication entitled *Dokumentensammlung über die Entrechtung, Ächtung und Vernichtung der Juden* (Collection of Documents on the Deprivation of Rights, Ostracism and Destruction of the Jews). This 254-page compilation was intended to fill in the background to Frankfurter's desperate action by offering a thoroughgoing review of anti-Semitic activities carried out by the Nazis since 1933.

The first section, 'The Fundamental Anti-Semitism of the NSDAP', reprints sections of the Party programme, a selection of quotations from *Mein Kampf* and items from the speeches and writings of the other Nazi leaders including Wilhelm Kube – '. . . Gemisch von Feigheit, Schmutz, Gemeinheit und Niedertracht, von Faulheit, Dummheit und Bosheit, dessen Superlativ Judentum heisst' (. . . That mixture of cowardice, filth, meanness and malice, of idleness, stupidity and wickedness, the epitome of which is Jewry', from an article in *Der Märkische Adler*, 3 June 1934).

The second section reviews the measures taken to bring about the economic and professional destruction of Jewry, while the third deals with ostracism. This section includes a number of press reports of German citizens receiving prison sentences for *Rassenschande*, literally 'race outrage', the Nazi term for Aryans having sexual relations with Jews and other non-Aryans (in the worst of the cases reported, the 'criminal' was condemned to 18 months). In relation to the boycott of Jews, there is this, from the *Frankfurter Zeitung*:

> The Hamburg Senate has decided to remove the Heinrich Heine memorial from the city park because it is an eyesore to many people. It will be stored, as reported, in some shed or other.[5]

The fourth section cites numerous examples of Nazi attacks on the Jewish faith and practice, and on synagogues and teachings. The fifth section deals with the treatment meted out to Jewish servicemen who fought in the First World War and the Jewish fallen, while the sixth section reviews the persecution of Jewish children.

The seventh section is a compilation of press reports of Jewish citizens who have been murdered or have committed suicide since Hitler's rise to power. The compilers freely admit the hopelessness of trying to arrive at accurate figures:

> It is intended only to offer a number of examples which, coming from reliable sources, are typical of their kind, especially in relation to the period in which they occurred (April 1933! – June/July 1934!).[6]

The section consists of a list of 44 documented cases of murder and 71 cases of suicide. It is obvious that this is nothing like a realistic total, but serves to highlight the difficulty of tracing victims of this sort of persecution.

The final section reprints the letter of resignation written by James G. MacDonald, the High Commissioner for Jewish and Other Refugees from Germany, to the League of Nations. MacDonald writes of the 'worsening situation' and 'a fresh wave of repression and persecution of a character not envisaged in 1933' (when he was appointed). He calls, in light of this, for 'a reconsideration by the League of Nations of the entire situation.' He leaves no doubt about the nature of the worsening situation:

> It is being made increasingly difficult for Jews and 'non-Aryans' to sustain life, condemned to segregation within the four corners of the legal and social Ghetto which has now closed upon them. In many parts of the country there is a systematic attempt at starvation of the Jewish populations.[7]

In the context of the period, the *Dokumentensammlung* represents one of the most substantial efforts to collate a systematic account of the bestiality of the new regime. It offered the outside world an early glimpse into the nature of the Third Reich. Yet it is undeniable that the revelations of the book could be dismissed (albeit unfairly) as exaggerated or invalid because they originated from a Jewish political organisation. It is certain, in any case, that the book did not reach a wide enough readership and did little to change the minds of those hostile to the Jewish interest.

A companion volume contained 62 pages of photographic evidence amassed by the JCIO. It was entitled *Photographische Dokumentensammlung über die Entrechtung, Ächtung und Vernichtung der Juden*. The Office had collected photographs since its inception, and had gathered an extraordinary collection of images documenting the persecution of the Jews in the years to 1939. During the war it was not possible to add to these, but from 1945 until the present day the Library has collected a photographic record of both Jewish life before the Nazi take-over, the war and the Holocaust.

The third major event in which the JCIO took a special interest was, of course, the Kristallnacht of November 1938. This allegedly spontaneous outburst of hatred against the Jews was in response to the murder of Ernst vom Rath, the third Secretary at the German embassy in Paris on 7 November. The murderer was Herschel Grynszpan, a desperate 17-year-old Polish Jew, whose parents were in the group of people expelled from Germany and herded into the no-man's land between the borders of Germany and Poland. The background to this was a steady build up of anti-Jewish measures which had been going on since March 1938, when the Germans annexed Austria in the so-called *Anschluss*.

An announcement was made by the Polish government on 6 October that all Polish passports would become invalid by a certain date unless marked with a special stamp, which could only be obtained within Poland. The Nazi regime interpreted this action as meaning that the Reich would be burdened with a large population of Polish Jews that they could not repatriate. Consequently, they announced that 'The Jews of Polish nationality in Germany will therefore, as a measure of precaution, be expelled from the Reich at the shortest possible notice.' As soon as this declaration reached Warsaw, the Germans began their initiative – the first major deportation of Jewish people in the regime's history. Between 15,000 and 17,000 people were rounded up and pushed across the border into Poland. However, in some places, where the Poles had border guards patrolling, this was impossible and the deportees remained stranded in the no-man's land between two nations. The locality where the deportees were subjected to the worst conditions was a town called Zbonzsyn. This is where Grynszpan's parents were trapped and it was their plight that drove him to his murderous act. The German name of this border town was Bentschen, it was the place where Alfred Wiener spent his formative years.

There is evidence to suggest that independently of the Polish passport measures, the Nazis were stepping up their anti-Jewish measures. Concentration camps like Dachau were being expanded and camp uniforms with the Star of David sewn on them were being readied for an influx of Jewish prisoners. In at least some areas, local Gestapo organisations were preparing lists of 'non-Aryans', most of whom were later arrested.

Grynszpan's murder of vom Rath coincided with the annual gathering of the Nazi elite in Munich to celebrate the anniversary of the 1923 attempt to seize power. When vom Rath died, the assassination was made use of to unleash a pogrom. Officially the Nazi position was that they were not ordering reprisals, but would not halt spontaneous expressions of outrage such as destroying shops and burning synagogues.

The pogrom raged for several days. Officially an end was called on 10 November, but this was disregarded in many places. The toll in lives and damage to property was enormous. In an initial report to Goering, it was stated that around 800 shops had been burned and 276 synagogues destroyed. How much of an underestimate this was can be seen from the fact that in Vienna alone around 5,000 businesses were destroyed. The German insurance companies estimated the damage at around 25 million reichsmarks — which threatened to make the pogrom something of an economic own-goal for the Nazis. More than 10,000 Jews were arrested and taken to Dachau in the month following the pogrom, and only slightly fewer to Buchenwald. In the absence of documentary proof it is presumed that a comparable number went to Sachsenhausen. Of these so-called Aktionsjuden (Jews taken in the 'action'), many hundreds were to die within months of arrest. Many were only released once they could prove that they were in possession of the documents that allowed them to emigrate.

The pogrom was followed by a package of measures designed to limit the economic damage and shift the attack on the Jews onto a more systematic footing. The Jewish community was to be be fined one billion reichsmarks (Goebbels had argued for a much higher figure). Other measures were designed to hasten the complete 'Aryanisation' of all Jewish property, to speed up Jewish emigration, to isolate the Jewish community in Germany from the general population and to abolish the only remaining official Jewish representative body.

In the wake of the pogrom, the JCIO gathered information and played its part in informing the world of the deepening crisis. While much of the statistical information in these accounts is preliminary and incomplete, what does emerge from these documents is an impression of the sheer scale of the action.

One document entitled only *The German Pogrom*, gives a fine sense of the controlled, indignant rage which must have permeated the JCIO office at this time:

> The German government deny their intention of establishing for German Jewry special residential quarters and municipal ghettos. Whether or no they actually did establish such quarters, seems however, entirely immaterial.
>
> Now that in towns without number, savage hordes have reduced Jewish dwellings to matchwood,
>
> Now that in a large number of cities, Jewish families have had compulsory notice served to quit on, or shortly after, January 1st,

Now that in various districts of Germany, such Jewish dwellings as have yet been left intact are crowded with families from destroyed houses, or refugees from the country,

Now surely it is bordering on hollow mockery for the German government to declare that they were not indeed intent upon establishing any ghettos.

The document ends:

In the 'Official Journal of German Jurisdiction', *Deutsche Justiz*, published by the Reich Minister of Justice . . . the Supreme Party Judge of the Nazi Party, Herr Buch, writes:

The Jew is not a human being. . .

That in fact he is treated worse than the lowest beast in Germany, has been realised by the civilised world, since 1933 and more especially since the pogrom of November 9–10.[8]

After the events of November 1938 Wiener must have begun to wonder how long he and his Information Office would be safe in Holland. The accelerating pace of events did not leave him guessing for long. The German invasion of Czechoslovakia in the spring of the following year made war appear inevitable. The Dutch government was becoming increasingly nervous about the JCIO's presence as well. When it was found that the historian and journalist, Konrad Heiden, had written his anti-Nazi account of the November Pogrom, *The New Inquisition*, with considerable help from the JCIO and had used their materials, it was felt that matters had gone far enough. Cohen was summoned by the prime minister, Hendrik Colijn, and asked about the Dutch translation of the Heiden book. Cohen answered enthusiastically that Heiden had written it at the JCIO and that they had published the book. This led to Colijn writing to the Office requesting them to stop the publication on the grounds that a particular passage, to which the book's printer had drawn the attention of the authorities, was apt to give offence to the Germans. In Cohen's words:

I felt I could not refuse the request, as the passage which had escaped our attention was, indeed, rather unfortunately worded. But I drew the consequences from this government intervention. If one book could be deemed sufficient to arouse the displeasure of the german Government towards the Netherlands, what was likely to happen if the library of the Jewish Central Information Office was discovered? After consultation with Dr Wiener, to whom the same thought had occurred in view of the approaching war (which he had foreseen), I suggested to my friends in Britain that they take over the Office.[9]

In any case, it was time to move on. Cohen suggested to Wiener that the way forward was for him (Cohen) to contact Neville Laski, the president of the Board of Deputies, with a request that the Board take over the bulk of the collection. Laski wrote back saying that he personally was happy with this, but that he was unwilling to act without consulting Sir Robert Waley Cohen. Eventually Cohen met with Waley Cohen at Woburn house, and the plan was agreed there.[10]

According to an application for compensation for loss of property which Wiener made to the Dutch government in 1951, the intention when he moved to London was to keep the Amsterdam office open permanently:

> It appeared to us that the National Socialists were trying to spread their physical and ideological influence to all countries, but especially the European ones . . . and that in spite of attempts to create a smoke screen they were visibly aiming to bring about a war sooner or later; Prof. Cohen and I therefore thought it advisable to divide the JCIO. In the autumn of 1938 we decided to continue the Amsterdam office on a smaller scale and to start a somewhat larger office in London. At the beginning of September 1939 the preparation of our London office was sufficient to allow us to open.
>
> It had been planned that in my capacity as Director of both offices I should devote a considerable part of my time to the work in London, particularly at the beginning, but that I should also be responsible for the Amsterdam office. My domicile and that of my family was to remain in Amsterdam.
>
> When at the end of August 1939 the outbreak of war between Germany and Great Britain seemed inevitable, I had to come to a vital decision. Was I to restrict myself to conducting the office in neutral Holland, leaving my collaborators who had moved to London and the work there without a Director, or was it my duty to take over the direction in London and to put our collection, so important for psychological warfare, at the disposal of the Allies? My duty and my conscience pointed unequivocally to the latter alternative, and therefore I went to London at the end of August 1939.[11]

From this it seems likely that Wiener intended Amsterdam to be either his permanent home, or perhaps his home until he could return to a liberated Germany. However other and stronger evidence exists, discussed fully below, that Wiener never intended to keep the Amsterdam office open after his departure and was probably not interested in settling permanently in the city at any point.

By the time the JCIO moved to London, it had a staff of 17. Its deputy director was Dr Kurt Zielenziger, like Wiener an old Potsdamer, who was known to him from Berlin days, when he was the city's deputy chief press officer and was an occasional contributor to the *CV Zeitung*. In fact the two were, according to Zielenziger's son, good friends.

Zielenziger was born in 1890, the son of Stadtrat Julius Zielenziger. He studied social sciences at Munich, Berlin and Freiburg iB; graduating 1912. In 1914 he published *Die alten deutschen Kamaralisten. Ein Beitrag zum Problem des Merkantilismus und zur Geschichte der Nationalökonomie*, based on his doctoral thesis.

Zielenziger worked in various chambers of commerce and 'einer grossen Kriegsorganisation', later in industry. Through all this, he was active as a journalist and scholar. In 1919 he became deputy chief of the Berlin Press Office and later the chief. The year 1926 saw the publication of his *Gerhart von Schulze Gaevernitz, eine Darstellung seines Wirkens und seiner Werke*. In the same year he was appointed Political Editor of the *Vossische Zeitung*. He specialised academically in the study of the Jewish contribution to the German economy, which led, in 1930, to his best-known book *Juden in der deutschen Wirtschaft*. He was also a contributor to the *Encyclopedia Judaica* and *Handwörterbuch der Staatswissenschaft*. He left Germany in 1933, taking his family to Paris. It was there that Wiener telephoned him to invite him to Amsterdam. As deputy director of the JCIO he was in charge of its day-to-day running. Profoundly German, Zielenziger had, in the words of his son, 'a certain discipline'. Although fond of travel, he got little opportunity while working with Wiener. He was, like Wiener, a German abroad, in no way able or willing to give up his national identity or characteristics. He was an even poorer linguist than Wiener, and never mastered the language of his adopted homeland.

When Wiener and the bulk of the JCIO materials moved to London, Zielenziger remained behind. According to his son, he tried to get the appropriate travel papers to come to London shortly before the German invasion. This turned out to be problematic because the Nazis had made him stateless. Apparently he had an appointment at the Amsterdam Police Department for 10.00am on Friday 10 May 1940 to get the necessary travel papers – but the Nazi invasion of Holland had begun at 3.00am that morning. Zielenziger and most of the JCIO staff (and also Wiener's wife and children) were stranded in Amsterdam.[12]

Documents in the Wiener Library's eyewitness account series tell a rather different story and are discussed below.

Kurt Baschwitz worked at the JCIO from 1935. Born in 1886 in Offenberg, Baden, Baschwitz had studied political science at Heidelberg, Berlin and Munich, before becoming the editor of the *Hamburger Fremdenblatt*, editor of the *Deutsche Allgemeine Zeitung* and assistant editor-in-chief of the Association of German Newspapers. In 1923 he published *Der Massenwahn: Seine Wirkung und seine Beherrschung* (Mass hysteria: its effects and control), a ground-breaking study which went through numerous editions. He was dismissed from his post at the Newspaper Association in 1933 because of his Jewish origins (Jewish-born, he was a practising Protestant) and fled to Amsterdam. He left the JCIO when offered a job at the Municipal University of Amsterdam, lecturing and writing on journalism. He was dismissed from this post when the Nazis invaded, spent a brief period in Westerbork and the remainder of the war underground. Post-war he resumed his career at the University, eventually becoming Professor of Journalism in 1952. He retired in 1957, continuing an active career as a writer until his death in 1968.

Also on the staff was Olga Bauer de Ginzberg, a language specialist of Russian descent with an aristocratic manner who was married to one of the leading Zionists of Spain, Ignacio Bauer. The Bauers had fled the Spanish Civil War, being unable to support either side because they were staunch royalists on the one hand and Jews on the other. Known to all as Madame Bauer, she read most of the foreign newspapers.

When Wiener was in London in 1938 he recruited two new members of staff. They were C.C. Aronsfeld, who was to have a long and distinguished career with the Wiener Library, and Louis Bondy. When Wiener recruited Aronsfeld in 1938, the young man was sent to W.G.J. Knop at Union Time Ltd. (Aronsfeld later reported in the Wiener Library Bulletin that he believed Union Time had been established by Robert Waley Cohen, the second-in-command at the Shell group of companies). Knop kitted Aronsfeld out with accreditation as a journalist researching issues relating to oil and rubber, and got him a four-week visa to Holland. Aronsfeld's routine was to spend a month in Holland, then get a series of two-week extensions to his visa, until the authorities hinted it was time to go back home. He would then return to London and apply for a fresh visa, and so it would go on.[13]

Wiener saw in Aronsfeld an intelligent and committed young man, but appears to have favoured the more glamorous Louis Bondy. Bondy was the son of a well-known journalist who had been living in Paris as second correspondent for the German newspaper *Deutsche Allgemeine Zeitung*. He was sacked from this paper after 1933 and found life in Paris increasingly difficult, so he left for Spain where work permits were unnecessary. There he translated the official bulletin of the League of Nations from German into French and scraped a living doing a variety of odd jobs including barman and beach photographer at the resort of Tossa del Mar. He came to London late in 1936. In 1964 he recalled how he met Wiener and what impression he made upon the young man:

> My first contact with him was when he phoned me in London during the winter of 1937/8 in reply to my application for a job at the Jewish Central Information Office in Amsterdam. Half an hour later I arrived at Ford's

Hotel, Manchester Street where Dr Wiener usually stayed and where he took up residence after the transfer of the office to London.

We shook hands and exchanged a few words. Then, quite abruptly, Dr Wiener bent down, lifted a huge parcel which had stood on a pile near him, asked me to hold it, heaped a second parcel of considerable weight on top of it, took a third one into his own hands and propelled me out into the street. He hailed a taxi, bundled me into it, followed, slammed the door and off we went on the way to the General Post Office. Only then did he explain to me that he had to post these packets urgently, was none too familiar with the required procedure and asked me – nay ordered me – to look after the dispatch. What characterises the unique qualities of Dr Wiener more than anything was the fact that I did not for one single moment resent being thus made use of by a complete stranger; on the contrary, I felt delighted at being drawn so quickly into the orbit of that delightful personality.

It was this charm and charismatic quality that allowed Wiener to demand so much of those who joined him at the JCIO. Bondy recalled:

Quite often I felt like grumbling when Wiener, who never spared himself, seemed to ask the impossible of his staff and on occasions made us work until midnight when an urgent task had to be completed. But soon I learned to respect and to admire his absolute dedication to the work he rightly considered of such tremendous importance. . .

And Bondy's devotion was further evidenced when romance came into his life:

When I married my first wife, Lisa, whom I had met at the JCIO and whom I was to lose so soon afterwards, we chose the 16th of March, 1939, as our wedding day, because it was Dr Wiener's birthday. And Alfred Wiener was my best man.[14]

Wiener's private secretary was Anneliese Bielschowsky, who worked for him from 1934 until he departed for England in 1939. She continued at the JCIO until the German invasion in the following May.

Also on the staff were Bernhard Krieg, the bookkeeper and cashier; Joseph Bettelheim, the office manager; Miss S. Delden and James Cohen, Krieg's assistants; Miss E. Mendelson, a typist; Miss C. Asser, Mrs Veltman and Miss N. Kohn who worked in the archives; Miss Leda, assistant secretary; Mrs Friedländer, a typist and Philipp Hart, the office boy.

By the time the Dutch phase of its existence was drawing to a close, the JCIO's collection consisted of around 8,000 books and pamphlets and many thousands of press cuttings.

Information about events in Amsterdam after Wiener's departure comes to us in a short report written by Joseph Bettelheim for the Wiener Library eye-witness accounts entitled *Die letzten Tage des Jewish Information Büros*. This is sufficiently important to quote in full:

> After people in Amsterdam were convinced that, sooner or later, war was inevitable, all the important materials of the Office were sent to London. It was decided to keep only a small library back in order to keep the service going as long as possible. At the beginning of April Prof. Cohen summoned the staff to a meeting and informed them that, to his regret, it would not be possible to keep the Office open in view of the threat of war. Present at the meeting were: Frl Bilschofkie [Bielschowsky], Frau Friedlaender, Frl Delden, Herr Dr Zielenziger, Herr Krieg, and Bettelheim. Since Dr Z., as the Director, said nothing after the Professor's announcement, Bettelheim declared that he thought he spoke for everyone when he said that everyone would do their duty up to the very last minute. Professor Cohen expressed his thanks and said he would do his utmost to secure the material basis for their work.
>
> The 10th of May 1940
>
> Herr Dr Z., Herr Krieg, and Bettelheim had agreed that on the day of the invasion they would meet at the Office as early as possible in order to discuss what should be done.
>
> Dr Z. and Herr Krieg arrived together at 5am and we began immediately to look over and destroy all the sensitive material which remained. Dr Z., who had completely lost his head, had to be told by Bettelheim that it would be better if he went home, because in his condition nothing would be achieved. It must also be mentioned that it was forbidden for all Germans, including the refugees to be out on the streets. Later Prof C. organised permits. It also emerged on this day that Dr Z. had kept the visas sent by Dr Wiener for the staff to go to London in his desk for weeks, without informing any of them of this. A bitter argument ensued in the course of which Dr Z. declared that he had had no interest in going to London. It also emerged that Herr Krieg had no means to pay the salaries. After a discussion with Prof Cohen, the latter said he would take care of it, which indeed he did after some days. On 13 May Bettelheim had to go to Prof C. to receive certain sums of money; in the course of this Prof C. suggested to B. that he, B., could if he wanted, still get to England that day, because in the course of the day a ship[15] was sailing. In reply to the question why he himself didn't go Prof C. announced that he had been appointed by the Germans to the leadership of the Judenrat and couldn't leave. B. also declined. Later it became known that the ship was bombarded by the Germans.
>
> We now had to work out what else we should do. It was decided to close

the office for a few days to await developments. The situation was very unpleasant for B., since he was living in the same building and feared being picked up by the Gestapo, because we had been referred to a few times in the Schwarze Korps, but we had presumably been forgotten about.

At the beginning of July, after discussions with Prof C. and Herr Krieg, B. was given the task of dismantling the Office. Herr de Hahn, of the Comité was instructed to sell off the furniture, stoves, floor coverings and so on, and to get as much for them as possible. Staff were also permitted to take things for themselves. B. made use of this, since he had to look for a new apartment. Since there was no motorised transport available, everything had to be removed in small hand-carts. B., who had found a new apartment, which had a large store-room, could accommodate everything that remained behind. Among these things were the entire archive of the Jewish Press Committee, the remainder of our Library, all the wood from the frames, and all the light-fittings. One day Prof C. summoned B. and told him that Snoek, the porter of the Comité, knew of the store-room where everything could be housed securely. This store-room was in the Brauersgracht, I cannot recall the house number. Dr Z., Herr K. and B. went there a few days later to look for any further material that might be dangerous and destroy it. One day Snoek went to Prof C. and told him the store-room was no longer safe, and suggested destroying everything there. Prof C. called for B. and told him about this. B. went to the Brauersgracht and discovered that everything had already been removed. Later it turned out that everything had been sold as scrap paper by Snoek.[16]

When Alfred Wiener received this report in June 1955, he made notes which he attached to the report (in fact his notes are about twice as long as the document itself!). In these he confirms all the significant details of Bettelheim's report, such as Zielenziger's tendency to panic in difficult circumstances and, above all, that Wiener secured visas for the staff of the JCIO to go to Britain and that Zielenziger deprived people of their chance to escape by hiding the documents in his desk until they were useless. Wiener further characterises Zielenziger as given to doing things in circuitous and even secretive ways. But he stresses the numerous strengths of his character, which made Zielenziger an appropriate second-in-command at the JCIO.

Wiener also detailed the plans he and Cohen arrived at in the wake of the decision to move the main JCIO office to London. He claimed that it was never his intention to keep the Amsterdam office open indefinitely, but to wind it down gradually and then close it. He also wrote that Zielenziger was not transferred to London, partly because he owned property in Amsterdam and had his family there, but also because his poor language skills made him unsuitable for working in London.

Wiéner added the important detail that his and Cohen's plan to shut down the Amsterdam office by stages was opposed steadfastly by Zielenziger: 'Es war ersichtlich sein Bestreben, und zwar ein keinesfalls zurechtfertigendes, trotz allem ein Sonderbüro neben dem in London, in Amsterdam bestehen zu lassen.' (It was plainly his endeavour to maintain a special office in Amsterdam despite everything, although this was quite unfeasible). He described the continuance of the Amsterdam office as 'totally unnecessary' and as an impossible financial burden. Wiener admitted that the Amsterdam office found a renewed usefulness with the outbreak of war, as a conduit for London-bound materials. But he added that he went to Holland in late February 1940, staying until 10 March, specifically to bring about the winding up or at least partial winding up of the office. Again he met with fierce opposition from Zielenziger. The whole issue was resolved in dramatic fashion with the German invasion – which guaranteed that Wiener's wish that the office close be fulfilled, though hardly under circumstances he could have approved of.

Wiener's document also takes up the matter of Zielenziger hiding the travel documents:

> I cannot remember the details, especially since the correspondence is either no longer available or has been mislaid. However, I know full well that long before the German invasion I took steps to secure documents to allow my colleagues to move to London. These measures were furthered by the fact that eight or ten days (or even longer) [earlier] an Englishman known to us who had the relevant connections and who had worked with us in London from the beginning, came to me and told me that I would shortly receive visas for my colleagues in Holland and also for my family. He would like to recommend that they all come to London. That was a warning from a significant quarter. I presume that I immediately took urgent steps with Dr Z. or elsewhere, to which Herr B. refers. For the sake of my family I sent a telegram to Lord Chichester, the Press Attaché at the British embassy at the Hague, who was known to me, but it apparently never reached him. My family had already been instructed several weeks earlier that British visas had been sent to them in the usual manner.

The Bettelheim-Wiener account of Zielenziger's actions in the last days of the JCIO has been commented on by his son, Eric Zielenziger. Mr Zielenziger points out that while:

> Jo Bettelheim was a trusted member of the staff . . . Bettelheim's report is very subjective: I knew him well and was friendly with him . . . My father was nervous, so were we all when the Germans marched in. So was everybody else! My father did NOT lose his head. In fact he kept his cool and

when the fight was over, Prof Cohen suggested he seek asylum for a few days at another address, just in case the Gestapo would appear for him! . . . The idea that my father kept travel documents in his desk is totally absurd. When Wiener signalled us to get travel papers we acted at once. As he says himself he did not know how the finances would work out and then he says that a knowledgeable person signalled him to get going and bring his 'folks' to London. My father was a loyal soldier. He respected Wiener for his talents and subordinated himself to his older 'Landsman'. That he engaged in 'Geheimnis krämereien' is absurd . . . My father never resisted a move to London. He knew some English and reaching England was the fondest dream of his life.[18]

The full truth of what happened at the JCIO in its last days may never be known. What is certain is that both Zielenziger and Krieg were robbed of their lives in Belsen under circumstances of unimaginable horror. Whether Zielenziger or anyone else could have saved them can now only be a matter for fruitless speculation.

NOTES

1. For Weltdienst and the *Protocols*, see Norman Cohn, *Warrant for Genocide* (London: Eyre and Spottiswoode, 1967).
2. 'World-Service (An International anti-Semitic Correspondence)', *Reports of the Jewish Central Information Office*, English edition, No. 2, Sept. 1934, p. 1.
3. See, JCIO, *Der Berner Prozess um die 'Protokolle der Weisen von Zion', 14. Verhandlungstag, Dienstag der 14 Mai 1935, nachmittags* (Amsterdam: JCIO, nd – a mimeographed report).
4. *Reports of the Jewish Central Information Office*, English Edition No. 5–6, Nov.–Dec. 1934, Amsterdam.
5. Der hamburgische Senat hat beschlossen das Heinrich Heine-Denkmal, weil es vielen ein Dorn im Auge sei aus dem Stadtpark zu entfernen und, wie mitgeteilt wurde, in irgend einem Schuppen zu lagern. *Dokumentensammlung über die Entrechtung, Ächtung und Vernichtung der Juden* (Amsterdam: JCIO, 1936) p. 139.
6. Es soll nur eine Anzahl von Fällen aufgezählt werden, die, aus sicheren Quellen belegbar, in ihrer Art und besonders in ihrem zeitlichen Auftreten (April 1933! – Juni/Juli 1934!) typisch sind. *Dokumentensammlung*, p. 205.
7. The original appeared as James Grover MacDonald, 'Letter of Resignation addressed to the Secretary General of the League of Nations', New York, *New York Times*, 1935, and the quotation is taken from this.
8. All the quotations are from *The German Pogrom: November 1938* (Amsterdam: JCIO, 1938), unpaginated.
9. 'The Early Days of the Wiener Library', *Wiener Library Bulletin*, Vol. 10 No. 1–2, 1956, p. 16.
10. Neville Laski was from a prominent Jewish family, and a member of the elite Cousinhood of Anglo-Jewry, which was losing its grip on power during the war years. He served as President of the Board of Deputies, and Vice-President of the Anglo Jewish Association. Robert Waley Cohen was also a leading member of the Cousinhood. He was the second-in-command at the

Shell group, president of the United Synagogue, and noted for his long-running feud with the Chief Rabbi, J.H. Hertz, about which of them had priority in the community.

11. Translation of a letter from Wiener to the Dutch Minister of Finance dated 17.12.1950, concerning his claim for damages, Wiener Archive, Wiener Library.

12. I am grateful to Mr Eric Zielenziger of Great Neck, NY for information about his father, Kurt Zielenziger.

13. 'They Warned Britain', *Wiener Library Bulletin*, 1964,Vol. XVIII, No. 1, p. 6.

14. Letter from Louis Bondy to C.C. Aronsfeld dated 18.2.1964, Wiener Archive, Wiener Library.

15. A marginal note indicates that the name of the ship was the *Bolivar*.

16. Als man in Amsterdam überzeugt war, das über kurz oder lang der Krieg unausbleiblich sei, wurde alles wichtige Material des Büros nach London versandt. Beschlossen wurde, nur eine kleine Bibliothek zurück zu behalten um so lang wie möglich den Betrieb aufrecht zu erhalten. Anfang April 1940 rief Herr Prof. Cohen das Personal zu einer Besprechung und teilte mit, das es ihm zu seinem Bedauern nicht möglich sei, angesichts der drohenden Kriegsgefahr den Betrieb aufrecht zu erhalten. Anwesend waren: Frl. Bilschofskie [Bielschowsky], Frau Friedländer, Frl. Delden, Herr Dr. Zielenziger, Herr Krieg und Bettelheim. Da nach der Erklärung des Prof. C. Dr. Z. als Leiter nichts erwiderte, erklärte Bettelheim: er glaube im Namen aller die Versicherung abgeben zu können, dass man bis zur letzten Stunde seine Pflicht erfüllen werde. Professor Cohen bedankte sich und teilte noch mit, das er alles mögliche tun werde um allen eine materielle Grundlage zu schaffen. Der 10 Mai 1940

Herr Dr. Z., Herr Krieg und Bettelheim wurden sich darüber einig, am Tage des Einmarsches so früh wie möglich im Büro zu erscheinen um zu besprechen was zu tun sei.

Dr. Z. und Herr Krieg kamen zusammen um 5 Uhr früh und begann man sofort alles vertrauliches Material, welches noch vorhanden war, zu sichten und zu vernichten. Dr. Z., der den Kopf vollkommen verloren hatte, musste sich von Bettelheim sagen lassen, es wäre besser wenn er nach Hause ginge, denn auf dieser Weise käme man nicht weiter. Dabei muss noch erwähnt werden, dass allen Deutschen, also auch den Flüchtlingen das Betreten der Strasse verboten war. Später sorgte Prof. C. für Passierscheine. An diesem Tage wurde auch bekannt, das Dr. Z. die von Dr. Wiener gesandten Unterlagen, um das Personal nach London zu bekommen, seit Wochen in seinem Schreibtisch liegen lies, ohne die Betroffenen davon in Kenntnis zu setzen. Es folgte eine scharfe Auseinandersetzung, wobei Dr. Z. erklärte, er hätte keine Interesse nach London zu gehen. Es wurde nunmehr auch bekannt, das Herr Krieg keine Mittel hatte, um die Gehälter aus zu bezahlen. Nach Rücksprache mit Prof. C. erklärte dieser, er würde dafür sorgen, was auch in einigen Tagen geschah. Am 13 Mai musste Bettelheim zu Prof. C. kommen, um einige Beträge zu empfangen, dabei machte Prof. C. B. den Vorschlag: er, B. könne wenn er wolle heute noch nach England gehen, da im Laufe des Tages noch ein Schiff ging. Auf die Gegenfrage warum er nicht selbst ginge, erklärte Prof. C. er sei nunmehr von den Deutschen zum Vorsitzenden des Judenrates bestimmt und könne nicht mehr fort. Auch B. lehnte ab. Später wurde bekannt, das dieses Schiff von den Deutschen bombardiert wurde.

Wir mussten uns nun klar werden, was weiter zu geschehen habe. Es wurde beschlossen, erst einige Tage zu schliessen, um die weitere Entwicklung abzuwarten. Für B. war die Situation nicht mehr angenehm, da er doch im Hause seine Wohnung hatte und befürchten musste von der Gestapo geholt zu werden, nachdem wir einige Male im 'Schwarzem Korps' zitiert wurden, aber scheinbar hatte man uns vergessen.

Nach Rücksprache mit Dr. Z. und Herrn Krieg bekam B. den Auftrag Beginn Juli mit der Auflösung zu beginnen. Herr de Hahn vom Comité wurde beauftragt, verschiedenes wie Möbel, Öfen, Bodenbelag u.a. zu verkaufen und zu sehen, so viel wie möglich dafür zu erhalten. Es wurde auch dem Personal gestattet, einiges für sich zu nehmen. B., der sich nun eine Wohnung suchen musste, machte davon Gebrauch. Da man keine Transport-Autos bekommen konnte, musste alles mit kleinen Handkarren weggebracht werden. B., der inzwischen eine Wohnung fand, konnte, da sich dort ein grosser Lagerraum befand, alles was noch vorhanden war, unterbringen. Darunter waren: das ganze Archief der Joodsen Pers. Kom.: der Rest unserer Bibliothek, das ganze Holz der Stellagen und alle Beleuchtungs-körper. Eines Tages lies Prof. C. B. zu sich kommen und teilte mit, das Snoek, der Portier des Comites, einen Lagerraum wusste, wo man alles sicher unterbringen konnte. Dieser Lagerraum befand sich in der Brauersgracht, die Nummer ist mir nicht mehr in Erinnerung. Dr. Z., Herr. Kr. und B. gingen einige Tage später dorthin um nochmals alles eventuell gefährliche auszusuchen und zu vernichten. Eines Tages kam Snoek zu Prof. C. und sagte der Lagerraum wäre nicht mehr sicher und er [schlug] vor, alles zu vernichten. Prof. C. lies B. kommen und erzählte ihm dies. B. ging zur Brauersgracht und musste feststellen, das schon alles abgeholt war und wie sich später herrausstellte ist obiges Material von Snoek als Alt Papier verkauft worden. Josef Bettelheim, 'Die letzten Tage des Jewish Informations Büros', unpublished document No. PIIIi 110a in the Wiener Library's eyewitness account collection.

17. Ich kann mich der Einzelheiten nicht mehr entsinnen, zumal die Korrespondenz entweder nicht mehr vorhanden oder im Augenblick nicht aufzufinden ist. Ich weiss aber genau, dass ich Schritte weit vor dem Einfall der Deutschen unternommen habe, um Unterlagen für eine Übersiedlung der Mittarbeiter nach London zu gewinnen. Diese Schritte wurden dadurch verstärkt, dass etwa 8–10 Tage, wenn nicht etwas länger, ein uns bekannter Engländer der die entsprechenden Verbindungen besass und mit uns von Anfang an in London zusammen gearbeitet hatte, bei mir erschien und mitteilte, ich würde für meine Mitarbeiter in Holland und auch für meine Familie sofort die nötigen Visas erhalten. Er möchte anraten, diese alle nach London kommen zu lassen. Das war natürlich eine Warnung aus erster Quelle. Ich vermute, dass ich damals sofort dringende Schritte bei Dr. Z. oder sonstwo noch einmal unternommen habe, auf die möglicherweise Herr B. anspielt. Meiner Familie wegen sandte ich den mir bekannten Presse-Attache der englischen Botschaft im Haag, Lord Chichester, ein Telegramm, das ihn ersichtlich niemals erreicht hat, Meine Familie war schon einige Wochen vorher unterrichtet worden, dass ihr auf gewöhnlichem Wege englische Visa gewährt worden sind. Alfred Wiener, notes attached to Josef Bettelheim's eyewitness account cited in note 16. Wiener's document is eyewitness document PIIIi 110b.

18. Personal communication to the author.

CHAPTER SEVEN

The War Years

LONDON

IN THE HISTORY of the Wiener Library, a certain amount of confusion surrounds its name. Since its founding, it has had three names: the Jewish Central Information Office, the Wiener Library and, most recently, the Institute of Contemporary History and Wiener Library. The assumption of the last name was a clear decision and a matter of policy. The adoption of the name 'Wiener Library', however, was more accidental. Officially, the name continued in London as in Amsterdam. However most of the organisations and departments making use of its resources preferred to call it Dr Wiener's Library and eventually this became simply Wiener Library. The name was officially changed to The Wiener Library after the war, in the course of sorting out the tangled legal status of the Library. For the sake of convenience, I will refer to it as the Wiener Library from the time of its arrival in London.

The story of the Library's move to London has been told in an interview given by the late Louis Bondy to former deputy librarian Tony Wells from which several interesting details emerge:

Q: At what point did either Wiener or the British Government decide that it was time to start shipping material to Britain?

A: Well, after March 1938, I think, we felt that Holland was an extremely unsafe place. Both in England and in Holland one anticipated war. There was beginning the sandbagging of public buildings in London and in Amsterdam people thought they might be able to maintain neutrality but it was very uncertain and unsafe and there was even in Holland a beginning Nazi movement with Mussert in Utrecht and so on, becoming quite menacing. So that then we decided that we wanted to go to England, because in case of war we knew we could be of more use here. And we certainly would be much safer.

Q: And was the feeling mutual? I mean, was the British Government also anxious to make sure that the Information Office should be saved?

A: Well, I don't think so. I think the original impulse came from us and once Wiener and I were the first here in London, – I was actually a bit before Wiener and started looking around for premises – and then Wiener came over after . . . the estate agents had found us this particular first floor in 19 Manchester Square, where we were very happy. Wiener immediately agreed that it was an ideal place, and it proved to be that . . .

Q: There's always been a story which some say is a legend, that the Library or the files were brought over by a British naval destroyer.

A: No, that is certainly not the fact. Actually, it fell to me, and it was one of the more disagreeable tasks, to clear all the material which arrived here in the docks, somewhere between Tower Bridge and London Bridge, in one of the big warehouses, and that's where we cleared it from and brought it to our premises . . . the transfer of the actual material was just an ordinary shipping arrangement and everything arrived safely and it was a terrible job getting it out, and getting it all into our premises but that was one of the main jobs we had at the time.[1]

The immediate priority was forging contacts with individuals and organisations that could help the Library continue its work and to build bridges with the government. The Library was of course known in London, having in a sense been conceived there. Undoubtedly there was goodwill towards it and a willingness to see it succeed. Wiener contacted Leonard Montefiore and the two men rapidly established a rapport which in time built up into something like a friendship. Montefiore acted as Wiener's guide round the labyrinth of Anglo Jewish organisations and committees.

Among the people they contacted early on were the Labour MP George Russell Strauss: A.G. Brotman, secretary of the Board of Deputies of British Jews: Sidney Salomon, the chairman of the Jewish Defence Committee: Leonard Stein, president of the Anglo-Jewish Association and the journalist and Independent MP Vernon Bartlett, who had acted as the London director of the League of Nations from 1922–32. Wiener also contacted his old friend Chief Rabbi Joseph Hertz.

The result of these contacts was to secure the immediate future by obtaining from the Jewish Board of Deputies a grant of £1,200 per annum. This gave Wiener the time he needed to establish the Library's reputation and usefulness and cast around for further funds.

Wiener rapidly made contact with the British government, specifically with the Foreign Publicity Department of the Foreign Office. The original contact had probably been arranged by Montefiore. In 1938 when Wiener first visited London, Montefiore had introduced him to Stephen A. Heald, head of

Information Services at Chatham House. Heald later wrote to Wiener with an account of that meeting:

> You described to me the contents of that unique library . . . and explained that the purpose of your visit was to make known the existence of this material to those who might be able to use it, and to examine the possibility of moving most of it to London before it was too late to get it away from Amsterdam.[2]

Heald was clearly impressed at what he learned about the Library's activities. As was his habit, Wiener followed up the introduction by sending Heald a number of letters with offers of materials, many of which Heald took up. By the time Wiener was setting up the Library in London, Heald had moved on to the Foreign Office and was able to furnish further introductions. The result was that in January 1940, the Library received its first payment from the British government of £100 for services rendered and the following month regular payments began. These were made:

> . . . in consideration of the Institute supplying material and services to all Government Departments and agencies nominated by the M. of I. (Ministry of Information), including the BBC, to the full extent of the Institute's resources, and giving priority to such work over any work done for private individuals.

The history of how the government subsidised the Library was summarised in this same document:

> Early in 1940, Dr Wiener represented that funds were running short and that it was unreasonable to expect his original private sources to go on financing him when HMG was reaping most of the benefit, free of charge. It was therefore agreed to pay him, as from February 1st 1940. . . a sum of £250 per month for three months. This subsidy was paid through the MoI, other departments contributing. It was revised at intervals (especially in connection with payments to Dr Wiener himself consequent on his departure for America in July [actually, it was August] 1940) but never exceeded £260 (of which only £180 went to the London office) until 1 August 1942 when, consequent on the decrease of grants from private sources, it was increased to £500 (£300 being for London). Responsibility for paying the London office was on 1st October 1942 transferred to PWE as the main user, and the system of collecting contributions from other departments discontinued.

The same memo reveals the private funding the Library enjoyed:

In February 1940 the Library was receiving a grant at the rate of £1200pa
from the Jewish Board of Deputies. In 1942 this was at the rate of £1372pa,
£414 being received from other sources outside HMG (including £200 from
Polish Government funds, £100 from a donor on the Board of Unilever and
£50 from the Board of Deputies of S African Jews. From 1st August 1942
the grant from the British Board of Deputies was reduced to £300pa; the
other payments were continued.[3]

Interestingly, Wiener does not mention these facts in a long letter he wrote to
Cohen on 4 January 1940, updating him on developments in London. He only
writes of how depressed he is about the financial burden Cohen is carrying on
behalf of the Library (by guaranteeing loans and so forth), and hints that he has
reason to believe that their joint work will not be wasted. He reports that the
Board of Deputies has just made over a further payment of £250 to bridge the
gap until the Library is established on a sound financial footing. He takes
encouragement from the fact that the Board has approached him concerning its
wish that Dr Gustav Warburg and the archive he had assembled at its Press
and Information Office should leave it and join the Library and he assumes that
it must be willing to pay for him to come.

The reason for the interest shown by government departments was simple:
in its preparations for war against the Nazis, the British government had
neglected to gather background material on the enemy and found itself lacking
even quite basic information about the Nazi leaders, military commanders and
institutions. There was also very little material on which to base propaganda
for use inside Germany. In Bondy's words:

We had an obvious role to play because we constituted the only collection of
material of a very far-reaching and detailed nature on the Nazis since 1933
and even before, that existed in Britain. There was nothing of that kind at all
available here.[4]

On the other hand, exploiting this unique material was problematic. The
fact that the JCIO was a specifically Jewish institution, set up on the orders of
a Jewish-organised conference and interested primarily in documenting the
Nazi attack on Jewry gave rise to potential conflicts of interest. The JCIO
might be expected to wish to publicise the persecution and suffering of
Europe's Jews – and this was in stark contrast with the policy of the government. The government's need was to gain access to the Library's resources
while limiting any of the activities of the Library which might be seen to clash
with its policies. This gave rise to tensions that were never properly resolved.
In documents preserved in the Public Record Office, there are countless

instances of government officials expressing suspicion and outright hostility towards the Library. Against this, the Library itself was unquestioningly loyal to the British government and its aims.

To understand the Library's work during the war years, it is necessary to enter the tangled jungle of departments and ministries responsible for overseas propaganda and subversion.

During the First World War propaganda had been in the hands of a department known as Crewe House, from its address. For ten years after 1918, the government carried out no overseas propaganda or subversion. Then the Travel and Industrial Development Association was set up to propagandize on behalf of British industry. In 1934 the British Council was set up to publicise the British way of life in general. From 1938 the BBC entered the field, broadcasting in foreign languages. In that same year the former head of the Foreign Office, Sir Robert Vansittart, produced a forthright report arguing the need for extended foreign propaganda. This was substantially rejected because it clashed with the government's policy of appeasement. Nevertheless, with the Munich crisis of September 1938, the issue came back on the agenda, with many arguing that any forthcoming war with Germany would be to a greater or lesser extent a war of ideas, with good opportunities to drive an ideological wedge between the people and their Führer. During the autumn of 1938 the newly set up Ministry of Information devised plans for foreign propaganda, and these outraged the Foreign Office, which argued that this was their territory.

Eventually, Neville Chamberlain, the prime minister, invited a Canadian propaganda expert, Sir Campbell Stuart, to set up a propaganda department in secret. Campbell went ahead only to be told after Chamberlain's meeting with Hitler in Munich ('Peace in our time'), that he should dismantle his embryonic department. By the spring of 1939 he was being told once more to build the department up, because it looked as though Hitler wanted war after all.

Stuart's department became known as EH – the initials of Electra House on the Strand where the department was based. In the event of war, it was decided to move department EH out of London to Woburn Abbey. However, for security reasons, its precise location was kept secret and so it gloried in the name of 'a certain department in the country.'

In 1940, when Churchill became prime minister, he decided to follow a more aggressive propaganda line. He ordered the setting up of a Special Operations Executive 'to co-ordinate all action by way of subversion and sabotage against the enemy overseas.' This was divided into SO1 (secret propaganda) and SO2 (sabotage). The two sections reported to the Minister of Economic Warfare.

This left the propaganda effort split: open propaganda was in the hands of department EH, reporting to the Ministry of Information, while secret propaganda was carried out by SO1, answering to the Minister of Economic Warfare. The confusion was increased even further by the fact that the Foreign Office got involved – because its Political Intelligence Department (PID) served as cover for the work of SO1.

Obviously this was a chaotic and thoroughly unsatisfactory situation, as was recognised by all concerned. Yet no one was able to resolve the problem: it turned into a lasting and rather absurd power struggle between two ministers, with Churchill and his aides reluctant to intervene. In 1941 Churchill tried to break the deadlock by replacing the Minister of Information and creating a three-man committee to support the work of the three ministers involved. This committee recommended the creation of a Political Warfare Executive (PWE) comprising sections of the BBC, the Ministry of Information and SO1. This plan was vigorously undermined by the head of Special Operations, but eventually propaganda and subversion was run under a single policy, albeit by two organisations: the PWE and SOE. These partners in lying and deception managed to get through the rest of the war without stepping on each other's toes too much. But achieving this had taken the British government the first two years of the war.

With the entry of the Americans into the war in 1942, intelligence, subversion and propaganda had to be co-ordinated among an even larger group of agencies. This had little effect on the Library, except that a further agency, PWI (Psychological Warfare Intelligence), entered the picture. A man with a lot to say about Wiener and the Library was the Oxford academic Michael Balfour, the Deputy Chief of PWD (Psychological Warfare Division), the agency running PWI. The Library's main contact at PWI was a former school teacher, Dr Thomas K. Derry.[5]

Like the government, the Anglo-Jewish community was not really ready for war with the Nazis. In brief, the community was living through a period of great change, which saw power being wrested from the old order of the Cousinhood, the elite of long-established wealthy families accustomed to having everything their own way. Those doing the wresting consisted of a newer elite of more recent immigrants. It was 'a contest between the old community and the new, between East and West'. In this contest, as one writer has observed, 'the ideological content of the struggles was of limited importance; it was the jockeying for position which was crucial.' Throughout most of the war, Anglo-Jewry was distracted to some extent from the task of helping Hitler's victims. The thing distracting them was the clash of egos. Consciousness of this failing may have played a role in shaping Anglo-Jewish attitudes towards the Wiener Library in the decades after the war.[6]

The Library's period of greatest usefulness coincided with the time when the war of the propaganda departments was raging in Whitehall. Thereafter its clients became increasingly independent and able to meet their own needs. From about 1943 onwards numerous memos were flying around government departments in which a variety of plans were suggested for withdrawing support for the Library (although they show a reluctance to let themselves appear too ungrateful and hard-hearted).

An indication of how rapidly the Library established itself as an important adjunct of the government's war effort can be shown by the fact that already in February 1940 Wiener estimated that 40 per cent of the Library's work was carried out on behalf of the PWE, while 30 per cent was for the Ministry of Information, 30 per cent for the BBC and other government departments and only ten per cent for private individuals. In March 1940 the PWE offered its assistance regarding the arrangements which Dr Wiener might wish to make for his Amsterdam branch in the event of a German invasion of Holland – another indication that the Library was considered valuable to the government.

A necessary consequence of working for the British government was that the Jewish character of the Library faded into the background to some extent. The authorities had little interest in documenting the fate of German Jewry, but wanted information of a kind that was immediately useful in the war effort. According to Louis Bondy:

> There was practically no Jewish content in our work as such. The Jewish content consisted mainly, in the later stages, of getting detailed stories of people who had escaped from the Nazis . . . and escaped from the concentration camps and so on. But the major work was entirely concentrated on finding material, practical material, for example details about the character and past of military commanders and their views on the Nazis and so on. There was quite a lot of that, the details of the Möhne Dam [one of the dams in the Ruhr area bombed by the RAF's 'Dam Busters'] when it was to be attacked by British planes and so on. And besides that, of course, we provided them with many political quotations, which were useful for leaflets that were dropped over Germany. . . [7]

Despite Bondy's recollection, the Jewish character of the Library was never forgotten: Aronsfeld was eventually able to launch a periodical of specific Jewish interest. Nevertheless it is important to note that the British government never showed the least interest in this aspect of the Library. The Jewish character of the Library is never referred to in the government correspondence preserved at the Public Record Office and it is well known that the government was concerned not to publicise the fate of European Jewry. The reasons for this were largely to do with government fears over increased domestic anti-Semitism if Jewish refugees were allowed into the country in large numbers, a possible upsurge in domestic fascism and the maintenance of its policy regarding immigration into Palestine.

The Germans moved into Holland in the night of May 9–10 1940 and the Dutch army surrendered four days later. The Nazis made efforts to win Dutch hearts and minds and the behaviour and policies of the invaders were initially restrained. Nevertheless panic spread among the Jewish population; many tried to get to the United Kingdom, some committed suicide in their terror. Margarethe Wiener, afraid that Wiener's activities would make them a target, took her children and hid for several days at the house of Wiener's cousin, Herbert Pick.

Losing the Amsterdam office was a blow to both the Library and the government, since the flow of printed materials out of Germany depended on it. This may be the reason why a later effort seems to have been made to rescue the Office from Amsterdam after the German invasion of Holland. Louis Bondy recalls:

> Later on the British Navy tried to evacuate the remaining members of our office from Holland and went as far as Ijmuiden to get Zielenziger and the other members of the Wiener Library in to Britain and that completely failed. Somehow the rendezvous didn't work out . . . [8]

However, according to a government report, 'No such arrangements were made, with the result that the Library was entirely cut off from its foreign contacts from May (1940) . . . ' The wording of this statement suggests that perhaps the authorities to some extent held Wiener responsible for his failure to act on behalf of loyal staff, not to mention his own family. In fact, as we have seen, Wiener tried to persuade his family to come to safety and had secured visas for his colleagues to come to London.

One priority in London was finding new staff to make good the loss of Zielenziger and Krieg. Chancing to meet Ernst Löwenthal, a colleague from the CV (Löwenthal had been deputy editor of the *CV Zeitung*) in Hyde Park one day, Wiener was introduced to Löwenthal's wife, Ilse. She had been in Berlin before the war, where she had been involved with the Reichsvertretung der deutschen Juden. Wiener's secretary at the time (Elizabeth Bondy) was seriously ill and he needed a stand-in. He offered the job to Mrs Löwenthal, who gladly accepted despite having doubts that she could meet the stringent Home Office criteria for getting a work permit. By January of 1940 she was on the permanent staff and she would remain until 1967.

In June 1940 the plan formed by the Board of Deputies to transfer Gustav Warburg to the Library was fulfilled. Wiener noted appreciatively that the extensive newspaper archive and book holdings Warburg brought with him 'have repeatedly contributed most valuable material needed for important and urgent orders'. Warburg remained at the Library until 1946, when he joined the Anglo-Jewish Association. Miss Friedlander, a bookkeeper and translator, also joined at the same time. When Wiener left for New York in August of that year he appointed Mrs Löwenthal as Warburg's assistant. Mrs Wolff (as she later became) recalls that Warburg had devised his own classification system for the collection and 'I shall never forget Dr. Warburg's uncomprehending face when the librarian of the London School of Economics inspected our collection and asked: "Do you classify by the Dewey method?" It was then I decided to become a librarian.'[9]

From August 1940, when Wiener left for New York, Louis Bondy became the *de facto* head of the Wiener Library. While this was initially understood to be a temporary arrangement, it in fact lasted for the duration of the war. It was left to Bondy to deal on a daily basis with the government officials, dealings which were not without their problems. A recurring theme of the letters and memos now in the Public Record Office is the frustration which the bureaucrats felt in their negotiations with the eccentric refugees of Manchester Square.

An unpublished report of the period details some of the services the Library provided to its clients:

> During the months of May and June alone . . . 617 cuttings from newspapers and periodicals were dispatched without special order. Over 400 cuttings were sent to different departments of the Ministry of Information. About 60 cuttings were sent to the BBC. Leading journalists have received about 250 cuttings. The Foreign Office has received more than 200 cuttings. About 80 cuttings were sent to the Royal Institute of International Affairs. The recipients of these cuttings have also received on loan a very considerable number of recent books, important periodicals, and other interesting material.

This document, known as the Big Report, provides further insight into the functioning and activities of the Library during the crucial early period of the war:

> New Government offices have got in touch with us, more particularly the Free French organisation, and a number of older connections have made much more intensive use of our collaboration. This was partly due to the complete reconstruction and the considerable enlargement of some of these departments, and also to the much increased supplies of important material

from enemy and other sources which have reached us through our Director
. . . from New York, as well as through the kind assistance of the Ministry of
Information and the Portuguese Jewish Refugee Organisation, from Lisbon.
Much interesting documentation has also reached us from the South
American countries, particularly from Brazil and the Argentine.

The report continues :

We have been called upon to furnish information on major issues, like
the arrival of the Deputy-Führer Rudolf Hess in this country, the Russian
invasion, and the new developments in the Middle East . . . When Hess
landed here, we immediately set out to compile a most extensive documentation designed to show this leading Nazi in his true colours. There was at
first a dangerous misapprehension that he was an honest, straightforward
man who had been driven into exile because of his moderation and his
opposition to official Nazi politics. It was of paramount importance to inform
Government offices and public opinion of the real situation without delay. At
4 pm on the day after Hess's arrival, we placed the dossier into the hands of
all leading Ministries and offices concerned with the problem. . . When
Germany invaded Russia, we compiled a special dossier on the period of
Russo-German friendship, dating from the conclusion of the Non-
Aggression Pact in August, 1939. We showed therein the great importance
Germany had attached to this friendship and the enormous economic,
political and military advantages the Nazis had derived from it. This documentation was used for the first comments of the BBC on the significance of
the new war, and was also used by the Ministry of Information and Foreign
Office.

The Big Report also provides us with a glimpse of the collecting policy,
which made the Library of such importance at this time:

It has been our aim to obtain not only the leading political and propaganda
publications which now appear on the continent of Europe, but also a
number of highly technical and specialised periodicals which may serve an
important purpose in showing the effects of the present war on economic and
industrial life, on health and justice, on education and on social conditions in
the countries under Nazi rule. The vast majority of these publications do not
reach any other institute or office in Britain, and it has therefore been of vital
importance to various Ministries to secure such material through us.

The same report goes on to discuss how the Library co-operated with newspapers and lists numerous articles which were based on its sources, and details

its co-operation with government departments. The Ministry of Information was the biggest client, particularly its reference division, photographic division, Middle East section and foreign publicity department. At the BBC the women's section of the German News Service was the leading client, but others included the European Services Organiser, the BBC Library European Records, Overseas Research Unit, Propaganda Research Records, and the German News Service. At the time of writing the report, 'A special department of the Foreign Office, whose headquarters are "somewhere in England" has . . . been one of the principal users of our material.' This was the Electra House organisation, responsible for overt propaganda activities. 'They have received all our reports on internal conditions in Germany, any cuttings referring to discontent or economic difficulties in enemy countries and almost all the rarer and more specialised periodicals and books. . . ' Chatham House, the Political Intelligence Department and the Ministry of Economic Warfare were also among the home clients.

Finally, the Big Report includes a complete list of visitors during the period numbering 150 and a list of orders for material which had been processed (45).[10]

The main published output of the Wiener Library was a periodical called *The Nazis at War*, first issued towards the end of October 1940. *The Nazis at War* contained more editorial presence than its Amsterdam predecessor and occasionally exhibited a touch of acerbic wit. Otherwise it followed much the same pattern as the *JCIO Reports*, reprinting extracts from the writings and publications of both major Nazi figures and organisations as well as those of local bodies and rank-and-file party members. *The Nazis at War* constitutes a fascinating commentary on the political developments of the war. The lead item in the 'Occupied Territories' section of the first issue is a poignant item concerning Holland under the Nazis, taken from a feature published in the *BZ am Mittag*, a Berlin daily newspaper:

> The traces of the war are hardly visible any longer in Holland, with a few exceptions. . . The journey through Holland is like a journey through peace. Only the people who live there haven't noticed it yet. They are by no means grateful to the German soldiers for treating their country with great consideration. On the whole they reject everything German, unless they are able to make money out of it.[11]

The object of *The Nazis at War* was to provide the British government and the Wiener Library's other clients with source materials for anti-Nazi propaganda.

While not containing editorials or commentaries of the selections reprinted,

The Nazis at War made its position clear by careful juxtaposing and headlining of the items. A good example is given by the following two quotations under the heading 'Contribution to Civilisation':

> 'There was a time when we were particularly proud of our intellectual achievements' (*Hamburger Fremdenblatt*, No 288, 14.10.41).

> 'Very shortly a Mulhouse Fashion School will be opened. It will, for the post-war period, give fresh guidance towards a new long-term cultural policy . . . The Fashion School is to carry the glory of Mulhouse to all parts of the world' (*Mulhouser Tagblatt*, No 176, 28.6.41).[12]

In this juxtaposition, the first quotation recalls the real cultural glories of the German past and invites us to think of Goethe and his ilk, and then sets this against the inflated small-town pomposity and philistinism of the second quotation with its glories of Mulhouse – a town few in the United Kingdom would ever have heard of. The message is very plain: under Nazi rule the great intellectual tradition of Germany has been reduced to triviality and vulgarity.

The Nazis at War contained hundreds of quotations by major figures in the Nazi Party; but some of the most interesting and important material was drawn from local sources and professional journals. An issue in February 1941 contains material relating to science and medicine which, with hindsight, seems to give fair warning of what the world could expect from the Nazis. Under the heading 'Nazi Learning: the Science of Prejudice':

> It is the sacred duty of the National Socialist doctor towards the State not only to persuade patients suffering from hereditary disease to allow themselves to be sterilised, but also to report them. Some doctors may say: what then remains of the patient's confidence in his doctor? But that does not release the doctor from his important obligation to do his duty as a watchful biological soldier. In the first place he has to defend the State and his nation and its future against asocial elements.
>
> Prof. Dr. Hanns Lohr, Director of Kiel University
Medical Clinic in *Die Medizinische Welt*, 1935.[13]

On the subject of writing history and the meaning of history, *Nazis at War* quotes Professor Walter Frank, who in his inaugural address to the Reich Institute for the History of the New Germany mixed absurdity and menace in equal measure:

> Even if we would, we could not be anything but an expression of the great era of Adolf Hitler. . . To be German means to be in earnest; to be German

means to be thorough; to be German means to have a conscience; to be German means to get to the bottom of things, even if it means getting wrecked. This belief has created the world renown of our nation and therefore we are resolved to regard every resistance against it as a rebellion of slaves, which must be quelled by the whip . . . when we have the strength to write history so that those who make history carry it with them in their kitbags, then we too shall have made history.[14]

The Big Report of 1941 contains interesting information about *The Nazis at War*:

This bulletin, which was started at the suggestion of the Ministry of Information and was published at approximately fortnightly intervals, has met with ever-growing attention. It is sent to our friends free of charge. The MOI distributes 60 copies to all internal departments, and 130 copies are issued to the regional offices of the Ministry throughout the country. The BBC, the Foreign Office, the Royal Institute of International Affairs, all the Allied offices with whom we collaborate, and about 100 other organisations and individuals in various countries also receive copies.[15]

From January 1942 the Wiener Library also issued a bulletin entitled *Jewish News*, intended 'to make accessible to the Jewish public such information of mainly Jewish interest as was not otherwise published in the Jewish press'. The idea for the periodical came from Aronsfeld, who felt that a great deal of the Library's interesting material was not being properly exploited, and that the Library was in danger of losing touch with its Jewish identity. *Jewish News* followed the same pattern as *The Nazis at War* and the editorial policy was ecumenical: 'A point was made of presenting the common interest of the Jewish and Christian cause. . . ' Among the items in its third issue was this story:

Cases of false pity and misapplied humanity to these Jews are by no means isolated. . . A case occurred in the Ameisenbergerstrasse. A German woman approached a Jew, stretched out her hand and said, 'It really takes more courage to wear that badge than to march into the war'. The problem of what to do with Jews . . . is easily solved. But it is more difficult to know what to do with a German woman who goes so far as to adopt an attitude of hostility to Germany . . . In these cases there can be only one solution: put her against the wall.

Stuttgarter NS Kurier.[16]

In the previous issue was an item from the Jewish Telegraphic Agency giving an early account of the horrors being carried out in Auschwitz:

At least 10 per cent of the 15,000 prisoners, the majority of them Jews, in the concentration camps of Oswiecim are dying each month. . . The majority of them die from hunger, exhaustion and the effects of flogging, which is inflicted daily, sometimes on individuals and sometimes on groups. There are also large numbers of suicides, which are carried out sometimes by hanging and sometimes by deliberately touching the live wire with which the camp is surrounded. A special crematorium has had to be erected because of the impossibility of burying the huge numbers of dead.[17]

The summer of 1943 saw intense wrangling in government departments in London over who should pay for the Library and Wiener in New York, and who should control them. In July 1943 Balfour wrote to W. Stewart Roberts:

I have felt for a little time that our relationship with the Wiener Library was not entirely satisfactory. Since the Department provides almost the whole of the Library's funds, I have regarded it as being under our orders to be operated at our convenience. The Head of the Library [meaning Bondy], however, has several times made it clear that he regards the subsidy as being paid simply in order to enable the Library to do its normal work.[18]

At different times during the war several schemes were proposed to remedy the situation. The central problem was always how the departments which funded the Library and drew on its resources could exercise control over its activities and staff, while avoiding any long-term commitment to its upkeep. Basically the authorities wanted to use the Library while they needed its materials and to sever the connection as early as practical.

In the event the government did cut off the Library at the earliest opportunity. In the meantime the price to be paid for its services was tolerating the annoying independence and freedom from constraint which it enjoyed.

However there were some schemes for bringing the Library under closer control, some thought up by men who also wanted to establish it on a more secure financial footing. One, proposed by Walter Adams (who worked hard for the Library's survival after the war), involved the creation of a European Information Library made up of the Wiener Library and (possibly) the Demuth Library,[19] another was to preserve its identity but move it closer to Bush House and so increase its accessibility. Both plans generated memos aplenty but came to nothing.

In the closing days of the war *The Nazis at War* catalogued the districts (Gaue) taken by the allies and reprinted earlier Nazi statements about the significance of each region for the Reich. It also documented the failures of the Nazis to set up popular resistance movements, such as the *Volkssturm* and

Werwolf. Concerning the former, it editorialises: 'The Volkssturm. . . was obviously a failure: white flags instead of fanatical resistance greeted the onward surge of the Allies'. It also published quotations from the *Werwolf* radio broadcasts and delights in pointing out the contradictions in the threadbare rhetoric, presenting the organisation as an elite, yet appealing even to children to join its ranks:

> The Werwolf movement is consciously and deliberately a minority.
>
> Only the best man can be a Werwolf leader. We suffer no careerists, no jobhunters, no dodderers glued to their positions, no bosses. . .
>
> German men and women, German boys and girls, join our ranks![20]

The final issue of *The Nazis at War* was published in mid-April 1945. By this time Dr Wiener and his Library were experiencing unexpected hardships. In the government departments served by the Library memos had been going back and forth for months about the ever-decreasing usefulness of the Library and the need for a painless and face-saving way of getting rid of the encumbrance.

Jewish News lasted into the early months of the peace in 1945. Its last numbers contain interesting items, such as George Orwell's view that there was 'more antisemitism in England than we care to admit', which 'the war has accentuated' and which he identifies as a symptom of 'the larger disease of nationalism'. The final issue dated 24 September 1945 focuses on the German press and contains some acid editorial matter:

> The violent anti-Jewish propaganda of the past has not as yet been countered by an effort equally determined to enforce the truth. Apparently the subject is not considered sufficiently important in view of the strictly observed policy of non-discrimination which causes the persecuted Jew to be treated like any persecuting German.[21]

Other items in this issue report on a radio broadcast in which it was stated that:

> As they [the Germans] looked back on the revolting record of the last 12 years, they found that antisemitism was the blackest page in German history, and what would they not gladly do today to have that page torn out and utterly destroyed?[22]

And a report on Berlin's first post-war piece of theatre, a production of Lessing's *Nathan der Weise.*

The Political Intelligence Department made its mind up in December 1944. A meeting was held in the office of John Wheeler-Bennett at which Walter Adams, among others, was present; it was resolved to give Wiener three months notice of the withdrawal of the department's full subsidy as soon as he returned from America. It was also resolved that an estimate should be made of what it might cost to maintain the Library as 'a consultative library only' (that is, one librarian, two assistants and the cost of rent, heating, lighting and cleaning), and that after the notice period had expired the PID might make a 'suitable but small' monthly payment to secure access to its holdings. Furthermore it was acknowledged that 'the material on national socialism was a valuable asset which ought to be preserved if possible in this country, and preferably in London.' As a long-term solution it was envisaged that 'interested bodies' be approached and offered the collection. The Board of Deputies, Chatham House and the University of London Library were suggested as likely candidates.

NEW YORK

In 1940 when Holland was invaded, the Library was cut off from the source of its materials. Wiener had already established some connections in South Africa, Australia and Latin America, simply as part of the network which kept the Office (both in London and Amsterdam) up to date. He suggested to Stephen Heald that it could no longer be taken for granted that his contacts in Portugal, Spain, Sweden and even Switzerland could send the desired materials direct to Britain, and that alternative supply lines via the United States should be established. It was generally admitted that Wiener's analysis was correct, and that funding should be made available to allow him to go to New York to set up new contacts.

A report he wrote for his bosses in the British government and at the British Embassy in Washington in February 1944 clarifies what he was doing there (Wiener refers to himself in the third person throughout):

> He succeeded in re-establishing connections with Switzerland within a short period of time and the figures given here are a convincing proof of the work accomplished.
>
> Material received from abroad in 1942

From Europe:	420 parcels		containing newspapers and periodicals
	80	"	books
From South America	40	"	newspapers and periodicals
	10	"	books
From the USA	400	"	books, newspapers and periodicals

Wiener was also approached by various other bodies who were looking for materials and expertise in European matters:

> Shortly after Mr Wiener arrived in New York in August 1940, he contacted the British Library of Information with official recommendation by Mr S.A. Heald, London. Messrs. A.A. Dudley and John Wheeler-Bennett took great interest in Mr Wiener's activities and he was frequently able to assist both gentlemen.
>
> In December of 1940 both gentlemen proposed that Mr Wiener enter into the British Press Services as special assistant on the Minority Press in the United States, and the consent of the British Embassy in Washington as well as the respective authorities in London were requested.
>
> In the meantime, Mr Wiener was asked to analyse the German, Italian and Hungarian press in the United States as well as to procure all newspapers in these languages. To assist him with this type of work, Mr Wiener employed translators and persons versed in these languages and it was his task to supervise their work.[23]

Wheeler-Bennett had worked at Chatham House before the war and so probably knew Wiener and would certainly have known Heald, who also worked there. He had been in New York since 1939, first on attachment to the British Library of Information and since early in 1940 at the British Press Service as assistant director. After the war he consolidated his already considerable reputation as an expert in international affairs and historian.

Two of Wiener's chief collaborators in New York were John F. Oppenheimer and his wife, as well as Jacob Picard, Emery Göndor and a Mrs Loeb. Wiener was an old acquaintance of Oppenheimer's, because they had been at the CV together. Oppenheimer was at that time known as Hans Oppenheimer and had been in charge of the advertising department of the CV newspaper. In addition he was one of the chief editors of the four editions of the Philo Verlag's *Lexikon*. He also worked at the Ullstein Propylaen Verlag (which had been founded by another Wiener contact, Emil Herz, the father of Ernest Hearst, later the editor of the *Wiener Library Bulletin*). Oppenheimer wrote of that time:

> We all worked for small salaries – more or less out of idealism. We were translators, researchers and 'handymen' all at the same time. Dr Wiener used my residence . . . in Sunnyside, Queens as 'Deckadresse' [P.O. box]. Almost every day packages of Nazi newspapers arrived. Part of the Wiener Library (shipped over from London) was stored in our apartment and in the basement of our building. These books were stored there long after the war had ended. When they finally were repacked for return shipment, it turned out

that maggots had feasted on the oil paper that lined the original crates. Hundreds of them crawled all over the place.

Oppenheimer describes how Wiener 'hunted New York and other cities incessantly for books valuable for the Library' and struggled without success to gain support and funding from American Jewish organisations.[24]

In early 1944, as the Library's London clients were complaining that its usefulness was coming to an end, Wiener in New York was writing a proposal for the expansion of his office and staff. Wiener complained of the excessive demands being made upon him:

> In order to keep things running smoothly, Mr Wiener, himself, is obliged to work far beyond the usual requirements, and although he is most happy to do so he feels he is unable to do so indefinitely, for reasons of health. It is impossible to work all day and every day into the early hours of the morning . . . working conditions under the present setup both as to staff and office have reached unbearable limits.[25]

He proposed a number of improvements and then went on to outline possible areas for expanded and new activity. In response Michael Balfour noted: 'In general I think it desirable to restrict Dr Wiener's activities rather than allow them to expand'. A couple of months later, in a letter to Walter Adams, Balfour made clear to what extent Wiener had overestimated his own indispensability to the British government:

> The value of the Library to this Department seems to me to lie in its pre-war material. As regards more recent material, our own sources are probably better, so that we are not particularly interested in keeping the Library up-to-date, especially as regards countries other than Germany. On the other hand, Dr Wiener obviously wants to come out of the war with as up-to-date a set of files and books as possible. Thus, our interests and his tend to diverge.

The same letter gives a clear sign of the impatience being felt with the unruly foreigner in some quarters:

> As Dr Wiener is not completely reliant upon our Department for funds . . . I do not think we can forbid him to engage in these activities [supplying American Government agencies] but . . . I do not think it would do any harm to remind him gently that he is very largely our servant and has got to do what he is told.[26]

The core of the problem was the fact that the British government had never formalised its relationship with the Library – one suspects out of anxiety about incurring a permanent financial drain. The precise nature of the relationship thus remained obscure and this led to conflicts which were never resolved.

In November 1944 Wiener was informed that the Political Warfare Mission of the British Embassy in New York would also no longer require his services. David Bowes Lyon wrote to him on the 27th:

> The opening up of new channels of supply from the Continent of German and other material has led my Department to review its existing sources of supply and to take various decisions, some of which immediately affect you. The Department has instructed me to inform you that it will terminate its financial support for your activities in the United States at the 31st January 1945 . . . In view of these decisions you will no doubt wish to take immediate steps to close down your New York office, to dispose of your stocks of books, and to make alternative arrangements with the other agencies in this country who have been using your services.[27]

Precisely how Wiener was informed of the decisions of other Library clients is not recorded. By the end of March 1945 he had been informed that all the subsidies to the Library would cease after three months, although a monthly subscription of 15 guineas would continue from PWI. This sum amounted to no more than a fraction of what was needed if the Library was to continue without cutting back its staff or services. Wiener did not even know where his own salary would come from, since the Library budget did not include him (because he had been paid out of the funds of the New York branch office). By the end of April it had been agreed that he could claim to be still in the service of the government and that his salary would continue to be paid through the British Political Warfare Mission.

Within days of hearing that his subsidies had been taken away, the war in Europe came to an end, and Dr Wiener and his Library entered upon the uncertainties of the post-war era.

NOTES

1. Taped interview with Louis Bondy, by Tony Wells, April 1989.
2. Letter from Stephen A. Heald to Wiener dated 7.5.1945. Foreign Office papers kept at the Public Record Office (FO 898/34/5).
3. Quoted in a document dated 2.12.1943, Foreign Office papers kept at the Public Record Office (FO 898/34/1).
4. Interview with Louis Bondy, see note 1.
5. For the British and Allied propaganda effort, see Charles Cruickshank, *The Fourth Arm:*

Psychological Warfare 1938–1945 (London: Davis-Poynter, 1977); Ellic Howe, *The Black Game* (London: Michael Joseph, 1982); and Daniel Lerner, *Psychological Warfare against Germany* (Cambridge, MA: MIT Press, 1971).

6. For a survey of these matters, see Richard Bolchover's at times scathing study, *British Jewry and the Holocaust* (Cambridge: Cambridge University Press, 1993), the two quotations are taken from pp. 37 and 42 respectively.

7. Interview with Louis Bondy, see note 1.

8. Interview with Louis Bondy, see note 1.

9. Ilse Wolff in *Wiener Library Newsletter*, 1989, No 13.

10. Alfred Wiener, Report on the Work of the Institute from 1.12.1940 to the 15.9.1941 (The Big Report), Wiener Archive, Wiener Library.

11. *The Nazis at War*, No. 1, 24.10.1940, p. 6.

12. *The Nazis at War*, No. 23, 31.10.1941, p. 5.

13. *The Nazis at War*, No. 10/11, 25.2.1941, p. 9.

14. *The Nazis at War*, No 10/11, 25.2.1941, p. 8.

15. Alfred Wiener, The Big Report, see note 10.

16. *Jewish News*, No. 3, 20.2.1942, p. 10.

17. *Jewish News*, No. 2, 29.1.1942, p. 6.

18. Minute from Michael Balfour to W. Stewart Roberts, dated 26.7.1943, Foreign Office papers kept at the Public Record Office (FO 898/34/1).

19. Fritz Demuth had been an economist and official in Berlin, working at the Berlin Chamber of Commerce. He emigrated to Switzerland in 1933, where he co-founded the Notgemeinschaft deutscher Wissenschaftler im Ausland. He came to Britain in 1939, where he founded the Central European Joint Committee, which was referred to by government officials as the Demuth Library in the same way as the Jewish Central Information Office was known as the Wiener Library. Post-war Demuth was involved in the retraining of PoWs at Wilton Park and in the running of the Luncheon Clubs.

20. *The Nazis at War*, No. 71, 17.4.1945, pp. 4–5.

21. *Jewish News*, No 46, 24.9.1945, p. 294.

22. *Jewish News*, No 46, 24.9.1945, p. 295.

23. Alfred Wiener, Report on the New York Branch Office of the Wiener Library – Jewish Central Information Office, London, 27.2.1944, Wiener Archive, Wiener Library.

24. Letter from John F. Oppenheimer to Walter Laqueur, see Ch. 4, note 5.

25. Alfred Wiener, Report on the New York Branch Office, see note 23.

26. Letter from Michael Balfour to Walter Adams, dated 21.4.1944, Foreign Office papers kept at the Public Record Office (FO 898/34/3).

27. Letter from David Bowes-Lyon to Alfred Wiener, 27.11.1944, Wiener Archive, Wiener Library.

CHAPTER EIGHT

'A New Type of Research Institute'

RELAUNCH

O NE MAN PLAYED a critical role in the history of the Wiener Library in the post-war period. Leonard Montefiore was every inch one of the Cousins, a member of the wealthy and influential Montefiore clan and the son of Claude Montefiore, the leader of the Liberal Jewish movement. He had been educated at Clifton and Balliol, then devoted himself to welfare work until called up for service in the First World War. In 1920 he was chosen by the Anglo-Jewish Association (his father had been its president) to represent it on the Joint Foreign Committee (with representatives of the Board of Deputies). From 1926–39 he served as president of the Association, then he became its treasurer. Later he acted as its vice-president. His expertise in matters to do with Jewish refugees made him a natural choice for working with the Central British Fund, the main British relief agency for refugees from Germany. After the war he became closely associated with the Wiener Library, acting as its second president and later as the chairman of its board.

It has been said with some justice that Montefiore lived in the shadow of his father. It is also true that he seemed perfectly at ease with this fact. He was no intellectual, but he was intelligent and realistic in his appraisal of people and situations. His approach to people was informal and direct, yet he unmistakably believed himself to be the superior of almost everyone. Many who knew him have commented that he was 'socially fastidious'. He could be scathing about other people ('the Brodetskys, Bakstanskys and Whatnotskys').[1] He hated being bored and would while away dull meetings by writing funny notes to those around him. His letters are short and invariably written on Smythson's blue note paper. A collection of them exists at the Wiener Library, and while being generally short on content they are playful and amusing (writing to David Kessler he referred to Wiener as 'King Alfred'). He spoke of himself as a museum piece ('I am the Berkeley Street Neanderthal man'), and his social outlook was indeed backward-looking and conservative. He and

Wiener developed a genuine respect and fondness for one another; there is no doubt that without Montefiore the Library would not have survived into the 1960s. Yet it is questionable whether Wiener was wise to render the Library so dependent on the whim of one man, particularly when that man was a member of a small and waning social elite with some pretty powerful enemies. Montefiore's patronage may have prevented the Library from going under, but it also stopped it establishing secure funding arrangements with bodies such as the Claims Conference and the Central British Fund. After his death this led to serious financial problems. Wiener was impressed at their first meeting by Montefiore's excellent spoken German and love of German literature. He must also have appreciated Montefiore's views on the position of Jewry in the Diaspora and on Israel. Montefiore had written:

> I do not agree with those who go about saying that assimilation has proved a failure. In this country it is thanks to assimilation, thanks to a steady allegiance to those principles by which emancipation and equality were won, that there is so little chance of Hitlerism. It is well to remember that those who stress the racial element in Jewish affairs . . . are merely echoing the opinions of Adolf Hitler in *Mein Kampf.* [2]

Later in his life these views softened, but only slightly. He maintained an unshakeable belief that while Jewish identity should be cherished and safe-guarded, the core of this identity was religious and not racial or national. When he visited Israel in the 1950s he could admire the achievements but not warm to the idea. Visiting a Zionist institution in Naples once, he wrote:

> The walls are covered with slogans in Hebrew, saying 'We are the only people in the world without a country', or 'Only speak Hebrew.' I felt slightly annoyed, because the first statement was false, and the second I had no wish to observe.'[3]

That Wiener got on well with a man so conservative, well-connected and rich need surprise no one. But it is important to note that Wiener's choice of Montefiore as a patron demonstrates how his reactionary views on the relative merits of West and East European Jewry were not altered by the Second World War.

Views on the nature of the relationship between the two men vary: some say that Wiener regarded Montefiore as a dilettante, and cultivated him only for the Library's sake. Others are sure the two enjoyed a genuine friendship – and the fact that the Library formed the entire context for their relationship is understandable in view of the emotional and social constraints of Montefiore's breeding. David Kessler recalls the two sitting in Wiener's office at the Library one evening after hours singing German student songs together.

In certain respects Wiener's return to London was not triumphant. It did not escape many that he had been safe in America, while they were facing shortages and danger at home and his family endured far greater hardships in Holland and Germany. At the Library, C.C. Aronsfeld recalls, Wiener was faced with the task almost of rehabilitating himself and rebuilding his personal credibility. He was also faced with the problem of guiding the Library through the very uncertain waters of the immediate post-war years.

Within days of arriving in London, Wiener was writing to Montefiore for help and advice. On 30 April he wrote concerning a meeting with Dr Thomas K. Derry in which Derry informed him of the withdrawal of his department's support:

> Unexpectedly he began to speak about the future of our relations. He told me we would receive in the next few days a letter discontinuing the existing agreement, with three months notice . . . On my asking him what amount would be in question, he gave me no definite answer, but I have the impression that not more than a few hundred pounds yearly, instead of about £4,600 yearly granted up to now.[4]

The months after the war were taken up with planning a strategy for survival. In some sense the Library faced its own *Stunde Nulu* and needed to carve out a new role for itself. Wiener did the rounds of friends and contacts to drum up support and take advice about the best direction in which to go. Specifically, he wrote letters to Leonard Stein, president of the Anglo-Jewish Association and A.G. Brotman, secretary of the Board of Deputies, in which he submitted a formal memorandum concerning the Library and asked for financial assistance and help in forming a board. Surprisingly, he met with a very positive personal response from the very people who, in their professional capacity, had just severed the Library's umbilical cord. He also gathered testimonials from the great and the good. Typical is the one sent by Arnold Toynbee, the director of Chatham House and Professor of International History at London University:

> It seems to me to be a library of very great, and probably unique, value for the study of (a) contemporary Jewish affairs, not only in Nazi Germany but in all parts of the world, and (b) Nazi Germany, not only in regard to the Nazi persecution of the Jews but in most other aspects as well.

Toynbee particularly praised the Library's collecting policy:

These fields have been interpreted in very broad terms by the scholars who have built the Library up, so that anyone pursuing his researches in the Wiener Library will be likely to find materials here for studying not only the more obvious main subjects but also many of their ramifications.[5]

During the spring of 1946 efforts were made to form a new board for the Library. This was necessary both in order to raise funds, and because the Library found itself in an anomalous legal position. With the dissolution of the Amsterdam office after the German invasion of Holland, it was found that the Library was not legally constituted. Wiener and Montefiore worked to bring together the board, hosting a lunch at the Savoy on 26 June. Present were Walter Adams, General M. de Baer, David Bowes Lyons, Professor S. Brodetsky, James Callaghan, MP, Stephen Heald, Gordon Liverman (Board of Deputies), Leonard Montefiore, the Marquess of Reading, Dr Eva Reichmann, Brigadier T. Robbins (Rio Tinto Company), Paul Rykens (Unilever), Lord Vansittart and others. Montefiore spoke about the potential for the future, and reviewed the Library's illustrious past (he also paid for the event). Walter Adams continued to promote his idea (first put forward during the closing stages of the war) that the Library should broaden its scope and become essentially a European studies library. Yet despite this high-powered event, the immediate financial benefit to the Library was negligible.

A few days before the Savoy lunch Montefiore wrote to Wiener, reviewing where matters stood in relation to fund-raising prospects. From this it emerges that, even at this early stage, Montefiore was actively using his position on the committees of Jewish organisations to find money for the Library:

> I enclose a hundred guineas as a sin offering for getting poor Aronsfeld dreadfully wet.
>
> Under the existing conditions a highly specialised library of this kind labours under great difficulties. So far as Jews are concerned we have other problems such as Concentration Camp orphans and so on more urgent, even in my eyes, than the library. The human being is of greater interest I suppose than the printed book. Of course a library like the London Library does not issue publications and saves that expense. On the other hand unless you issue publications like Chatham House the mere existence of a collection of books, pamphlets and newspapers becomes museum like and is dead.
>
> I am not at all sure what my colleagues of the JCA Council would say if I asked for a further grant this year, I am very much afraid they would say No.
>
> You might ask Stein whether he would feel inclined to raise the question once more at the July meeting of the Council; in some ways it is easier for a member of the Council to do so than the President.[6]

The reference to Aronsfeld concerns a visit the two had paid somewhere in Bond Street one rainy day. Returning to the Library, Aronsfeld had wanted to hail a taxi but Montefiore refused, saying that he couldn't bear to waste money on such unnecessaries and the two returned on foot.

Paul Rykens of Unilever had supported the Library during the war, hence his presence on the board. Wiener now felt that this connection might offer a way out of the Library's problems. In July he reported to Montefiore on a meeting he had had with Rykens:

> I only touched on the financial problems of the Institute very lightly . . .
> I told him I was not interested in getting just a few hundred pounds, but I should like to consider just how Unilever might materially assist the Institute. I told him that I had an idea in my mind which was not yet fully developed, this idea being that in some way or other Unilever should make a foundation 'Unilever Research Institute' similar to 'The Welcome [sic] Institute of Medical Research'. Such a gift would be worthy of Unilever and be of course of great propaganda value. [7]

Wiener put a considerable amount of work into drawing up a submission to Unilever. In it he spoke of the Wellcome Institute and the Nuffield Trust as models of public-spirited work for the human good and proposed that:

> Unilever with their world renowned name and great influence would perhaps sponsor and make a foundation of this Institute to commemorate, if thought suitable, the Allied Victory in World War II and to those who fell in defence of freedom, in particular to the employees of Unilever.[8]

Nothing came of this scheme. An interview with Brigadier Robbins of Rio Tinto Zinc on 19 July also yielded little. He himself was happy to put in 50 guineas and thought that he could come up with 50 names of people who could be persuaded to make a similar 'subscription', provided that the Institute succeeded in becoming more widely known to the public. (Montefiore responded, 'fifty people paying fifty guineas each: well you might, but its a d—d sight easier to say it should be easy than it is easy to secure the fifty')[9] Gordon Liverman thought something could be done but 'my influence in regard to the BoD Funds is not as strong as it has been'. (Montefiore: 'Well: Liverman seems friendly anyway')[10]

Proposals were also drawn up for the Nuffield Foundation and the Carnegie Endowment for International Peace and neither of these yielded anything useful.

In spite of setbacks and obstacles, by the summer of 1946 the Library was prepared to relaunch itself. It did so in some style, with a lavish 24-page

1. Alfred Wiener and his father outside the family shop in Bentschen

2. Alfred Wiener (far right) with comrades-in-arms during World War I

3. Jan van Eijkstraat, Amsterdam; the JCIO occupied the first floor [far left], while the Wieners lived on the ground floor below

4. Members of the JCIO staff in Amsterdam. On the far left are Margarethe and Alfred Wiener

5. David Cohen, first President of the JCIO, seen here [second from left] attending a Joodse Raad meeting

6. The Wiener Library at 19 Manchester Square. The Library occupied the first floor

7. Louis Bondy, who was in charge of running the Library during the war years, while Wiener was in the US

8. C.C. Aronsfeld [left], editor of *The Nazis at War*, *Jewish News*, and the *Wiener Library Bulletin*; Eva Reichmann [right], Director of the Library's research department

9. Members of the staff on the balcony of Manchester Square. The building opposite is the Wallace Collection

10. Friends and colleagues; [from left to right] Susanne and Werner Rosenstock, Ilse Wolff, Alfred Wiener, Eva and Hans Reichmann

11. Leonard Montefiore shortly before his death, in the Library's Devonshire Street reading room

12. [from left to right] Alan Montefiore, President of the Wiener Library, Walter Laqueur, Director of the Library 1964-92, and Tony Wells, former Deputy Librarian, at the opening of the Library's exhibition *From Enemy to Ally: Germany 1945-49*

13. HRH the Duke of
Edinburgh at the
Library's fund-raising
Dinner of 1987, with the
Appeal Committee's
Vice-Chairman,
Lewis Golden

14. [from left to right]
Present Director David
Cesarani. former
Librarian Christa
Wichmann, Chairman of
the Executive Committee
Ernst Fraenkel and
Committee member
Ellen Schmidt.

brochure (including four pages of illustrations) entitled *The Wiener Library: Its History and Activities 1934 – 1945*. The object was obviously awareness-raising, the style heroic:

> The Institute seeks to provide in Great Britain a Jewish centre where the great traditions and vital work of the destroyed or decimated Continental communities can be taken up and maintained from a specific European point of view. The Institute is eminently suited for this high task. It is conscious of its great responsibility towards the millions who have perished in the most atrocious persecution in history, and even more to the survivors who face the future with hope reborn and at the same time with immense anxiety.[11]

The brochure continues:

> If the Institute may be likened to a tree with two branches growing out of one single trunk, each trunk can be studied separately with fruitful results; the Jewish scholar will find ample material on every aspect of Jewish life with the exception of purely religious or philosophical questions, the student of world affairs will be in a position to trace back the totalitarian movements of our epoch to the very origins as well as to examine their structure, growth and downfall.[12]

Wiener shrewdly saw in this bifurcation a strength rather than a weakness:

> In combining these two studies the Institute has completely departed from the usual course. It will be found that this procedure has opened entirely new ways of approach. Jewish affairs are not self contained. In their political, social, cultural, economic and human aspects they are largely a function of the surrounding world.[13]

The high style adopted for this brochure occasionally spills over into bombast. Discussing the need to re-establish connections with Europe's Jewish organisations, it reads:

> This alone will enable the Institute to become again in the fullest sense of the word what its name expresses: a Central Jewish Information Office. This role may well make itself felt in connection with peace negotiations and the re-planning of the world.[14]

A more realistic appraisal was given in the first issue of the Library's new publishing venture, the *Wiener Library Bulletin*:

> The aim is so to develop the Institute as to enable conscientious students of Central Europe to carry on their studies, particularly on the subject

of fascist and racist activities . . . The achievement of this aim is, unfortunately, hampered by the lack of many requirements. Hundreds of new friends are needed to swell the Institute's membership, which is as yet small indeed. Co-operation is needed from organisations, libraries and scientific institutions with a view to providing the Institute with an annual subsidy.[15]

The Library's struggle for survival was to be longer and more arduous than anyone could have foreseen at this point. Nevertheless by the end of 1946 Wiener was optimistic and in expansive mood. He felt confident that the Library was succeeding in transforming itself from a quasi-official body to an academic institution. He had gained friends in the Jewish press, notably David Kessler of the *Jewish Chronicle*, which publicised the Library's work enthusiastically. Kessler eventually became closely involved with the Library, serving as the Chairman of its Executive Committee. Wiener had also visited other academic libraries and persuaded the editors of the *Aslib Bulletin* to publicise the Library. He looked into leasing more space for the Library and reported to Montefiore on the steady trickle of new memberships.

Support for the Library among Jewish organisations around the world remained strong. In the United States the American Jewish Committee and the American Joint Distribution Committee continued to subscribe (the 'Joint' even raising its level of support). B'nai B'rith, Washington and the 'Anti-Diffamation Ligue' (in Wiener's curious orthography) also continued their support. Community groups in Australia, New Zealand and South Africa were joining. At home the Board of Deputies and Anglo-Jewish Association and several lodges were members. Departments of the Foreign Office continued as clients, notably the German Control Office, as did the BBC. In total 26 organisations paid subscriptions to the Library.

Early in 1947 Wiener prepared a monthly financial statement for Montefiore, to show what the Library's position was:

Bank Account JCIO	ca £60.0.0
Bank Account WL	£300.0.0
Petty Cash	£20.0.0
Sub Total	£380.0.0
Unpaid Bills	£12.0.0
Total	£368.0.0
Estimate of Payments in February	
Salaries	ca £230.0.0
Taxes	£38.10.0
Rent	£32.0.0
Bulletin	£30.0.0
Bills	£30.0.0

Montefiore responded in characteristic fashion:

> Yes: it is 'Knapp' [German, meaning 'tight'] to say the least of it. . . I enclose cheque for £300.[16]

This submisson of carefully prepared accounts and generous response from Montefiore was so regularly repeated that it became the pulse of the Wiener Library.

NUREMBERG

In the meantime, the Library's work went on. Considerable effort was made to assist in the preparations for the Nuremberg War Crimes trials and the Library was able to supply material to the United Nations War Crimes Commission, the British War Crimes Executive and the US Chief of Counsel. Writing in the first issue of the *Wiener Library Bulletin* in November 1946, after the conclusion of the trials, General M. de Baer, the Belgian Commissioner of the United Nations War Crimes Commission stated that:

> It may be said that it is thanks to the Wiener Library that the criminal decrees, regulations, orders and circulars of the Nazi rulers were made known in this country, and that from 1942 it has been the centre of documentation on German matters. Documents which could be found nowhere else were available there. The help it has given has been invaluable in the preparation of charges against the leaders of Nazi Germany. . . [17]

The Library played a pioneer role in helping to bring war criminals to justice. In Britain only the BBC was able to furnish large numbers of documents to the War Crimes Trials authorities – mostly records of broadcast speeches. The Wiener Library's holdings constituted a unique body of evidence. Without it the trials could not have succeeded as they did. It should be remembered that, at this time, Simon Wiesenthal's documentaton centre in Linz had yet to be established and the great man still to begin his Nazi-hunting career.

In acknowledgement of the Library's contribution to the success of the War Crimes Trials, Mr Justice Jackson, the US Chief of Counsel invited the Library to send a representative to Nuremberg 'to take part for a short time in the proceedings.' Wiener chose not to go himself, but sent Louis Bondy. Bondy used the trip to visit several German cities, buy materials for the collection and gather impressions of how life was being lived amid the ruins of the Reich. These were issued by the Library as the third in a series of reports entitled *Europe 1946*. This report gives a peculiarly vivid snapshot of the post-war conditions and attitudes. Writing of the people Bondy noted:

> . . . I found no trace anywhere of a feeling of guilt, or the consciousness that every individual, or at least many of them, must bear part of the responsibility for the war and its attendant misery. Some with whom I spoke were only too ready to admit the guilt of some individual high-up Nazis – hardly ever Hitler – but this guilt consisted, in their mind, not in having loosed the war, but in having lost it.

And he found people clinging pathetically to the remnants of their recent past:

> A young girl who happened to be seated at my table in a Frankfurt cafe, and whom I asked what kind of insignia she wore in her button-hole (she wore it turned inside so that it was impossible to recognise) proudly turned her lapel and showed it to me. It was the Nazi party badge. As I was eager to collect all such Nazi insignia for our Institute, I asked her not why she wore it, but whether she would give it to me. At this she indignantly replied that she would not dream of parting with it as it was very dear to her.

And he noted that Germans who had resisted the Nazis expressed bitterness and disappointment at post-war developments:

> One of the neatly dressed Frankfurt policemen, some of whom even carry arms, complained that he, as a Socialist and genuine anti-Nazi, felt thwarted in his reawakened republican instincts by the fact that the owner of the factory in which he worked during the war and who was an out and out Nazi had been transferred to another factory where nobody knew him and again put in charge, while some of the anti-Nazi men who had worked under him were now unemployed and despairing of the justice of the allies.[18]

Turning to the trials, Bondy had little to say of the proceedings themselves, but recorded his impressions of the prisoners, commenting that they were 'a sad-looking lot'. Only Goering retained an air of authority and was almost alone among his co-defendants in not having lapsed into apathy. Bondy's views of Julius Streicher, in whom he had a particular interest, were recorded later in his book *Racketeers of Hatred*:

> . . . [he] looks an inoffensive and tired old man. He wriggles uncomfortably on the wooden bench, stares unseeingly into the large courtroom, and his jaws move interminably as if he were chewing. Those who watch him often remark that it seems impossible to believe that he has ever done any harm.[19]

Contemplating the state of shops he considers what is nearest to a Librarian's heart, the book trade:

The number of book shops is still fairly large, but most of them sell only the few booklets and periodicals which appear currently. . . There are, however, exceptions, especially in Berlin, where more than a hundred book shops are again open. Some second-hand booksellers who were lucky enough to save their stocks have thousands of books left, amongst them rare and valuable volumes, but in the majority of cases they are reluctant to part with them as their trust in the present German currency is almost nil . . . Would-be sellers often demanded not money but goods for their books and said that they would not part with them unless they were certain to get coal, and, even more often, potatoes in exchange.[20]

During this trip Bondy also took a series of remarkable photographs showing conditions in Germany as well as pictures of displaced persons camps and portraits of some of the individuals working with DPs. These photographs were made available to the public by the Library in February 1946, immediately after Bondy's return to London.

The Library later received further acknowledgement of its help to the trials authorities when a large percentage of the documentation generated by the trials was deposited there. These documents constituted invaluable raw materials for historians of the Third Reich and the fate of European Jewry.

And so life went on. In the spring of 1947 the Library's landlords at 19 Manchester Square unexpectedly served notice to quit. This led to several months of frantic searching for alternative accommodation. (While the crisis was in full flood Montefiore donated £500 to cover moving costs, solicitors' fees and so on.) Wiener approached the Central British Fund with a request that the Library be allowed to take over the Rose Hertz Hall at Woburn House. This was briskly rejected as 'unsuitable'. In the event the landlords changed their minds and the Library remained at Manchester Square for another ten years.

THE WIENER LIBRARY BULLETIN

Among the Library's most successful publishing ventures in the post-war era was the *Wiener Library Bulletin*. Begun in November 1946 it was issued bi-monthly until July 1965, when it underwent major reorganisation and then continued until 1983. From its second issue until the summer 1966 issue, it was edited by C.C. Aronsfeld (the first issue had been put together by Louis

Bondy), thereafter by Ernest Hearst (Aronsfeld's brother-in-law), who had acted as assistant editor from 1965 until 1975 when Robert Wistrich became joint editor. Wistrich took over from Hearst in 1976 and edited the *Bulletin* until its demise in 1981. The 1983 50th anniversary special was edited by Walter Laqueur.

The *Bulletin* struggled into life. The first issue was eight pages long, the second only four. Thereafter its length varied between six and eight pages, gradually expanding to 12 pages and more. Its tentative and halting beginnings reflect the problems scholars faced in researching the Nazi era in the post-war years.

Immediately after the war many people wanted to put the recent past behind them and forget about the hardships and atrocities. Partly as a result of government policy, the appalling sights that had greeted the liberators of camps like Belsen and Buchenwald were interpreted in ways that distorted the truth. It was not widely realised that the overwhelming majority of those exterminated in the camps had been Jews, selected for the 'crime' of their birth. Most people lacked a conceptual framework to make the information about the camps meaningful. Many thought that what had gone on there was only a continuation of the sort of cruelties exposed during the 1930s. Furthermore it was not understood that the camps found in Germany were fundamentally different from those liberated by the Red Army in Eastern Europe. The truth about the Nazi genocide only emerged very gradually and was assimilated even more slowly. Above all the fact that what is now called the Holocaust was a specifically Jewish tragedy emerged during the 1950s and 60s (in certain ways it is still being argued over). In the United Kingdom, there was virtually no forum for this debate other than the *Wiener Library Bulletin*.[21]

The *Bulletin* covered a wide range of topics, and was never marred by parochialism. It followed the development of communities of Jewish refugees around the world, tracked the activities of what one article called the 'International of Anti-Democracy' and reported on the reconstruction of democratic Germany.

As early as March 1947 it reviewed the progress made in investigating the ghettos and concentration camps established by the Nazis and called for a new, analytical approach. Arguing that all existing accounts were of three basic types – presentation of basic facts about the persecution, eulogies for the victims, or accounts from memory – it suggested that what was needed:

> . . . is this: to describe the internal life of a ghetto or concentration camp in such a way as to expand and enrich the field of social science. Again and again the question must be asked: what happens as a result of each order and prohibition? How do community and individual behave in the face of

increased oppression? How much scope remains, within the steadily narrowing confines of existence, for any self-chosen activity? More important than what happens is the way it happens. The procedure of a 'normal society' will have to be referred to for comparison with this highly abnormal society; the dwelling of an ordinary citizen, for example, with the accommodation in a camp. Only by confrontations of this kind will it be possible to arrive at something like a psychology of the camps, in which terrible destinies were fulfilled under often unfathomable circumstances – destinies from which have sprung impulses that will reverberate through the history of this age.[22]

What is interesting here is the vision of the writer (Aronsfeld) in asking at least some of the questions needed in order to set the camp experience in a proper sociological and historical context. The early issues of the *Bulletin* also highlight how, at this time, even those closest to the story of Nazi genocide were less interested in memorialising the victims than in taking positive steps to see that their number should not be added to. That said, memorial work was reported, particularly if it was being carried out in Germany itself.

An interesting feature of the *Bulletin* under Aronsfeld was the attention paid to race issues in a broader sense. The Wiener Library had never before turned its attention to the racist attitudes prevalent in Britain and America, especially those directed against black people. Thanks to Aronsfeld such questions began to creep onto the Library's agenda and this represented an important opening out of the scope of the Library's activities at a time when concerning oneself with such problems was far from fashionable. The first mention of this subject came in 1948 in the second issue of that year in an article entitled 'Black Man's Burden', which cited a review in the *Observer* of a novel by Sinclair Lewis. In Issue 5 of 1948, the question was given much greater attention. Under the title 'Negroes in Britain' the *Bulletin* printed a lengthy review of a sociological study of race relations in Britain by K.L. Little of the London School of Economics. The review carefully noted the dichotomy between the attitude of the government and official bodies and the much less savoury attitudes found amongst ordinary people. The government was anxious to avoid 'any reproach that, when we blame Hitler for his poisonous doctrine of the Herrenvolk, we have a similar doctrine lurking in our own hearts.' But at street level things were rather different:

> Dr Little cites the example of a bank manager living in a select part of the town, who strongly objected to the idea of two African students occupying the house next door, and added, partly in apology, 'Oh, I know these days we are all supposed to be equal.'[23]

The *Bulletin* continued to take note of events and publications which had a bearing on the race question in Britain and other countries throughout its lifetime.

But the main business of the *Bulletin* and indeed the Library continued to be Germany, Nazism and the post-war development of democracy and anti-democracy. It followed and contributed to the academic debate about Nazi Germany and the Holocaust. It reviewed all the major books covering the subject. The names of many eminent historians, politicians and thinkers are to be found in the pages of the *Bulletin*, including Hugh Trevor Roper, John Wheeler-Bennett, Alan Bullock, Robert Weltsch, Lionel Kochan, James Callaghan, Gerald Reitlinger and many others.

It is noteworthy that one of the earliest systematic studies of the roots of Nazi ideology was by the Wiener Library's Eva Reichmann: *Hostages of Civilisation*, published in 1950. Two years later Alan Bullock published his acclaimed *Hitler: A Study in Tyranny*. He was another academic with a long association with the Library, yet his work ignored the centrality of anti-Semitism in Hitler's world-view, as the *Bulletin* did not hesitate to point out.

One seminal work, Reitlinger's, was carried out largely at the Library, a debt the author acknowledged generously. *The Final Solution* was among the very first systematic academic accounts of the fate of the Jews under Hitler. Widely ignored and with only very modest sales, it nevertheless laid the groundwork for a vast amount of later research. It was reviewed in the *Bulletin* by Louis de Jong, the director of the Netherlands State Institute for War-Documentation, who stressed that while studies of particular countries had been carried out, 'There exists no other book in which the tragedy of European Jewry as a whole is described in such abundant detail.'[24] The book has gone on to become a classic.

The same issue of the *Bulletin* which reviewed Reitlinger carried an item on its front page highlighting the paucity of work being done on the Holocaust. Entitled 'Let There Be Research' the editorial focused on the failure of the work being done to be systematic and scholarly:

> Many of the books published during the last few years in Britain and USA are undoubtedly instructive, and it would be wrong to dismiss as negligible the German literature of post-war memoirs. But it is probably only fair to assume that few of the authors were actuated by a desire for scientific research. Frequently the trained reader has the impression that the house is being built from the roof downwards. The main reason more often than not is inadequate familiarity with the sources. To be sure, the sources are not easily traced, not even those which have been printed, for in the majority of instances, no sign posts have yet been fixed.
>
> Some sign posts are being set up by the Wiener Library – in this Bulletin

as well as in the catalogue series of which Nos 1 and 2 have so far appeared
. . . But the source material available in the Wiener Library, much of it
unique, calls for systematic exploitation. The next step, therefore, must be to
enable the Library to carry research into those fields of the Hitler period
which have hitherto been little or not at all explored.[25]

Among the specific areas identified requiring research was the Pogrom of
November 1938 – which had been ignored by writers up to that date. The
Library actively encouraged and to some extent sponsored studies in this field.
Lionel Kochan's ground-breaking study on the Kristallnacht, for instance,
entitled *Pogrom*, was carried out at the Library with Wiener Library sponsor-
ship (funded out of Claims Conference money). In this way the Library not
only reflected and reviewed progress in the academic study of the Holocaust,
but played a crucial role in shaping it. The intellectual force at the Library
driving this work was C.C. Aronsfeld. Modern scholarship on Nazi Germany
and the Holocaust owes a debt to Aronsfeld that has been poorly acknowledged.

Only a very few books published in the 1950s concerning the Holocaust
made a large impact on the general public. One was *The Scourge of the
Swastika*, by Lord Russell of Liverpool. Its success was based on graphic
depictions of Nazi sadism. It is not now held in high regard, but was seen as
valuable at the time in arousing widespread interest in the subject. Leonard
Montefiore reviewed it for the *Bulletin*. He pointed out a number of errors, was
conspicuously unable to praise it for extending scholarship and recommended
it to 'those who need to be reminded of Nazi crimes.'[26]

The greatest publishing success to come out of the Holocaust was, of course,
The Diary of Anne Frank. This book was completely ignored by Aronsfeld at
the time of its publication, presumably because he did not see it as constituting
a significant contribution to the scholarly study of the Holocaust. Nevertheless
this book developed a life of its own: it has been uniquely successful, being
adapted for the stage and cinema, and these manifestations were taken note of
in the *Bulletin*.

Throughout the 1950s and the first half of the 1960s, the *Bulletin* tracked the
development of Holocaust scholarship and reviewed its products. In 1961
A.J.P. Taylor published his *Origins of the Second World War*. This volume
triggered an angry controversy, because Taylor attempted something
approaching a defence of Hitler, including claims that he did not directly order
the Final Solution and was unaware of its being carried out. The book was
widely criticised in the press; in the *Wiener Library Bulletin* it was lambasted
under the heading 'History as She Never Was'.

EYEWITNESS ACCOUNTS

The *Bulletin* was only one branch of the Library's post-war publishing activities. From a historian's viewpoint the most interesting and significant publications were the eyewitness reports of Nazi persecution, which the Library began to assemble almost the moment at which the war in Europe ended. It is impossible to overestimate the importance of these early published testimonies by Holocaust survivors – certainly the first of their kind in the United Kingdom, probably in the world.

The first of these remarkable testimonies was issued in May 1945, just days before the end of the war. It was written by Mordecai Lichtenstein, who visited the Library shortly after he was liberated from Auschwitz. A Polish Jew born in the town of Bendzin, near Katowice, Lichtenstein was a partner in a timber business. Having unsuccessfully tried to escape the German advance, he found himself stranded in Bendzin. His report is remarkable in its detailed description of life under Nazi occupation, transportation to the camp, the selection process, the quarantine, life in the prisoners' sick bay and all the grotesque minutiae of cruelty, torment, suffering and death. The conclusion graphically illustrates the sad fate of the survivor, adrift in a foreign culture, unable to find out what has happened to relatives and friends and carrying the burden of unbearable knowledge:

> Now I am here, I live in the elegant flat of a friend from Bendzin, I am free, but I cannot feel happy. My parents-in-law were gassed, my younger brother, his wife and their little daughter gassed, my brother-in-law Moses hanged, and his wife and her friend died from typhus in the women's camp. I lost sight of my second brother and my brother-in-law Wolf during the shooting near Laband, and I do not know whether they have survived that assault. Worst of all, however, I do not know anything about my wife's fate. I only know that the women were evacuated from Auschwitz like ourselves and taken across the Oder.
>
> I am very grateful for the hospitality this country has offered me, but whether a man of my experiences will ever be able to enjoy life again, that remains to be seen. At the moment I cannot believe it.[27]

The second of these 'personal reports received by the JCIO from eye-witnesses of the persecution of Jews under Nazi rule', was entitled *The Persecution of Jews in Holland 1940–1944: Westerbork and Bergen-Belsen*. Its author was Dr Israel Taubes and his report was a very systematic account of the Dutch experience of Nazism. It paints a vivid picture of the life from which Wiener escaped, and to which his wife, children and colleagues were condemned. Taubes describes the Nazi invasion and the efforts of people to flee the country:

> Thousands of Dutch men and women raced to Ijmuiden, a small fishing harbour, trying to get across to England, in small steamers and fishing boats. It was almost too late when the Dutch Jewish Aid Committee (Comité voor Byjzondere Joodsche Belangen – the Committee David Cohen had founded with A. Asscher) began to organise a few buses. . . Only very few Dutch Jews managed actually to reach England.[28]

Taubes's report offers an excellent account of the dilemma of David Cohen in his role as joint leader of the Joodse Raad, once the Nazis stopped prevaricating about its true purpose:

> On July 4th, 1942, SS Sturmführer Lages sent for the leaders of the Jews, Asscher and Cohen. He told them that a certain number of Jews were needed for 'labour service' in Germany. All between the ages of 16 and 40 were wanted, both men and women. Such words as 'Evacuation' or 'Deportation' were never used. Lages explained that it was simply a matter of a new labour force and nothing else. . . They were given three lists and had to promise to give exact addresses and to return the lists before midnight . . . This call-up was directed at non-Dutch Jews only. The lists were completed upon German orders in the Secret Department of the Jewish Council, with the result that about 4,000 non-Dutch Jews were to make up the first transport for 'police-organised labour services in Germany'. . . the fact that only foreign Jews had been called up caused violent indignation amongst these people. Since the Germans never admitted any distinction between Jews, Messrs. Asscher and Cohen were publicly charged with having sacrificed the foreign Jews.[29]

For the Germans, it was a triumph of strategy: spreading division and conflict among the victims, and thereby making them more confused, panic-stricken and manipulable. For Cohen and Asscher it was an impossible situation. Whatever action they took would lead to condemnation from one quarter or another. Dr Taubes's report continues and describes the journey to Bergen-Belsen, his own experience being rather less horrific than that of others because he was on the Palestine Exchange Register. His report ends on a happy note, with his arrival in Haifa, after many false starts and a long and arduous journey.

The third report was by Max Mannheimer, a 27-year-old man whose parents had left Germany before 1933 and settled in Amsterdam. It was entitled *Theresienstadt and from Theresienstadt to Auschwitz*. Mannheimer had been educated there and had worked as a senior clerk in a bank. He was active as a volunteer in the Joodse Raad and was arrested in December 1943, having lived underground since May, when he learned that he was being sought.

Mannheimer provided a detailed description of Theresienstadt and the life in the model camp of the Nazis, set up to serve as their alibi. There is a fine rage in his testimony:

> Was it not an example of humanity to set up a kindergarten, to permit Jews to go to a cafe or listen to a music band?
> Humane indeed, if you call it humane to deprive decent, innocent people arbitrarily of their freedom, to strip them of everything but the clothes they had on, to feed them on a diet which enabled only the strong to survive, to isolate ordinary people and some who had won world fame, completely from the outer world, behind guarded ghetto walls, sealed off from life.[30]

And he reported how 'all the time I could not help imagining that we were interred in a mass grave on which people were dancing.'

Mannheimer went on to describe the transport to Auschwitz, how the SS forced the prisoners to write postcards to their families describing the good conditions and food, and he laid stress on the fact that 'the whole responsibility for the murder of my poor fellow-prisoners lay with the Commanding SS officers. Where no orders to massacre were given . . . no-one was shot.'

The fourth report in the series consisted of three letters written by survivors who had been deported from Germany to the Riga Ghetto and had ended up in Sweden. These letters contain gruesome accounts of the hardships suffered on the journey, the appalling brutality of the SS in Riga, the terrible conditions in the Ghetto and in the Kaiserwald and Salaspilz camps nearby.

The fifth report was by Paula Littauer and detailed her experiences of persecution in Berlin and Brussels. It contains some relatively heart-warming reflections on the attitude of Germans. Of being forced to wear the yellow star, Littauer said:

> Being clearly marked, we were exposed to every kind of malice and jeering insult. A large proportion of the German people certainly did not approve of this persecution; but Hitler's ardent followers did wholeheartedly.[31]

She also reported that upon being forced to leave her flat, she realised later that she had left all her savings in a hiding place. Returning, she naturally could not find them. Calculating that it must have been the workmen who cleared the flat, she plucked up courage to face them and ask for the return of the cash. Somewhat to her surprise they agreed. They told her that they had only given back the money because she had not involved the police: they detested the police every bit as much as they hated the Nazis.

The final report, by Dr Jacob Jacobson, concerned the daily life in Theresienstadt (Jacobson began his account of being arrested with the dry remark, 'It was an unpleasant day') and featured an annex by the former president of the JCIO, David Cohen, on the behaviour of the Russian liberators of Theresienstadt. Cohen writes of 'This liberation – a miraculous, almost unbelievable event,' and that 'tirelessly, the Russians brought food and medicaments. One lorry after another arrived. . .'

The *Jewish Survivors' Reports*, as the series came to be known, was the first attempt to capture eye-witness accounts of the Holocaust, but the effort was not systematic. The Library staff simply seized such opportunities as presented themselves. Later, beginning in the mid-1950s, a properly funded systematic effort was made to gather such reports under the auspices of a new research department at the Library, of which Dr Eva Reichmann was the head. By the early 1960s over 1,200 had been secured. They remain among the Library's most harrowing yet valuable holdings and their number has been added to steadily over the years.

Collecting the testimony of survivors was regarded 'as a safeguard against any future attempts to falsify the events of those years'. This is a remarkable instance of the foresight of the Library: in the 1950s the phenomenon of so-called revisionism or Holocaust denial was little known, yet from the 1960s on it became an important issue.

The eyewitness accounts were to be collected systematically, with a team of interviewers tracing, contacting and persuading survivors to take part. It ran from the mid-1950s until the mid-1960s. The methods used for collecting the early reports were described in the *Bulletin* in 1955:

> Only occasionally the reports will be drawn up by the authors themselves; usually the eye witnesses are visited by one of the Library's interviewers for one or more conversations. During these the interviewer tries to elicit as much information as possible and, on the strength of it, writes the report. This is submitted to the interviewed person to ensure that it contains no mistake or misunderstanding, and is subsequently incorporated into our archives. For the purposes of reference, it is analysed, catalogued and cross-indexed.[32]

The opportunity which the Library gave to survivors to bear witness and record their experiences was very precious. In the immediate post-war era, survivors endured a degree of social isolation which some have described as causing them greater suffering than they had experienced in the camps. In the United Kingdom, the revelation of the horrors of Belsen and the other camps liberated by the Allies served to arouse violent anti-German feelings which, grotesquely, were often directed at German victims of the camps. The government's policy of covering over the fact that the Jews were the main victims of persecution meant that few people understood the nature of their trauma. Furthermore the political unrest in Palestine fuelled anti-Jewish feelings. This served to compound the Anglo-Jewish tendency in the post-war years towards introspection and anxiety about its own identity. The combination of these facts left Jewish refugees comprehensively out in the cold. The extent of their isolation can be gauged from the fact that in Hampstead, one of the classic refugee havens, a petition was organised in 1945 calling for the removal of 'aliens'.[33] In this sort of atmosphere, the importance of the Library as a social centre and as a place to which severely traumatised people could turn for validation cannot be overestimated.

In the slow emergence of the Holocaust as a field of academic study, the *Wiener Library Catalogues*, compiled and issued between 1949 and 1978 played a highly significant role. The seven volumes (eight, more properly, since the 1960 edition of the first catalogue is in fact an entirely new book) constituted, at their respective times of publication, pretty well the most comprehensive bibliographies available in their field – a proud boast for what was actually just a listing of the Library's own holdings. Like the *Bulletin,* they were a driving force behind the systematizing of scholarship on the Nazi era and the establishment of contemporary history as an academic discipline. While no longer able to make any claim to completeness, the catalogues still provide an excellent way into the subject and document very many publications long out of print and now scarce. The *Catalogues* were published by Vallentine Mitchell, a house closely associated with the Jewish Chronicle. This fact is indicative of the interest taken in the Library by David Kessler, the *Chronicle*'s chairman. At one time the *Bulletin* was also printed by Vallentine Mitchell. The Library also continued to issue other mimeographed reports on various subjects, chiefly Jewry and Germany.

During this period Alfred Wiener and his Library also enjoyed some moments of great personal satisfaction. One of the greatest came in 1949, when Thomas Mann, together with his wife, Katia and daughter, Erika, were making a semi-official tour of Europe and agreed to visit the Library during their 10-day stay in Britain.

Wiener and Montefiore worked together on introductory speeches and the drawing up of a guest list and their excitement is almost tangible in the notes they exchanged at this time:

Thanks for putting in the remark on Erika but, I am afraid, it appears now this would over-emphasise her importance unless you do not say a few words more about T.M. himself whom we consider the most outstanding living representative of all that is valuable and lasting in German civilisation.

May I also suggest that 'novelist' is perhaps not doing him full justice; what about writer and thinker?[34]

The occasion focused public attention on the Library when it needed it. It was widely noted in the press (the *Manchester Guardian* rather unkindly referred to the Library as 'a chamber of horrors'). The visit took place on 18 May, witnessed by a selection of the Library's friends. Mann gave a short speech, part of which was translated and printed in the *Bulletin*. Montefiore introduced him remarking laconically, 'So, after you have looked at Dr Thomas Mann, whose presence has drawn you here, spare a few moments please to look at our books.'[35]

Mann replied that seldom in the history of civilisation had there been such degradation of humanity as during the time documented by the Wiener collection. He praised the Library's work during the war and spoke about the importance of its future. He concluded:

> . . . Germans should remember, and from the remembrance they should draw the impetus to make good their failings. The German authors will have a lot to do before they have written up a library to compare with this one for truth and justice.[36]

But despite occasional highlights like Mann's visit, the daily reality of trying to maintain the Library began to wear Wiener down. By 1950 he was sufficiently disheartened by the continuing financial difficulties and by his failure to attract a decent level of support, that he was ready to contemplate sending the Library out of Britain to get it off his hands. This is not to suggest that he had lost faith in its importance or value. He recognised these as clearly as ever, and he wanted a permanent settlement of its future. But he was now 65 years old and doubtless wanted to reduce his work-load and settle his affairs.

NOTES

1. Selig Brodetsky was a mathematician and the first East European immigrant to serve as president of the Board of Deputies; Lavy Bakstansky was the secretary of the Zionist Federation. The two men were key players in the power struggle between the Anglo-Jewish elite and the immigrant 'upstarts', which characterised Anglo-Jewish life during the war years.
2. Quoted in Leonard Stein and C.C. Aronsfeld (eds), *Leonard G. Montefiore 1889–1961 In*

Memoriam (London: Vallentine Mitchell, 1964), p. 14.

3. Leonard Stein and C.C. Aronsfeld (eds) *Leonard G. Montefiore* , p. 16.
4. Alfred Wiener to Leonard Montefiore, 30.4.1945, Wiener Archive, Wiener Library.
5. Arnold Toynbee, Testimonial signed and dated 25.8.1945, Wiener Archive, Wiener Library.
6. Letter from Leonard G. Montefiore to Alfred Wiener, 12.6.1946, Wiener Archive, Wiener Library.
7. Letter from Alfred Wiener to Leonard G. Montefiore, 13.7.1946, Wiener Archive, Wiener Library.
8. Draft application to Unilever, Wiener Archive, Wiener Library.
9. Letter from Leonard G. Montefiore to Alfred Wiener, 22.7.1946, Wiener Archive, Wiener Library.
10. Letter from Leonard G. Montefiore to Alfred Wiener, undated, Wiener Archive, Wiener Library.
11. *Jewish Central Information Office, The Wiener Library, Its History and Activities 1934–1945*, London, The Wiener Library, p. 3.
12. *Jewish Central Information Office, The Wiener Library, Its History and Activities*, p. 3.
13. *Jewish Central Information Office, The Wiener Library, Its History and Activities*, p. 3.
14. *Jewish Central Information Office, The Wiener Library, Its History and Activities*, p. 12.
15. 'Achievements and Aspirations', *Wiener Library Bulletin*, Vol. I, No. 1, Nov. 1946, p. 1.
16. The financial statement is contained in a letter from Alfred Wiener to Leonard G. Montefiore, 7.2.1947; Montefiore's reply is 10.2.1947, Wiener Archive, Wiener Library.
17. M. de Baer, 'Nuremberg and the War Criminal', *Wiener Library Bulletin*, Vol. I, No. 1, Nov. 1946, p. 3.
18. L.W. Bondy: *Report on a Recent Journey to Germany* (London: nd).
19. L.W. Bondy, *Racketeers of Hatred* (London: Norman Wolsey, 1946), p. 257.
20. L.W. Bondy: *Report on a Recent Journey* .
21. For a survey of the post-war scene, see Part II of Tony Kushner, *The Holocaust and the Liberal Imagination* (Oxford: Blackwell, 1994), an excellent, if in places rather Whiggish account.
22. 'Concentration Camps to be Investigated by Social Science', *Wiener Library Bulletin* , Vol. I, No. 3–4, 1947, p. 15.
23. 'Negroes in Britain: The Challenge of Racial Prejudice', *Wiener Library Bulletin* Vol. II, No 5, 1948, p. 27.
24. Louis de Jong, 'The Extermination: A Standard Work from Source Material', *Wiener Library Bulletin*, Vol. VII, No. 3–4, 1953, p. 17.
25. 'Let There Be Research', *Wiener Library Bulletin*, Vol. VII, No. 3–4, 1953, p. 15.
26. Leonard Montefiore, 'Lord Russell's "Scourge of the Swastika"', *Wiener Library Bulletin*, Vol. VIII, No. 5–6, 1954, p. 30.
27. *Jewish Survivors Report: Documents of Nazi Guilt* No 1, M. Lichtenstein, 'Eighteen Months in the Oswiecim Extermination Camp', London May 1945, p. 15.
28. *Jewish Survivors Report: Documents of Nazi Guilt* No 2, Dr Israel Taubes, 'The Persecution of Jews in Holland 1940–1944, Westerbork and Bergen-Belsen', London, June 1945, p. 1.
29. Dr Israel Taubes, 'The Persecution of Jews in Holland 1940–1944, p. 16.
30. *Jewish Survivors Report: Documents of Nazi Guilt* No 3, Max Mannheimer, 'Theresienstadt and From Theresienstadt to Auschwitz', London, July 1945, p. 7.
31. *Jewish Survivors Report: Documents of Nazi Guilt* No 5, Paula Littauer, 'My Experiences during the Persecution of the Jews in Berlin and Brussels 1939–1945', London, Oct. 1945, p.2.
32. 'Eye Witness Accounts and Original Documents', *Wiener Library Bulletin*, Vol. IX, No. 5–6, 1955, p. 43.
33. For this, see Tony Kushner, *The Holocaust and the Liberal Imagination*, pp. 220–21.

34. Letter from Leonard G. Montefiore to Alfred Wiener, undated, Wiener Archive, Wiener Library.
35. 'Thomas Mann at the Wiener Library', *Wiener Library Bulletin*, Vol III, No. 3–4, May–July 1949, p. 19.
36. 'Thomas Mann at the Wiener Library', p. 19.

CHAPTER NINE

Jerusalem

T HE PLAN WIENER and Montefiore conceived for settling the Library's
future was to incorporate it into the collection of the Library at the
Hebrew University in Jerusalem. In view of his highly critical attitude to
Zionism before the war, this may seem a surprising choice. But it would be
unfair to assume that Wiener's post-war view of Palestine and, after 1948, the
state of Israel, would necessarily reflect his earlier opinions. The world after
the war was not the same; Wiener and all Jews recognised this. It is striking,
for instance, how little bitterness and how much warm comradeship is in
evidence in the relations between Wiener and former opponents such as Robert
Weltsch. Furthermore, Wiener was deeply disappointed by the disregard
which the Anglo-Jewish community as a whole showed for his Library, in spite
of generous support offered by some individuals and organisations. Israel
appeared to him the only place in the world where his life's work would be
valued, maintained and built upon.

The negotiations with the Israelis were to prove extremely complex and
trying. They dragged on for five years. The outcome was decisive for
the Library's future. Indeed it is not putting it too strongly that this was a
defining moment in the Library's history. Wiener got caught up in matters
of high politics and struggled to resist very powerful institutions which
happily would have taken over the collection while ditching the Library's
identity and ending its autonomous existence. Wiener, by standing out against
these pressures, committed the Library to a future of financial hardship
and uncertainty. He also sacrificed any hope of a quieter life: the work and
worry of keeping the Library going would be with him almost to the day of his
death.

He travelled to Israel in 1950 to open negotiations with Werner Senator, the
chief administrator of the Hebrew University. Agreement was reached quite
quickly between Wiener, Senator, Kurt Wormann, the head of the Library at
the University, and Gershom Scholem, Professor of Jewish Mysticism and the
Kabbalah at the University and the one-time librarian, that moving the Library

to Jerusalem was a good idea. In a Memo dated 6 November 1950 Senator detailed the basic plan:

1. Some kind of official relationship should be established between the Hebrew University and/or its Library and the Wiener Library. This may find expression, for instance, in the nomination of a University representative to the Board of the Wiener Library.

2. The University should support the Wiener Library by an annual subvention of £1,000–1,500 (sterling) for a number of years, say ten.

3. After that period the University will, by virtue of the annual payments, have acquired the Wiener Library, it being understood that then the University would be free to transfer the Library to Israel. It might be stipulated in the agreement that the University may have this right after a period of seven years, but that the University is bound to make a decision on the transfer after the lapse of ten years.

4. Upon expiration of these ten years a pension is to be paid to Dr Wiener. He is now 65. It appears that there are no further legal or moral commitments towards the staff to any considerable extent.

My recommendation is that the University take this opportunity of acquiring a probably unique library of historical and contemporary value along the lines set forth above.

A few days later Senator wrote a long letter to Wiener with certain clarifications:

The purchase price will amount to £15,000 payable in equal annual installments over the above period of ten years. . . The above annual installments will be used for the general purposes of the Library, and it is clearly understood that until transfer is effected the University will not be called on to meet any of the expenses or obligations of the Library beyond those annual installments.[1]

But the same letter set out the first of the many problems, namely who actually had title to the Library and whether or not Wiener was entitled to dispose of it. Clarifying this took over six weeks and Wiener then wrote optimistically to Kurt Wormann expressing the hope 'daß wir jetzt, wie ich hoffe, energisch vorwärts kommen' (that we can now move forwards energetically). It was not to be.

By 29 October 1951 a resolution was slipping away. The Israeli economy was experiencing a downturn, money was tight. Everybody appeared to be having second thoughts. Walter Zander, the secretary of the Friends of the Hebrew

University in London (the organisation that was actually to pay the money to the Library) used a conversation with Wiener in April of 1952, to raise once again the question of why Wiener wanted to sell the Library in the first place. Wiener replied that it was because he and Montefiore were now both old and in the event of their deaths the Library's future would be completely uncertain. It might be sold off at auction or broken up in other ways. In any case its loss would be a loss to Jews everywhere.

In October 1952 Norman Bentwich, the chairman of the Friends of the Hebrew University, wrote to Senator arguing strongly that buying the Library was inappropriate. He claimed that much of the Wiener Library's holdings would merely replace books the University Library had lost to 'worms and rats' and would presumably suffer the same fate. Wiener was by now convinced that the Friends (or at least Bentwich) were out to block the deal ('ich habe für solche Situationen ein deutliches Gefühl' 'I have a distinct feeling for such things.').[2]

Bentwich was however unable to halt negotiations and on 16 November 1952 Senator wrote to Wiener that 'the permanent Committee of the Executive Council of the Hebrew University has now finally confirmed the previous decision about the acquisition of the Wiener Library'.

Yet now Wiener announced unexpectedly that he had hopes of winning substantial backing from the Jewish Trust Corporation, and that since this would make the Library an even more attractive package for the University, he begged leave to follow through on the possibility and suspend the negotiations with Jerusalem.

The Jewish Trust Corporation (JTC) was set up in 1950, following the model of the American Jewish Restitution Successor Organisation. The JTC's function was to serve as the legal successor to heirless and unclaimed Jewish property recovered within the British zone of the former Third Reich. Wiener made his approach to the CBF requesting that they pass a portion of the funds allotted to them by the JTC to the Library but his request for £5,000 in the short term and a ten-year grant of £6,000 per year was rejected.

This diversion turned out to be a tactical mistake. The delay dragged on for months and meanwhile circumstances changed to such an extent that the opportunity to close a deal was to all intents and purposes lost. By the end of October 1953 the JTC matter was not settled and Wiener, after again reviewing his options, had decided to go after a share of the money being collected by the Conference on Jewish Material Claims Against Germany.

This Conference was, in the words of Nahum Goldmann, its president, 'a phenomenon without precedent in Jewish life.' It had been established after representatives of some 23 Jewish organisations concerned with the Jewish refugee problem met in October 1951 with two objectives:

To obtain funds for the relief, rehabilitation and resettlement of Jewish victims of Nazi persecution, and to aid in rebuilding Jewish communities and institutions which Nazi persecution had devastated.

To gain indemnification for injuries inflicted upon individual victims of Nazi persecution and restitution for properties confiscated by the Nazis.[3]

The cause was taken up by the Israeli government, which opened negotiations with the government of the Federal Republic early in 1952. In September of that year two agreements were signed, one between the two governments and one between the Germans and the Conference. The Conference secured a commitment from the Germans to provide a total of DM 450 million ($110 million) over an agreed period of time. This was to be used to help Jewish victims resettle and rebuild their shattered lives. Most of the money was spent resettling people who chose to make their homes in Europe, other than in the Soviet Union. But about 20 per cent was set aside for 'cultural and educational reconstruction' and with the encouragement of his friends and allies, Wiener decided to apply for some of this money.

In total the Conference distributed almost $19.5 million to educational and cultural institutions during the 1950s and 60s. It was spread among 250 organisations, over half of them Jewish schools in Europe which the Nazis had destroyed and which were rebuilt and stocked with Conference money. Under the heading of Commemoration and Documentation of the Jewish Catastrophe, four institutions received funding; the Yad Vashem Authority, Jerusalem; the Yivo Institute, New York; the Centre de Documentation Juive and the Wiener Library.[4]

But for Wiener, making the decision to ask for Claims Conference money was a very different matter from actually getting any. He found the whole experience frustrating. According to Walter Laqueur:

> Wiener was an excellent diplomat but also somewhat naive; he seems to have believed the funds would be distributed mainly according to merit and importance. The idea that political pull and manoeuvring would play the decisive role and that self-advertisement and public relations would be crucial seems not to have crossed his mind. Politically the Wiener Library had little support; on the contrary, a German Jewish institution was always slightly suspect in view of the traditional antagonism towards German Jewry among those of East-European background.[5]

A second complication arose from the establishment and rapid growth of the Yad Vashem organisation. On 15 January 1954 Wiener saw an article in the *Jewish Chronicle* concerning two developments in Israel. The first was an agreement signed between the Yivo Institute and Yad Vashem to work together on a project to establish a memorial to Holocaust victims. The second concerned an arrangement that Yad Vashem had made with the French Centre de Documentation Juive, under which Yad Vashem would pay the Centre some $400,000 in return for copies of its documents. The money would come from the Claims Conference.

Initially Wiener regarded these developments as potentially helpful to his efforts to settle the Library's affairs. He got assurances from the director of Yad Vashem, Benzion Dinur, that it recognised the importance of the Library, that it was content with the negotiations between it and the Hebrew University, that it would support Wiener's application to the Claims Conference and that Yad Vashem felt it a duty to assist the Library to secure its budget.

Wiener's application consisted of a four-page account of the Library's history and activities and a paragraph headed Our Urgent Wants: .

> For an extension of our premises, the acquisition of new office equipment, the filling of certain gaps in our collections, the removal of our books from their present state of 'Dispersion', etc, we would need a first allocation of £5000. For the future maintenance of the extended Institute and the implementation of projects as outlined above, we would apply for an annual amount of £6,000 for at least ten years.[6]

In the event the Library was offered $15,000, roughly half what it had asked for. Wiener was incensed. When he met with the director of Yad Vashem in May 1954 he told him that he intended to turn the money down. Later he sensibly changed his mind stipulating that he and Montefiore understood the $15,000 to cover only the last six months of 1954, a ruse intended to force the allocation for 1955 up to $30,000. (By way of comparison, the Yad Vashem Authority received an allocation of over $211,000, the Yivo Institute got almost $112,000 and the Centre de Documentation Juive was granted $150,000).[7] The following year Wiener put in an application for £23,000, then reduced his request on the advice of a contact at the Claims Conference and was again affronted when the allocation for 1955 came through at just $16,000.

The agreement Yad Vashem had signed with the Yivo Institute meant that, together, the two institutions had considerable leverage at the Claims Conference. There seems little doubt that Yad Vashem and Yivo officials, particularly Yivo's Mark Uveeler, were very keen to acquire the Wiener's books. However preserving the identity of the Wiener Library was apparently not their priority.

By July 1954 Bentwich in London was strongly recommending to Wormann that the University should let Yad Vashem pay for at least half the Library. He saw no harm in the University having no exclusive rights over it. Wormann also saw how things were developing and wrote to Wiener:

> As you know, our government and the Claims Conference are extremely interested in building up Yad Vashem rapidly. The international Jewish organisations are very active in support of these plans, and Dr Nahum Goldmann is personally a great supporter of Yad Vashem.[8]

The message was clear: if Yad Vashem had set its sights on the Library, few people were going to stand in its way. In summer of 1954 Wormann wrote to Scholem that:

> Prof Dinur told me shortly afterwards when we met that he would like to take over the Wiener Library for Yad Vashem. . . Dinur would naturally like to include the library in Yad Vashem's building complex, since it is, in his view, a particularly valuable reference library for all archival research.[9]

Wormann nevertheless assured Wiener that Dinur and Schenabi of Yad Vashem were happy to contemplate joint ownership with the University and understood that in order to satisfy Wiener the Library would have to be located on the University's campus.

By the end of January 1955 an agreement had been reached in Israel that Yad Vashem and the Hebrew University would buy the Library jointly, and that it should transfer to Jerusalem in 1960. The scheme favoured by Wormann was for the Library proper to be housed at the National Library and for the archives of documents and press cuttings to go to Yad Vashem. This arrangement was formally agreed in March and the University's solicitor was instructed to draw up a new contract. Wiener declared himself satisfied.

But in May 1955 the general secretary of the Yivo Institute, Mark Uveeler, came to see Wiener, tactlessly telling him that he intended to secure the Library exclusively for Yad Vashem, and that Nahum Goldmann would be 'helpful to the utmost extent' in bringing this about. Wiener was terribly alarmed about this, writing to Wormann in an uncharacteristically heated manner about the plans of Yad Vashem and Yivo for 'world domination', which would leave the Library in ruins. Wormann and Scholem replied, urging Wiener to calm himself and to concentrate on bringing the deal to a conclusion. But between themselves they were almost as dismayed as he was.

Wiener himself was becoming ever more unhappy, insisting that the Yivo Institute and Yad Vashem were trying to undermine his life's work with their political shenanigans:

I cannot take the treatment we have experienced from the Claims Conference and especially from Yivo and Yad Vashem as lightly as your letter suggests. It is, from our side, a question of work and research projects which are quite simply being sabotaged by dishonesty, carelessness and ill-will. Something has occurred, which is just as unsatisfactory as what has already happened. I am neither over-sensitive in such matters, nor am I lacking in understanding for the position of others, even where that position is one I don't like. However, I do not understand all this and I am not prepared to suffer and to watch as good, clean and honestly executed work is deliberately prevented from coming to its proper end.[10]

On 20th October 1955 Zander forwarded to Wormann a telegram from Mr Hoffman (negotiating on behalf of the University):

Attended Yad Vashem meeting re Wiener stop Committee unanimously endorsed agreement with university stipulating Library housed Harhazi-caron stop Following today's conversation Dinur Believe possible eliminate now clause rehousing stop Suggest continuing negotiations Wiener stop.[11]

Scholem wrote to Wormann on 8 November and explained how the University had been boxed into a corner. The Yad Vashem people (he argued) regarded the Library as the one concrete element in their programme. They could not afford to 'lose' it to the University.

Scholem saw no possibility of resisting Yad Vashem short of Wiener refusing to sign a contract taking the Library off the University campus. He explained that Dinur was unconcerned at this possibility and seemed to rely on the pressure the Claims Conference would bring to bear on Wiener. In this supposition he was mistaken, and by the time he realised it and was prepared to compromise, Wiener had given up the entire project.[12]

In April 1956 Wiener wrote a personal letter to Wormann's wife. In it he told her that all these developments had thrown him into confusion:

Now there is a chaos that I cannot find my way out of.[13]

And indeed he didn't. Instead he entered upon his 70s knowing that the future of the Library would continue to be uncertain. He probably understood that he was unlikely to secure it within his lifetime.

In conducting the negotiations with Jerusalem, Wiener had been characteristically discreet, not to say secretive. Most of the correspondence was conducted from his home address and he did not discuss the plans with the Library's staff, although Montefiore was of course kept fully informed and his views canvassed. Aronsfeld had no idea of what was afoot. Wiener repeatedly asked his correspondents to exercise discretion. Whenever it emerged that rumours about the negotiations were circulating in London, he flew into a near-panic.

The whole episode of these negotiations demonstrated to Wiener and his supporters that there was no whole-hearted support for the Library in the larger Jewish world, anymore than there was among Anglo-Jewry. Certainly Wiener had friends at the Hebrew University and certainly many people were willing to help him. But the specifically German identity of Wiener's collection was an embarrassment and inconvenience to many of those who recognised the quality of the collection and would have liked to acquire it. This reflects the extent to which the German Jewish non-Zionist and assimilationist milieu was vilified and despised after the war by the Zionists, who came to dominance in Israel and the United States. This prejudice and unwillingness to recognise the achievements of German Jewry in combating Nazism remains, in my view, a bottom-line reality to this day. It explains why the Library struggled so hard through the 1960s and 70s and why many today remain keen to see it absorbed into a university or slowly transformed into an Anglo-Jewish institution.

NOTES

1. David W. Senator to Alfred Wiener, 28.11.1950, Wiener Library correspondence, Jewish National and University Archive, Jerusalem; I am most grateful to Mr Rafael Weiser, Director of the Department of Manuscripts and Archives, The Jewish National & University Library for arranging for the Wiener Library correspondence kept there to be microfilmed and made available to me.

2. Norman Bentwich to David W. Senator, 16.10.1952; Alfred Wiener to Kurt Wormann 17.10.1952, Wiener Library correspondence, Jewish National and University Archive, Jerusalem.

3. *Twenty Years Later: Activities of the Conference on Jewish Material Claims against Germany* (New York: Conference on Material Claims against Germany, 1972), p. 9.

4. Yad Vashem (Martyrs and Heroes Remembrance Authority) is the Israeli national institution for Holocaust remembrance; Yivo is an abbreviation of Yiddisher Visenshaftikher Institut, the world's largest organisation for Yiddish research; the Centre de Documentation Juive was founded by Isaac Schneersohn in 1943 during the Nazi occupation, to gather documents concerning the Holocaust.

5. Walter Laqueur, 'Dr Wiener and his Library', *Wiener Library Bulletin*, Special Issue, 1983.

6. Draft application, Wiener Archive, Wiener Library.

7. *Conference on Jewish Material Claims against Germany, Report 1954*, (New York: Conference on Material Claims against Germany, 1954), p. 83. Over the period 1952–72, the Conference allocated $86,000 to the Wiener Library. Yad Vashem received $2,787,000, the Yivo Institute received $790,000, and the Centre de Documentation Juive got over $300,000. See *Twenty Years Later, (*note 3 above), pp. 61–6.

8. Wie Ihnen selbst bekannt ist, ist sowohl unsere Regierung wie die Claims Conference an dem schnellen Aufbau der Yad wa-shem Organisation ausserordentlich interessiert. Die

internationalen jüdischen Organisationen unterstützen diese Pläne sehr tatkräftig, und besonders Dr Nahum Goldmann ist persönlich ein grosser Förderer von Yad wa-shem. Kurt Wormann to Alfred Wiener, 28.7.1954, Wiener Library correspondence, Jewish National and University Archive, Jerusalem.

9. [Prof Dinur] hatte kurz danach mir bei einer Begegnung auch direkt gesagt, dass er die Wiener Library für Yad wa-Shem übernehmen möchte . . . Dinur möchte aber natürlich gern die Bibliothek selbst in den Gebäudekomplex von Yad wa-Shem einreihen, da sie seiner Meinung nach für alle archivalischen Forschungen eine besonders wertvolle Handbibliothek sein kann. Kurt Wormann to Gershom G. Scholem, 27.7.1954, Wiener Library correspondence, Jewish National and University Archive, Jerusalem.

10. Die Behandlung aber, die wir durch die Claims Conference erfahren und insbesondere durch Yivo-Yad Vashem, kann ich so leicht nicht nehmen, wie es aus Ihrem Briefe heraus zu klingen scheint. Es handelt sich dabei für uns um Arbeit und Forschungsprojekte, die durch Unwahrhaftigkeit, Lässigkeit und Übelwollen einfach sabotiert werden. Inzwischen hat sich wieder manches ereignet, das ebenso unerfreulich ist wie das bereits Geschehene. Ich bin weder empfindlich noch in solchen Sachen sentimental, noch fehlt mir Verständnis für das Verhalten anderer, auch wenn mir das Verhalten nicht gefällt. Hier aber bin ich mit meinem Latein zu Ende, und ich bin nicht gewillt, dass alles einzustecken und zu sehen, wie absichtlich gute, saubere und ehrlich getane Arbeit nicht zu ihrem Rechte kommen soll. Alfred Wiener to Kurt Wormann, 26.6.1955, Wiener Library correspondence, Jewish National and University Archive, Jerusalem.

11. Wiener Library correspondence, Jewish National and University Archive, Jerusalem.

12. Gershom Scholem to Kurt Wormann, 8.11.1955, Wiener Library correspondence, Jewish National and University Archive, Jerusalem.

13. Nun ist ein Chaos aus dem ich mich nicht mehr herausfinde. Wiener Library correspondence, Jewish National and University Archive, Jerusalem.

CHAPTER TEN

The End of the Wiener Era

DEVONSHIRE STREET AND UNEXPECTED CALM

ONE OF THE factors which eventually allowed Wiener to extricate himself from the Jerusalem negotiations was an improvement in the Library's financial outlook. This was partly because Claims Conference money was trickling in. But he had also been busy cultivating German government departments whenever he visited the country, and this diplomacy began to bear fruit as the federal government started to make regular contributions to the Library.

If Wiener saw himself released from one unpleasant situation with the end of the Jerusalem negotiations, he was soon plunged into another. In 1956 the landlords at Manchester Square had again given the Library notice to quit the premises, since they were scheduled for demolition in 1957. In the last number of the *Bulletin* for that year the following forlorn notice appeared:

AN URGENT APPEAL

The Director of the Wiener Library regrets to announce that owing to the large-scale rebuilding scheme now in progress in the vicinity of Manchester Square, W., the Library will have to be removed from its premises where it was established after its transfer from Holland in 1939 and has remained ever since.

New premises will have to be found by March 1957, and in view of the difficulties of obtaining suitable accommodation an urgent appeal is made to all friends kindly to notify the Director of any address, preferably in the W1, WC1, NW1 or NW3 districts of London, large enough to afford sufficient space for the Wiener Library collections.[1]

Temporary accommodation had been found at 18 Adam Street, off the Strand, in an Annex of the Royal Society of Arts, but a considerable part of the Library's material had to be put in storage. Once again the lack of support for the Library threatened its existence. Ironically another Jewish Library in

London, that of Jews College was also moving home at this time. A press cutting in the Wiener Library's archives tells an interesting story: the Jews College Library attracted over £200,000 to support its move; the Wiener Library appealed in vain.

It was thanks to the effort of the Librarian, Mrs Ilse Wolff (formerly Mrs Löwenthal), that the premises at 4 Devonshire Street were found. She was shown the house by an estate agent and immediately felt that this was the right place. Through Montefiore, the Allocations Committee of the CBF was requested to buy the lease, since the terms of reference of that committee allowed it to do so. In due course a decision was taken and the lease purchased, and the CBF became the Library's generous landlords. At first the freeholders of the property, the Howard de Walden Estate, were unwilling to allow the building to be used for a library, insisting that it be used to house medical practices. Eventually they were persuaded otherwise and they have never since expressed any reservations about this decision. In the CBF's decision-making one again detects the quiet work of Montefiore using his influence for the Library's benefit. He was, after all, its acting chairman at the time.

The money from the Claims Conference was not available for the general support of the Library, but was intended to fund a number of specific projects including the publication of an annotated catalogue of the Library's holdings, the cataloguing of the Nuremberg War Crimes Tribunal documentation and, above all, the collecting of the eyewitness accounts. Eva Reichmann's research department was charged with processing the Nuremberg documents and with conserving materials which were deteriorating. Over the following years the Nuremberg documents were comprehensively indexed and annotated, and similar work was done on the mounting volume of eyewitness material.

Another sphere of the Library's activities was co-operating with the effort of Jewish victims of the Nazi regime to reclaim their property. The issue of restitution and indemnification went back to January 1943, when the Allied governments issued a declaration of their 'rights to declare invalid any transfers of, or dealings with, property rights and interests situated in the territories which have come under the occupation or control of the government with which they are at war.' After the war various pieces of legislation were enacted to restore property and compensate victims for their suffering and loss. Organisations to pursue these claims were established and all of them sooner or later found themselves turning to the sources in the Wiener Library. The Library enjoyed a particularly close and cordial relationship with the United Restitution Organisation, one of whose directors was Wiener's close personal friend, Hans Reichmann. The usefulness of the Library lay, to a large extent, in its holdings of local and specialist literature and periodicals of the Nazi era. These often contained vital evidence of ownership or proof of an individual having held or been dismissed from a particular post. For many years the Library employed a specialist lawyer, Frantisek Hajek, to assist with these researches.

Some time late in 1956 a decision was taken to make the Library into a limited company. Although superficially this seems a minor administrative matter, it was significant in that it brought David Kessler into a formal relationship with the Library, since he became a member of the Executive Committee. Kessler was the South African-born chairman of the *Jewish Chronicle* and the founder and chairman of Vallentine Mitchell. He had supported the Library since he first met Wiener in 1946 and built up a good personal relationship with Wiener in the coming years. Their correspondence from the years 1957–59 shows a rapid transition from Dear Dr Wiener, to Dear Wiener, to Dear Alfred. Evidently Wiener had confidence in Kessler, seeing in him the best hope for continuity and stability. In the period after Montefiore's death, Kessler would be the decisive influence in shaping the course of the Library.

In 1957 the Library recruited a new member of staff, Helen Kehr. Kehr was a British woman who had recently returned to live in London after several years in South Africa. Her husband, Erich Kehr, had been a colleague of Wiener's at the CV and the couple had remained in Germany throughout the war, Kehr suffering arrest and a period in a concentration camp. He had died in South Africa. Mrs Kehr worked as assistant to Mrs Wolff in the Library, collaborating with her on the compilation of the Wiener Library catalogue series, the editorship of which she eventually took over, when Mrs Wolff retired. Mrs Kehr remained at the Library until 1979, retiring shortly before her 80th birthday. Her 'retirement' was spent initially in compiling a bibliography entitled *The Nazi Era*, with her former colleague at the Library, Janet Langmaid. It was published in 1982 by Mansell.

By 1958, after so many turbulent years, the Library had entered a period of unexpected calm. Settled into its new home in Devonshire Street, with a greater degree of financial security than it had known since the end of the war, Wiener and his colleagues were free to build on the formidable reputation of its collection. Ilse Wolff oversaw the compilation of the Wiener Library published catalogues, so important in establishing an academic discipline of 'Holocaust studies'. C.C. Aronsfeld edited and wrote most of the *Wiener Library Bulletin*, Eva Reichmann supervised the gathering of the eyewitness reports and organised the Nuremberg documents and toured Germany speaking to youth and Christian groups. In 1958 she and Wiener attended a three-day conference at Bad Nenndorf, near Hanover, on contemporary history and the Nazi era. Both spoke to the conference, Wiener on research projects and problems of contemporary history from the viewpoint of the Wiener Library, Reichmann on Jews in the Weimar republic.

The year 1958 was also the Library's 25th anniversary. This was marked by commissioning a book of essays on a variety of topics related to the Library's activities. Contributors included Alan Bullock on the problems of writing contemporary history, James Joll on Germany and the Spanish Civil War, Louis de Jong on Nazi-occupied Holland, Léon Poliakov on racism and Alfred Wiener on how the German Kirchenstreit of 1933–38 was perceived in England. The collection was published in 1960 under the title *On the Track of Tyranny* and was presented as a Festschrift to Leonard Montefiore on the occasion of his 70th birthday.

In October 1958 the Library received the honour of an unofficial visit from the Federal Republic's president, Professor Theodor Heuss, during his State visit. This took place at the president's own request, and although a private event, was widely regarded as the high-point of his time in Britain. Heuss had not received a particularly warm reception in Britain. *The Times* noted that most people 'felt that something was happening, for reasons of high policy, above their heads. They could accept it, but they could not pretend to rejoice.' Nevertheless Heuss's decision to take in the Library was regarded as 'exemplary', if only by the *Observer*. In the Jewish press the Library received some criticism, the *Jewish Echo*'s 'London Letter' contributor being especially blunt:

> I am sorry that the Wiener Library continues to make capital out of the visit of Professor Heuss. . . He is clearly a 'good' man but his visit to this famous Library . . . was clearly a publicity stunt. Some clever public relations man thought it up as a useful gimmick during the visit of the German President and it was exploited to the full. . . A German-Jewish journalist referred to a distinguished and outspoken critic of the visit as a 'pipe-smoking, belching ruffian.' It is in this context that I object so much to the Germans whitewashing themselves with the Wiener Library brush.[2]

The *Wiener Library Bulletin* noted that in the coverage of the visit, the press largely ignored the issue of the Jews of Germany and the Holocaust.

In 1959 the *Wiener Library Bulletin* announced the establishment of the Germania Judaica Library in Cologne. This had been set up privately with the financial backing of the city and state authorities. Wiener strongly encouraged this institute, providing the young library with materials and sitting on its Academic Advisory Council from 1961. The GJL was to a large extent modelled on the Wiener Library and throughout the 1960s and 70s the two institutions co-operated closely. The first issue of its periodical *Germania Judaica*, carried an article about Wiener and one about the Library.

THE EICHMANN TRIAL

The last great event of Wiener's time as director was the trial in Jerusalem of Adolf Eichmann. Eichmann had been captured at the end of the war and held by the Americans in an internment camp. Being a discreet bureaucrat, his name and deeds were not known at the time and he was able to escape. With the aid of a Vatican passport, he made his way to Argentina, where he lived safely until 1960. In May of that year the Israeli secret service tracked him down and kidnapped him, taking him to Jerusalem to stand trial. The hearings lasted from 2 April to 14 August 1961, with Eichmann being sentenced to death on 2 December. The sentence was carried out on 31 May 1962.

The Library provided background materials to the prosecution as it had done for the Nuremberg Trials. It was rewarded with a good deal of press attention, including a large item in the *Daily Mail*, describing the Library as 'a terrifying room in London W1' and calling Wiener 'a keeper of the mutilated German conscience':

> While the rest of the world has been forgiving and forgetting, Dr Wiener, with his assistant director, Mr Caesar Aronsfeld, and their staff, have gone on piling up the indictment. . . Sixty thousand books on the nation which went mad – and papers, documents, photographs pointing the finger at a man who first drew breath in the land which is now Israel, and who devoted his life to the extermination of its people.[3]

(The reference to Eichmann having first drawn breath in Palestine is, of course, a journalistic inexactitude: in fact he was born in Solingen, Germany, grew up largely in Austria and visited Palestine only in 1938 as part of a fact-finding mission into the Final Solution)

On 9 July 1960 the head of Israeli security, Chief Superintendent Abraham Selinger, had visited the Library to collect documentation relating to the Eichmann case and to meet former concentration camp inmates.

At the Library the Eichmann trial was very much Aronsfeld's event. He gave numerous press interviews and wrote a large article on the Library for the *Scotsman*. It was he who helped Commander Seligman amass the evidence linking Eichmann to specific crimes. The biggest article was published in the *Toronto Daily Star* in November 1960. It describes the items taken by Selinger for the prosecution's case and the efforts that the Library was making to trace survivors presumed to be living in the United Kingdom. Aronsfeld also showed the paper a letter from Eichmann to the Anatomy Department of Strasbourg University offering a supply of skeletons, and correspondence between Eichmann and concentration camp officials about the 'installation of gassing machines'.

The Eichmann trial is sometimes portrayed as marking a turning point in general attitudes towards the Holocaust. Yet while it served to bring the issue to the attention of a younger generation and spark off some heated controversy, it did not fundamentally change public perceptions. Throughout the 1960s the Holocaust remained a marginal and faintly disreputable subject, both in society at large and, more importantly, in schools and universities. It is interesting in this context to recall that a standard work on the subject such as Raul Hilberg's *The Destruction of European Jewry* was rejected by numerous publishers in the late 1950s, only appearing the year Eichmann was tried. Hilberg was heavily criticised by German refugee leaders for stressing Jewish passivity in face of Nazi persecution, a point also taken up by Hannah Arendt in her *Eichmann in Jerusalem.*

The *Bulletin* followed both the trial and the prosecutions of war criminals in West Germany which it triggered, publishing lists of people prosecuted. Yet it declined to comment in any way on the death sentence, or to acknowledge execution of it. Instead, it carried an article entitled 'Auschwitz Doctor at Large', concerning the discovery of a notorious Nazi doctor living in Ghana. For the Wiener Library, the conclusion of the Eichmann trial marked the end of only one piece of unfinished business.

COPING WITH LOSSES

At the time of the Eichmann trial Gertrude Levi worked at the Library, having joined in 1959. She was herself a concentration camp survivor and in her book *A Cat Called Adolf,* she recalled her time at the Library:

> I . . . quite enjoyed the work at the Library and found it extremely interest-ing, though somewhat harrowing . . . as the only person on the staff who had survived the concentration camps, I felt I was being used as a guinea-pig supplying information to journalists . . .
>
> I became depressed. At the Wiener Library there was a curious atmosphere; the staff were marvellous in personal relationships. Birthdays were celebrated and when someone was ill, all were sympathetic and helpful. Yet workwise they seemed to spy on each other and there was a good deal of jealousy among the personnel. As time went by, I found the atmosphere unpleasant and felt that I had to get away from the Library. [4]

Levi left in 1964 complaining of the poor pay and unhealthy atmosphere.

In the spring of 1961 Wiener announced his retirement as director of the Library, although he agreed to continue 'to attend to certain financial as well as representative matters connected with the Library.' In fact, he merely gave up day-to-day work. Nevertheless his decision underlined the fact that changes were on their way for the Library. The search for a new director had already been going on for at least a year, with various suggestions and approaches being made, none of them successful. No new director was appointed and eventually the Executive Committee settled on an interim measure. C.C. Aronsfeld took over as acting director, in charge of the Library. This was an arrangement which satisfied no-one. Aronsfeld had no ambitions to become Wiener's successor, yet his efforts to see the Library through an uncertain period brought him into conflict with the Executive Committee, especially its chairman, David Kessler. But finding a new director was a problem which took quite a long time to sort out.

Wiener, in his semi-retirement, continued to travel and speak publicly. In November 1961 he was in Germany, addressing students of the Theological Faculty at Göttingen on the subject of '2,000 years of German Jewry'. He gave the same talk to the West Berlin College of Education. At around the same time he was involved in a commission for the history of Frankfurt Jewry, representing the Library.

On 23 December 1961 Leonard Montefiore died. At the age of 72 he had been in good health and his death surprised and shocked many. Wiener wrote an obituary for the *Bulletin,* which appeared early the following year. In it he called Montefiore the 'father of the Wiener Library' and remarked that he:

> . . . chose to make himself barely conspicuous and always took exquisite care to cause no inconvenience. Consideration for others was the hallmark of his character, he seemed to be showing it even in his death, passing away suddenly, almost casually, sparing himself and others the trials of illness and death.[5]

Montefiore's death precipitated a crisis for the Library. Not only had its most generous benefactor died without leaving any provision for it in his will, but without him the Library lacked its most important friend inside the Anglo-Jewish community. Aside from what he himself gave, Montefiore habitually used his influence with the various committees he sat on for the Library's benefit. Without him funding was a great deal harder to come by.

Wiener was keen that David Kessler succeed Montefiore, perhaps because Kessler had consistently used his influence on the *Jewish Chronicle* to publicise and help the Library and would in this way help draw in sympathy and money from the Jewish community at large. Yet while Kessler was a staunch supporter of the cause, he had less time to devote to it, less personal wealth and perhaps a different view on what was for the best.

After his appointment Kessler took a cool look at the situation and reported to one of his correspondents that 'the death of Leonard Montefiore . . . left a serious gap in the financial structure.' But he also noted that the Library had had a certain success in raising money on its own behalf:

> I have been looking at the amount of money the Wiener Library has raised in this country during the last five years. I find that it amounts to a sum of £60,000 or an average of £12,000 per annum.[6]

He was optimistic that the Library's financial situation could be stabilised. A few weeks earlier he had written to Professor Max Beloff, a member of the Executive Committee, that 'the financial situation is, of course, serious, but not desperate.' What he came to see as its best hope was a tripartite arrangement involving the Claims Conference, the Allocations Committee of the CBF and the Library itself. In the same letter to Beloff he concedes that 'if my expectation of support from these organisations is wrong, the position certainly turns from serious into desperate.'[7]

Beloff, for his part, in a letter dated October 1962 urged Kessler to work towards the Library being taken over 'part and parcel' by University College London or the LSE, because 'Anglo-Jewry would never support it.'

In fact the Claims Conference continued to fund some of the Library's projects for many years, but correspondence housed in the *Jewish Chronicle* archives at Southampton University makes clear that the relationship between the Claims Conference and the Wiener Library was never an easy one. With the appointment of Mark Uveeler, who had been at the Yivo Institute during the time Wiener was negotiating with Jerusalem, as the Claims Conference secretary, the difficulties increased. It was he who in the first instance dealt with and approved the Library's applications for grants. Uveeler had difficulty with the Library and while he doubtless recognised the value of the collection, seems not to have been enamoured of its personnel or management. There seems little doubt that he put obstacles in the Library's way when it asked for help. In private meetings he apparently encouraged Kessler's plan of asking the Conference to fund the Library's work under two heads, its general running costs and its special projects. But when Kessler submitted a formal application on this basis, Uveeler reacted with surprise and outrage, claiming that this request was unwarranted and could not be approved.

The Library had already honoured Montefiore with a Festschrift in 1960 (*On the Track of Tyranny*) and now paid further tribute with a publication for private circulation. Containing some characteristic writings by Montefiore himself, it also contained reminiscences of his friends and colleagues. It was edited by Leonard Stein and C.C. Aronsfeld and appeared under the title *LGM* –Montefiore's initials.

Wiener himself was now approaching the end of his life. He undertook fewer public engagements, suffered a good deal of illness, and devoted his diminishing reserves of strength and energy to grappling with the mounting problems of the Library. In May 1963 he was in Germany, talking to officials of the German Interior Ministry about the Library's needs. He secured immediate funding of DM25,000 to help out the 1963 budget and an assurance that this would constitute only a part of what the ministry would grant. But the Germans wanted assurances that in Wiener's words:

> . . . it [the Library] continue to be run in that spirit which my relationship to
> the German people has determined from the very start.[8]

In this connection, the Germans placed some importance on Aronsfeld's appointment as acting director. Yet even German support did not constitute a long-term answer to the Library's troubles. The problem was that the Germans were as unwilling as everyone else to assume full and permanent responsibility for the future of the Library, while, also like everyone else, wanting to control its destiny almost entirely in return for the little they did give. Steering a course through all the conflicting interests of the Library's supporters was a full-time job and one requiring a deft touch. At the time there was no one but Wiener with the skill and commitment to do this.

A financial statement of income and expenditure for 1963 shows where matters stood. The largest block came from the Library's German supporters, chiefly the Interior Ministry and the Forschungsgemeinschaft (Research Council). The biggest single contribution was from the Allocations Committee of the Central British Fund, £5,333 plus a further £440 grant for book purchases. Predictably one of the smallest sources was from other UK organisations, less than £1,000 for the year. Expenditure stood at £17,826. A surplus of £4,000 looked good on paper, but in fact the Library had considerable debts.

Wiener's death in February 1964 brought to a head the quest for somebody to take over the directorship of the Library. Both Wiener and the Executive Committee were of the opinion that Aronsfeld was not suitable in the long run. Only a 'fully qualified director of academic standing' (Wiener's words in a letter to Kessler dated January 1963) would do. Aronsfeld was probably not very disappointed with this decision. It would have suited him if a new director had been appointed swiftly, someone as like Wiener as possible and committed to continuing the work of the Library as it had been carried out for many years.

For the Committee, where to turn up such a man was a ticklish problem. As already noted, even before Wiener's death, approaches had been made to a number of people, but no one suitable had emerged. Aronsfeld continued as a safe pair of hands as far as the day-to-day running of the Library was concerned, but it became clear that he could not accommodate the changes which the Executive saw as vital. As early as 1962 he had clashed with Kessler on the question of how to go about raising funds. Aronsfeld had wanted to try an approach to wealthy individuals, Kessler was set against this because he had reservations concerning Aronsfeld's competence in approaching potential donors and argued that the main effort should be directed at the Claims Conference and Allocations Committee. Aronsfeld wrote at the time 'I did not force the argument but consider Mr Kessler's views highly disappointing and unsatisfactory.'

In the wake of Wiener's death the conflicts between them came to a head. Before the end of February 1964, Aronsfeld submitted a memo to the Committee detailing his anxieties. The Executive was determined to reduce the Library's budget and force it to live within its means. As a first step, the section dealing with the Nuremberg documents was done away with. Aronsfeld was determined that only by maintaining and increasing the budget could the Library continue to fulfil its past role as an active information bureau:

> . . . the closing of one section, inasmuch as it is a symptom of a policy, will only be a first step. If no financial expansion is undertaken, further sections must expect to be closed, more staff may have to be dismissed, the Bulletin may be discontinued, until at last little is left except a lifeless collection of books and miscellaneous files and records which can no longer be kept up-to-date.

Aronsfeld made it clear that only a continuation of the Wiener Library as Wiener and he had built it up since the war would satisfy him:

> [If] the Library is to be kept as hitherto on a shoestring or even less . . . it will merely be a shadow of its old self, operating for a while under false pretenses and sure to be found out before very long. I feel I owe to you, as my directors, the conscientious confession that having served Dr Wiener and willing to serve you, I would not wish to be associated with such an under-taking.

And to conclude he spelled out his lack of confidence in the Executive:

> While Dr Wiener was alive, I was doing my duty cheerfully and with confidence, knowing that the utmost was being done to keep the Library in a fit working condition. I devoutly hope that I shall be able to go on doing my duty in this assurance, but I would not be fair or sincere if I were not to tell you frankly now that I am having very serious doubts.[9]

In April 1964 Aronsfeld was in Berlin where he attended a memorial meeting for the Warsaw Ghetto being held by the Jewish community of Berlin. There he collected the Heinrich Stahl Prize for 1964, awarded to the Library in honour of Dr Wiener by the Berlin Community. In his address the chairman of the Jewish Executive, Heinz Galinski, spoke of the Library as 'the first scientifically-run research institute for contemporary history in Europe and as such . . . an invaluable source of incontestable facts and data during the war years'.

While in Germany Aronsfeld also went to Bonn to meet Dr Treue of the German Forschungsgemeinschaft. He reported back on this meeting that Dr Treue was negotiating with the Volkswagen Foundation concerning the Library, and that the figure of DM1 million was being spoken of. Aronsfeld again complained of Kessler's policy, because Kessler appeared lukewarm to this news.

Kessler was at this time hoping to persuade the Wolfson Foundation to endow a chair at University College London, which would be linked to the directorship of the Library.

This scheme stretched back to before Montefiore's death and originally involved Montefiore, UCL's Provost Sir Ifor Evans, Israel Sieff and James Parkes, founder of the Parkes Library. Parkes was at this time also worried about the future of his library. He had a long-standing association with Sieff, who had supported the Parkes Library generously. The negotiations were aimed at merging and housing the two ailing libraries at UCL. For various reasons the talking dragged on and Parkes cast about for other solutions, eventually committing his library to Southampton University, where it remains to this day.

This left the Wiener Library and the College. UCL remained interested in acquiring the Library and the Library regarded UCL as an acceptable partner, with long-established Jewish connections and substantial Jewish holdings in its Mocatta Library. It was envisaged that the Wiener Library might occupy a status something like the Warburg Institute – independent and self-standing, yet secure in the university structure. However the major difference between the Warburg and the Wiener was that the Warburg came to UCL with an endowment which made it self-financing. The Wiener had no such luxury, as Kessler had written to Beloff, who strongly supported giving the Library to the College:

We can be quite clear that no monetary assistance whatsoever is to be obtained from that source. They would be delighted to have the Library under their aegis but they are in no position to contribute financially or to find space for the books. Any connection with UCL would therefore be an advantage primarily from a prestige point of view, and this would be particularly important if we were able to obtain the services of a Director of professorial standing.[10]

The person of professorial standing Kessler actually had in mind was the German-American historian George Mosse. Mosse had written to Kessler in April 1963 that 'I would be interested in the position and I would consider the post very seriously.' But Mosse also had concerns about the Library's financial position and pointed out that he would be rash to give up a permanent job in the United States for a post that only had funding to meet his salary for a five-year period. Beloff pointed out to Kessler that Mosse 'would only come if the post could be combined with a chair at London, and I think this would apply to any alternative candidate of any merit.'[11]

The Wolfson Foundation, which made a grant to fund the director's salary for five years, insisted that this was conditional on the Library forming closer ties with the University of London. In response to this Professor Leonard Schapiro, who had been appointed Professor of Political Science at the LSE in 1963, was brought on to the Library's Executive Committee.

In the end the proposed merger with UCL foundered because the Wiener Library was too big to fit into UCL's existing library space, came without an endowment and insisted on retaining its identity and a large measure of independence. The College suggested that the Library come up with money towards constructing a new building to house it. The Library argued that if it could raise money for a new building for UCL, it could raise money to support itself and would have no need of the College's help. With the failure of this scheme, any interest Mosse had had in the directorship evaporated. Nevertheless he recommended that Kessler consider Walter Laqueur.

Laqueur was German-born, had gone to Palestine in 1938 and had worked as a political journalist for various newspapers in the Middle East from 1944–55. He had then come to London to take up an appointment as editor of *Survey*, a quarterly journal of East European affairs, and to write scholarly books. He was already a man with a string of well-regarded books to his name, had edited *Soviet Cultural Scene 1956–57* with George Lichtheim and recently written *Nasser's Egypt*. He was also at this time engaged in writing *Young Germany* and a volume of reminiscences and meditations on Germany, *Heimkehr*. The Library was known to him and he had contributed occasionally to the *Bulletin* on various topics.

Kessler happened to be at the Library one day and saw Laqueur there. Kessler approached Laqueur and invited him to a meeting at the *Jewish Chronicle*. There they discussed the possibility of his taking over and Laqueur expressed himself keen on the idea. He was then interviewed by the Executive

Committee at 25 Furnival Street and formally offered the job. He describes his salary as having been 'very modest', but was assured that funding for it was secure for five years. This was acceptable to Laqueur and he was duly appointed on 6 July 1964, although his arrival at the Library was delayed by an operation.

The appointment of Laqueur was made by Kessler and the Executive Committee without reference to Aronsfeld or the Library's staff. Aronsfeld was furious about it and wrote to Kessler of the 'incredulity' and the 'strongest resentment' felt by the staff. George Mosse was more friendly. He wrote to Laqueur that 'I am absolutely delighted that you have accepted the Wiener directorship. Without flattery, you know what can be done, are a scholar and a first rate organiser as well. In short, this is wonderful!' He also wrote a generous letter to Kessler approving of Laqueur's appointment and offering assurances that he was not offended at being passed over.[12]

Laqueur was energetic and ambitious. He swept into the Library like an aggressive new broom and rapidly set about re-creating the Library in his own image.

A last anecdote belongs to the pre-Laqueur era. In March 1964 a fictional story appeared in the American magazine *Man's Story*. The title of the piece was 'The Captive Maidens' and it was illustrated with lurid and titillating photographs. It began:

> I thought I had learned to live with it until that day a year ago when I found myself walking down Devonshire Street. I still have no way of knowing what was preying on my subconscious mind. It may have been the London Times announcement of the execution of Adolf Eicmann (sic) in Israel.
>
> Whatever it was, it drove my footsteps inexorably to the little building with the sign Wiener Library. I moved among the more than 50,000 documents which chronicle the savagery and torture that was Nazi Germany.
>
> Somebody once said of the library, 'Here you will find yourself wading ankle deep in blood.'

There followed a preposterous story of spies and jackboots and torture chambers. The concluding paragraph began:

> Yes, it's all there in the library on Devonshire Road (sic) for anyone who is interested to read.

It is, I feel, a tribute to the apparent infallibility of the network of contacts which the old-style Wiener Library had, that even this ludicrous article was tracked down and duly submitted to be entered in its files.[13]

NOTES

1. 'An Urgent Appeal', Wiener Library Bulletin, Vol. X, No. 5–6, 1956, p. 35.
2. 'London Letter', *Jewish Echo*, 9.1.1959.
3. Stanley Bonnet, 'Eichmann', *The Daily Mail*, 25.5.1960.
4. Trude Levi, *A Cat Called Adolf* (London: Vallentine Mitchell, 1995), p. 151.
5. Alfred Wiener, 'Leonard G. Montefiore', *Wiener Library Bulletin*, Vol. XVI, No. 1 1962, p. 3.
6. David Kessler to R.N. Carvalho, 15.1.1963, Archives of the Jewish Chronicle, Hartley Library, University of Southampton. I am grateful to the archivist, Chris Woolgar, for allowing me access to these important papers.
7. David Kessler to Prof. Max Beloff, 17.10.1962, Archives of the Jewish Chronicle, Hartley Library, University of Southampton.
8. daß sie [the Library] in dem Geiste weitergeführt werde, der mein Verhalten zum deutschen Volk von Anfang an bestimmt hat. Confidential memo from Alfred Wiener to members of the Executive Committee and C.C. Aronsfeld, 3.6.1963, Wiener Archive, Wiener Library.
9. C.C. Aronsfeld, A Memorandum to the Directors of the Wiener Library, Feb. 1964, Wiener Archive, Wiener Library.
10. See note 7 above.
11. Prof. Max Beloff to David Kessler, 16.7.1963, Archives of the Jewish Chronicle, Hartley Library, University of Southampton.
12. C.C. Aronsfeld to David Kessler, 5.7.1964; Prof. George Mosse to Walter Laqueur, 5.7.1964, Archives of the Jewish Chronicle, Hartley Library, University of Southampton.
13. Diana Lawson, 'The Captive Maidens in the Nazi's House of 1,000 Deaths', *Man's Story*, Vol.5, No. 2, March 1964, Wiener Archive, Wiener Library.

CHAPTER ELEVEN

Walter Laqueur and the Institute of Contemporary History

WITH THE APPOINTMENT of Laqueur a period of uncertainty came to an end. He was a man with clear ideas about what the Library ought to become if it was to survive in a changing world and he had the authority to push his agenda through. Unfortunately the Library was up against the old financial problems, a fact the Executive had neglected to discuss with him at his interview. Although the existing budget was being met, on a year-by-year, hand-to-mouth basis, the fact was that the Library's expenditure was rising. Throughout the 1940s and 50s the budget hovered between £5,000 and £8,000. In the year Laqueur took over it had reached £20,000 and by the end of the 1960s this was to more than double. To make matters worse, in 1964 the money from the Claims Conference came to an end, although a smaller amount was paid into the Library by the Memorial Foundation for Jewish Culture.

Small wonder then that Laqueur was forced to make fund-raising a priority. He was aware within the first month that the Library was in serious financial trouble. Among his first actions as director was to write an article on the failure of the Jewish community in Britain to support the Library. It appeared in the autumn edition of the Journal of the Association of Jewish Ex-Servicemen. One is tempted to wonder why Laqueur did not choose the *Jewish Chronicle* in which to place his appeal. Laqueur felt that the *Chronicle* was not the appropriate place in which to lambast the Anglo-Jewish community. He also had no objection to letting Kessler see that he was now in charge and was intent on doing things in his own way. The *Ajex Journal* was probably an appropriate way of reaching those who ought to have been the Library's natural constituency.

Laqueur's article began by reviewing the Library's past achievements and the recognition it had earned among leading members of the academic community. He went on:

All this is very gratifying, but this support and recognition has unfortunately not been matched by similar enthusiasm on the part of those who should have been most vitally interested in the work of the Wiener Library, namely the Anglo Jewish community. With a few notable exceptions . . . it has been almost totally ignored by the Jewish public in this country.

This attitude has provoked concern and even shock on the part of non-Jews, and is extremely short-sighted. For anti-Semitism in this country and abroad is unfortunately not a thing of the past; whenever an upsurge of anti-Semitism occurs the Wiener Library finds itself in very great demand as the only research centre able to provide the facts and the information to cope with a sudden crisis. But once the immediate emergency passes the fate of the Library is regarded with indifference or worse.

After reviewing and dismissing the possibilities for attracting funding from abroad, Laqueur gets down to brass tacks:

If we do not get the assistance [we need] we shall have to discontinue the Bulletin and curtail activities for which the Library has been traditionally known.

It would be a great shame and, I fear, a great chance missed by Anglo-Jewry. On so many occasions in Jewish meetings, public and private, speakers stress the need for vigilance in the never-ending struggle against anti-Semitism and intolerance. I have no doubt that these fine declarations are genuine; support for the work of our Institute seems to me an obvious way to match words to deeds.[1]

This article may have roused a conscientious few to act on the Library's behalf; certainly it served to announce to the Jewish public that the Library now had a director of energy and ambition, unafraid to bruise sensibilities in pursuing the interests of his institution. But the apathy of the community at large seemed intractable. And although he had stated the unsatisfactory nature of getting support from America, the *Bulletin* was only able to continue because the Anti-Defamation League of B'nai B'rith, New York became its co-publisher. Laqueur rapidly came to favour a policy of pursuing funding from the United States, Europe and the United Kingdom, and felt that the Library should be able to raise around a third of its requirements from each territory.

While Laqueur was lashing the indifferent public in the *Ajex Journal*, he was also unveiling a programme of expansion to the audience of the *Bulletin*. He recognised that 'the Third Reich still figures as the central theme of our time' and that it would go on forming the core of the Library's concern. But:

At the same time, the Library has always been more than a collection of books and newspaper cuttings. It is in fact an Institute for the study of contemporary history. Since the main problems facing us in 1964 differ in many essential respects from those twenty or thirty years ago, the focus of such an Institute has to be adjusted in accordance with the changes taking place in the world around us.[2]

So the main thrust of Laqueur's effort was to maintain, in fact build up, the relevance of the Library's work to the contemporary political scene. This did indeed indicate some fairly radical changes in collecting policy, opening out the focus of the Library to take in the entire question of the East–West divide, the Middle East and the Cold War.

Laqueur also announced that the *Bulletin* would get a facelift, and that there was a plan for a new publication, the *Journal of Contemporary History*, which would back up the work of the Institute of Contemporary History. In addition, the Library would organise and host research seminars and occasional conferences. All of this was going to cost money and Laqueur made no bones about the budgetary needs. He envisaged the Library's budget going immediately to £50,000 per year.

The Institute of Contemporary History was founded in 1964, initially under the name Institute for Advanced Studies in Contemporary History. 'Contemporary history' was a coinage intended to distinguish its subject matter from that of modern history – since modern history takes in events going back as far as the seventeenth century, while the Institute would seldom deal with anything before about 1870. It was seen as a research-led institution and would take up the neglected field of twentieth century European history including totalitarianism, but looking beyond it as well. By May of 1965 the Institute was a functioning reality with a well-defined academic outlook:

> The approach of the Institute is interdisciplinary. Its advisory board includes historians, political scientists, sociologists and social psychologists. Every effort is made not to overlap in activities with similar institutes in Europe. The Institute is not concerned with current political events as is Chatham House, for instance, it is not exclusively devoted to the study of National Socialism as is the Insitut für Zeitgeschichte in Munich. The independent, non-governmental character of the Institute enables it to sponsor and carry out projects which are not usually tackled by university departments and, while maintaining the highest academic standards, will not appeal exclusively to professionals.

In political terms the Institute was founded on the assumption that:

> . . . though the era of European supremacy has ended, Europe continues and

will continue to play a leading role in world affairs and perhaps even more markedly in the realm of new ideas. The primary object of the Institute's research programme is to broaden the understanding of the forces and mechanisms affecting the emergence of this new Europe and its relationship with the rest of the world.

Laqueur's long-term ambition for the Institute was that it 'serve as the nucleus of an international association of contemporary historians.'[3]

Laqueur scored an early and important victory with the finances. He successfully lobbied government departments in Germany and succeeded in getting regular and substantial amounts from the Cultural Department of the Foreign Ministry. This was a major achievement because although the Library had been getting money from the German government for some time, Laqueur's efforts resulted in a long-term commitment on the part of the Cultural Department to provide around one-third of the Library's budget. Furthermore, unlike most other donors, the Cultural Department did not tie its contributions to specific works: the money formed part of the regular budget. In the summer of 1965 two new staff members were appointed to the Institute. Jane Degras came from Chatham House, and acted as assistant editor of the *Journal*, while also continuing to work on *Survey*, where she had met Laqueur. George Urban, a freelance writer and broadcaster (he later became the director of Radio Free Europe) joined to take charge of special projects. This chiefly involved organising the Institute's conferences and lecture series.

In the summer of 1965 the *Bulletin* in its old form came to its last issue. Aronsfeld wrote an elegaic article which was not without a tinge of bitterness. The *Bulletin* had been under his control for almost 20 years. Although its circulation was always small (around 2,000 issues), its reputation was as the authoritative source of news in its field. This was largely Aronsfeld's personal achievement. It was natural that he would have resisted change, particularly since it narrowed the scope of his reporting and reduced the opportunities for him to contribute.

Aronsfeld wrote bravely in the introduction to the revamped *Bulletin* that its 'academic research will be in keeping with the standards which have been set in the past 19 years ever since the *Bulletin* first appeared.' But his heart wasn't in it anymore. He disagreed with Laqueur's policies and it can hardly have been easy for him to take direction from a newcomer and someone who, in his eyes, perhaps lacked commitment to Wiener's original ideals. He edited the *Bulletin* for another four issues and then gave up. The new editor was Ernest Hearst, Aronsfeld's brother-in-law.

By the end of 1965 Laqueur was able to report substantial progress with his plans. Sufficient new funding had materialised to enable the first issue of the *Journal of Contemporary History* to be planned for the end of the year. A new research unit was established for the study of contemporary Jewry, the first volume of an annual publication was planned, and a research project covering modern European history got under way.

Aronsfeld left the Library altogether at the end of 1965, going to the Institute of Jewish Affairs, a branch of the World Jewish Council, where he served as senior research officer and editor of the journals *Patterns of Prejudice* and *Christian–Jewish Relations*, from their inception until June 1985 when he retired at the age of 75.

Obviously Aronsfeld's departure marked something of a watershed in the Library's history. He was the longest-serving member of the staff and only Ilse Wolff, the chief librarian, had a service record that approached his. She herself would resign from the Library within a year of Aronsfeld owing to a serious illness. Unlike Aronsfeld she felt quite content working with the new director. She felt regret that he had never seen her 'normal' self, because she was already ill when he joined, and her health declined steadily. Aronsfeld went on to a life of renewed intellectual fulfilment, also as a writer – he produced two major contributions to his field, *The Text of the Holocaust* and *The Ghosts of 1492*.

The Wiener Library Bulletin continued until 1981, first under the editorship of Ernest Hearst, later under Robert Wistrich. It evolved steadily, particularly under Wistrich, a young, multi-lingual and very ambitious academic and it became much more of a 'heavyweight' academic journal. In addition to the quarterly issues, he prepared larger special issues on topics including *European Anti-Semitism 1890–1945* (1976), *The British Mandate in Palestine* (1978). These have been judged to be major contributions to scholarship and were favourably reviewed in the press. He remained at the Library until late in 1980 and went on to have a successful academic career.[4]

The *Bulletin* continued as a joint publication with the Anti-Defamation League until early in 1968. This arrangement ended as the focus of the *Bulletin* gradually moved away from anti-Semitism and its coverage ranged over a wider field. Thereafter, financial considerations forced the decision to issue only two numbers per year, although nominally it continued as a quarterly, with each being a double issue. Two years after it had ceased publication there was a special issue of the *Bulletin* to mark the 50th anniversary of the founding of the Library.

The Journal of Contemporary History ranks as one of Laqueur's most lasting achievements at the Wiener Library. The first issue appeared in January 1966, carrying a short editorial justifying itself: 'After centuries of Eurocentrism the pendulum has swung to the other extreme, and current fashions have led to a neglect of contemporary Europe.' The editorial attempts to counter the traditional historical view that contemporary history is not possible, either for lack of documentary evidence ('the contemporary historian of Europe and America in the sixties is more likely to be confronted with a surfeit'), or for lack of detachment ('distance in time also involves remoteness, lack of immediacy, difficulty in understanding the quality of life of a period that is hard to describe and define'). And the editors promised to make no particular effort to avoid controversy, although they declined to court it as well.

The early issues of the *Journal* were strangely anonymous, giving no information about editors or institutional affiliations. It was not until issue 3 that Laqueur and George L. Mosse were identified as the editors, operating with the assistance of Jane Degras and Ernest Hearst.

Press reaction to the new *Journal* was mixed. *The Times* wrote that 'it should be as legitimate to write – and read – contemporary history as any other sort of history', provided one did not fall into the trap of trying to learn practical lessons from it: 'It is safer to say that history has no lessons than to claim to have discovered one of them.' The *Daily Telegraph* took precisely the opposite view, arguing that while contemporary history is temporary history, certain to be revised later, nevertheless studying it may help prevent 'laughable errors'. On the other side of the political fence, the *New Statesman* praised its clarity of thought but felt that it lacked ambition. The *Guardian* dismissed the *Journal* for merely reflecting the Library's 'preoccupation' with fascism. The *Frankfurter Allgemeine Zeitung* regretted the absence of a study of the fascistic tendencies of the countries of the Middle East, Indonesia and Africa.

It was apparent to Laqueur from an early stage that the Library could not survive indefinitely on its own. In January 1966 he made a renewed appeal to the Wolfson Foundation, but this was rejected. The possibility of a tie-in to London University also came to nothing, as had the earlier effort to endow a Chair at University College London. However, he was in contact with several British and American universities. Meanwhile the financial situation was tightening up. In a memo to the Executive Committee written in early 1967, he set the situation out:

> For 1967 we shall have an income of about £45,000, but with various grants ending that year (and they have to be spent in 1967!), we can expect at present only about £18,000 for the subsequent years. This is not sufficient to guarantee the survival of the Institute even on a modest scale.

By 'modest scale' Laqueur meant calling a halt to all research work and retaining only a skeleton staff. He estimated that on this basis the Institute could go on for 'a year or two' provided the budget could be kept at £20,000.

So £18,000 per year which 'we can expect at present' clearly meant the death of the Library altogether. Laqueur argued that:

> . . . full independence can be a reality only on the basis of an assured minimum income. This, unfortunately, we do not have. It is of course possible that during 1967 we shall succeed in obtaining new grants . . . but we cannot take this for granted, nor would it provide a long-term solution. In the circumstances, there seems to be no other way than an affiliation with a university. . .[5]

This was to form the basis of the Library's efforts to secure its future throughout the remainder of the 1960s and into the 70s. In particular Laqueur was anxious to preserve the option of linking up with more than one university, especially if one of them was in America.

The first proposed affiliation was with the University of Reading. The idea was first floated in 1965 by Dr Stuart Woolf, who lectured at Reading and knew the Library well from researching there. By January 1966 Laqueur sent a detailed memo to Woolf, outlining how the two institutions might co-operate. Reading was a young university, with a very active graduate school of Contemporary European Studies and anxious to build up its academic reputation. Negotiations progressed quite fast. In September 1966 a meeting was held at Reading involving Laqueur, Professor Leonard Schapiro of the Wiener Library's Executive Committee, Marion Bieber from the Institute and Reading's vice-chancellor, H.R. Pitt, its bursar and Professor A.G. Lehmann, who was the chairman of the University's Graduate School of Contemporary European Studies. This meeting led to the drawing up of a statement, drafted by Laqueur and Lehmann, setting out the basic points. After an initial association between the two bodies, the Library would become an Institute of the University, and when the opportunity arose, a third party would be sought, preferably an American university. The Library's academic staff would join the University. Laqueur would 'enjoy a standing' at the University. The University would contribute £5,000 per annum to the Library's budget during the initial period. The Library's Executive Committee would be made up of not more than one-third by members of the University.

While certain details were discussed further and revised, this early statement contains the essence of what in fact took place. By July 1967 a formal agreement was drawn up between the Library and the University to come into effect in October. The agreement recognised the close ties between the Library (in fact the Institute of Contemporary History) and the graduate School of Contemporary European Studies. The agreement was to be for a five-year period, after which it would have to be renegotiated.

This affiliation was to bring a number of benefits to the Library. In financial terms it was worth £5,000 per year and this was sufficient to keep the Library safe for the immediate future, even if it could indulge no extravagance. Academically it allowed for an expanded programme of seminars and conferences and the consequent raising of the Library's profile, both in the United Kingdom and internationally. The University's representatives on the Executive Committee were H.R. Pitt, Professor P. Campbell, Professor A.G. Lehmann and Professor H.S. Thomas. Stuart Woolf was co-opted to serve as the Institute's assistant director – although this was largely an honorary title and involved him in very little work or decision-taking.

With the affiliation, Laqueur had taken a first step towards getting the Library incorporated into Britain's university system. According to the plan, it would now be less reliant on individual acts of philanthropy and its long-term financial future would begin to look up.

In the course of the next few years, Laqueur worked hard at forging similar partnerships with other institutions. He focused his efforts largely in America, where he had been a visiting professor at Johns Hopkins, research fellow at Harvard and a visiting professor at Chicago, and had built up a sound network of contacts and supporters. Officially, his goal was the tripartite arrangement envisioned in the deal with Reading. In reality, it is likely that he would have agreed to an exclusive deal with a willing university, even if this meant jettisoning Reading.

There was, during the 1960s, a widespread interest among American academic institutions in establishing bases in Europe. This was especially the case among the newer universities, which had fewer resources in terms of library materials and needed ways of attracting students. Linking with an established European institution and being able to offer summer schools and study opportunities in Europe was an obvious and attractive way to boost enrolment and expand research facilities.

One of the first to give such an arrangement serious thought was the University of California, Riverside – but this was soon overtaken by negotiations with Brandeis University, which was by far the strongest candidate for possible co-operation. In a letter of November 1965 to the president of Brandeis, Dr Abraham Sacher, Laqueur enlarged on his vision for such co-operative ventures:

We would offer our American partner full co-sponsorship in all our activities, which would be reflected in all our operations, including the name of the Institute. Furthermore, we would also offer a number of research fellowships of a year at least, for young scholars and graduate students who could make their base of operations the Institute itself. They would have an office, access to the Library, and the possibility of secretarial assistance . . . Our resources and personnel, including myself, if that should be desired, would be available not only to visitors but also to our American partner – in other words, there could be exchange visits, teaching, loan of source materials etc. [6]

It is clear that Brandeis was the favoured choice for Laqueur, for 'the simple reason that Brandeis would presumably be interested in co-sponsoring both our Jewish and our general activities whereas other universities are, pre-sumably, interested in our general work only.'[7] Like Reading, Brandeis was a recently established university, founded in 1948, and was keen to carve out a reputation for itself and to build up its bibliographic resources.

What Laqueur was offering Brandeis was a partial or total take-over. This would leave the Library intact in London and offer the new owners a European base from which to conduct research, hold summer schools and extend their influence. Sacher visited the Library in person and discussion of the proposal continued for some time, but ultimately yielded nothing, for reasons that lay with Brandeis.

Meanwhile the Institute of Contemporary History was successfully building up an international reputation. In October 1966 it held an international con-ference on the subject of the study of contemporary history in Europe. This attracted a host of renowned scholars including Alan Bullock, M.R.D. Foot and George Mosse. The two-day conference ranged widely over topics and issues of interest to historians, from the haphazard procedures by which source material is either preserved or destroyed, to the role of ideological commitment in writing history, to the vexed question of co-operation with contemporary historians from the Eastern bloc countries.

Laqueur himself made an attack on the dullness of so much writing in history, which left many of the imaginative fields as the preserve of journalists. He called for historians to stop concentrating on footnotes to history and to address issues of interest and concern to a wider reading public. George Mosse criticised the narrow scope of much writing in history and argued that developments in the modern world, such as large movements of populations, require interdisciplinary approaches involving social psychology, sociology, anthropology and so on. Both were agreed that it was time for historians to 'stop writing the same book over and over again.' Many of the papers were later collected and published in a volume entitled *Contemporary History in Europe*, edited by D.C. Watt. It appeared in 1969.[8]

This event marked the beginning of a stream of seminars and conferences staged by the Institute, which attracted large audiences, first-class participants and good press reactions.

D.C. Watt served as organiser of a second conference, held in October 1967.

This covered the subject of *New Approaches in the Social Sciences and Their Application to Contemporary History*. Several papers from this conference were later published in the *Journal*. In 1968 Laqueur issued a report of the Institute and Library's activities since 1964. Apart from the launching of the *Journal* and the revamping of the *Bulletin*, it listed two completed research projects. The first was by Bernard Krikler, entitled *Anglo-Jewish Attitudes to Nazism*, the second was entitled *Jewish Students in British Universities*. New research projects included a symposium on the Holocaust under the joint auspices of the Institute and Brandeis University, a study of the persecution of the Gypsies under the Nazis – a ground-breaking piece of research by G. Puxon and D. Kenrick, based largely on the Library's own holdings. It was published in 1972 under the title *The Destiny of Europe's Gypsies* and Dr Isaiah Friedman undertook a study of Zionism, published in 1977 under the title *Germany, Turkey and Zionism*, which remains a standard work on the subject. A study of Belgian fascism was also researched but not published. The work of the new academic unit for contemporary Jewish studies also went ahead. In 1967 its publication *Explorations* was in print. *Explorations* was seen initially as a one-off publication, with the potential to become an annual if successful. Its focus was contemporary Jewish themes such as Ideas, Arts, Sciences; The Community; The Past Recaptured; and so on. It was edited by Murray Mindlin with Chaim Bermant and its advisory board consisted of Julius Gould, John Gross and Dan Jacobson. With contributions by Albert Goldman, Isaac Bashevis Singer, Chaim Bermant, Dannie Abse and others, it was a brave attempt to provide the British scene with a serendipitous and eclectic compilation of literature, criticism, reminiscence and perhaps a touch of controversy. *Explorations* was well-received by the critics, but was not a financial success. No second volume appeared. This was partly due to political events in the Middle East, which simply drained the project of its sense of purpose. While Israel fought for its survival, the production and publishing of cultural reminiscences and artistic efforts may have appeared something of an indulgence.[9]

The connection with Dan Jacobson had benefited the Library in another way, by introducing Bernard Krikler to the Library. Krikler later served as a contributor to *A Dictionary of Politics*, which was compiled at the Wiener Library under the editorship of Walter Laqueur. Krikler co-ordinated most of the research and copy-editing of the entries and wrote many himself. Others involved in this major project included Ernest Hearst, Ze'ev Ben Shlomo and Geoffrey Pridham.[10]

By the time this project was completed and in print in 1971, Krikler was the Institute's assistant director. This post combined most of the functions formerly carried out by Marion Bieber, but also involved supervising the Institute's activities during Laqueur's enforced absences at Brandeis.

Krikler later played an important role in setting up the Wiener Library Appeal Fund.

The Institute also organised series of public lectures and seminars on topics related to contemporary history. From 1965–66, the lecture series included speakers of the calibre of Hugh Trevor-Roper, Arthur Schlesinger, Alan Bullock, Asa Briggs, Sir William Hayter and Stephan Hurwitz. Public lectures were replaced in 1967 with seminars. The first series was entitled *Contemporary Germany* and included speakers such as Richard Lowenthal on *Germany between East and West*, Erwin Scheuch on *Neo-Nationalism* and Ralph Dahrendorf on *Germany's Crisis in Education*. The second series, running 1967–68, was entitled *Socialism in Western Europe in the 20th Century*, while the third, *Generations in Conflict in Historical Perspective* included papers on *English Youth Movements, 1908–39*, *Social and Intellectual Origins of the Hashomer Hatzair Youth Movement, 1913–20* and others on Italian fascism and youth and Polish youth in the 1930s.

Later publications include the seminal *Fascism, A Reader's Guide*, edited by Walter Laqueur and organised and supported by the Wiener Library with funding from the Volkswagen Foundation. This volume remains in print almost 20 years after its first publication and continues to offer an introduction to the subject to students around the world.[11]

Less visible than these public manifestations of the Institute and Library's prowess but perhaps even more significant, were a series of improvements being carried on in the Library itself during the 1970s. These included major reorganisations of whole sections of the book holdings and the recataloguing of thousands of volumes. Many of the non-book collections had previously been accessible only through the personal knowledge of the Library staff. Now they were indexed and catalogued and made available to all users. The Library's collections of unpublished materials, such as the documents donated by the Nuremberg trial authorities, were only now fully indexed. A systematic programme of indexing all the periodical holdings was launched and hundreds of volumes of periodicals were bound, thus protecting them and conserving them for future use. The team of people working on this included Frantisek Hajek, Janet Langmaid, Helen Kehr and Christa Wichmann.

Of these people, Christa Wichmann remained longest at the Library, retiring in 1994 from the post of chief librarian. She joined the Library in August 1966. She had known of the Library's existence while still living in Germany and felt a keen interest in its work. Initially she joined on a one-year contract, during which time she worked closely with Helen Kehr on reorganising and indexing the press archives. Her contribution was such that she was kept on beyond her contract and by around 1970 she was effectively in charge of the Library. She went on to guide the Library through the extraordinarily difficult period in the late 1970s and early 80s and made an essential contribution to its revival in the years since the transfer of books to Israel.

The Library also got to grips with new technology, buying a microfilm reader and acquiring significant microfilm holdings, most importantly, the *Hauptarchiv* (Central Archive) of the Nazi Party and other Nazi material.

After 1967 a Middle Eastern Document Centre was opened, with a member of staff available full-time to undertake research of queries raised by members of the public. The collection, based on books, journals, periodicals and newspaper cuttings included materials in French, Russian, Hebrew and Arabic and rapidly became a widely-used resource.

Work also continued on the *Wiener Library Catalogue* series. Three new catalogues appeared in the 1960s and 70s: Number 5 (*Prejudice: Racist, Religious, Nationalist*), London 1971; Number 6 (*German Jewry, Part II*), London 1978; and Number 7 (*Persecution*), London 1978. All three were edited by Helen Kehr, who had also worked extensively on the earlier volumes.

NOTES

1. Walter Laqueur, 'The Future of the Wiener Library', *The Ajex Journal*, Autumn 1964, No 2.
2. Walter Laqueur, 'The Wiener Library's Future: A Programme of Expansion', *Wiener Library Bulletin*, Vol. XVIII, No. 4, Oct. 1964, p. 43.
3. 'Five Year Programme of The Institute for Advanced Studies in Contemporary History', unpublished document, May 1965, Wiener Archive, Wiener Library.
4. During his time at the Library Wistrich wrote a pamphlet, *The Myth of Zionist Racism*, arising out of the controversy around a UN resolution which condemned Zionism as racist; he served as editor of a special issue of the *Journal of Contemporary History* concerned with *Theories of Fascism*; he edited *The Left against Zion*, based on pieces published in the *Wiener Library Bulletin* and some commissioned especially for the book; by the time he left the Library he was at work compiling *Who's Who in Nazi Germany*; in later years his published works included *The Jews of Vienna in the Age of Franz Joseph* (which one writer has called 'monumental').
5. Walter Laqueur to the Executive Committee, 11 Jan. 1967, Wiener Archive, Wiener Library.
6. Walter Laqueur to Abraham L. Sacher, 11.11.1965, Wiener Archive, Wiener Library.
7. See note 6 above.
8. DC Watt (ed.), *Contemporary History in Europe* (London: Allen & Unwin, 1969).
9. G. Puxon and D. Kenrick, *The Destiny of Europe's Gypsies* (London: Chatto Heinemann for Sussex University, 1972); Dr Isaiah Friedman, *Germany, Turkey and Zionism* (Oxford: Clarendon Press, 1971); Murray Mindlin (ed.), *Explorations* (London: Barrie and Rockcliff, 1967).
10. Walter Laqueur (ed.), *A Dictionary of Politics* (London: Weidenfeld and Nicolson, 1971).
11. Walter Laqueur (ed.), *Fascism, A Reader's Guide* (London: Wildwood House, 1976).

CHAPTER TWELVE

Crisis and Merger

T HE MIDDLE EAST conflict, and in particular the Six Day War, had a considerable effect on the Library's efforts to secure funding. For example,
Laqueur had called a press conference in late May or early June 1967 to draw
attention to the financial plight of the Library. With the events of 5 June, any
hope of press coverage and a good response from the public evaporated.

The reaction of world Jewry to the War was fervent. Prior to 1967 the existence of Israel was a fact in the background of many people's lives. It was only
when its continued existence was under immediate threat that many realised
how important they felt it to be. In the aftermath of the War, thousands of
people went there to help. Donations for Israel, which had stood at $50 million
for the year 1966/7, rocketed to $350 million in the period 1967/8. For each of
the following two years, donations totalled around $250 million, and the Jewish
Agency took over responsibility for a significant part of Israel's social services
and higher education budgets. As the tension dragged on with hijackings, air
raids, commando raids and the rest, philanthropy in the Diaspora continued to
be directed towards Israel and interest began to wane in what was perceived as
a small and largely backward-looking academic institution in safe and leafy
London.

The affiliation with Reading was to have been the first stage of integration of
the Library into the University structure. Yet no one really knew what the
successive stages should be, or how to get there. It was unclear whether the
activities of the Institute and Library should gradually wind down, or whether
an effort to raise money to fund the continuation of long-running projects like
the *Bulletin* should be strengthened. From the minutes of an Executive
Committee meeting of April 1969 it is plain that the Executive was deadlocked.
Laqueur explained that there was not enough money to carry through a full
programme and requested guidance on where to prune. Kessler suggested
setting up a sub-committee to look into this. He asked Vice-Chancellor Pitt
when Reading could be expected to make its plans known, since the sub-
committee could not exercise its function without clearance from the

University. Pitt replied that he would try to expedite matters but could promise nothing. Laqueur was left with the problem of running the Library for another period of several months with inadequate funds and no clear decisions having been taken or likely to be taken.

In the course of that summer the log-jam gradually broke up. A plan to link a professorship in Contemporary History at Reading to the directorship of the Library became a financial possibility, when the Wolfson Foundation agreed to make funds available. Before September the position was offered to Laqueur. However, he turned the offer down. He was adamant that with two full professorships already, he did not want a chair in the United Kingdom. This was certainly a blow to the affiliation and to future plans. While the Committee looked for another candidate, he prepared to resign. Eventually the Committee lit on George Mosse, as Kessler had done in the early 1960s, when the plan to merge with UCL was being explored. Mosse was approached and went so far as to attend a selection committee meeting at Reading, but then turned the offer down, arguing that insufficient funds were available to run the Institute and Library properly.

Nor was this the only problem. In contemplating the future of the affiliation, the University felt that the best plan was for the Library to cease its independent existence in London and move on to Reading's campus. But Laqueur insisted that the Library retain an autonomous standing within the University, since this had for decades been a central plank of all thinking about the Library's future. The University countered that this would require raising funds for a new building to house the collection, since no existing building was suitable. It would be the responsibility of the Library to raise these funds. This demand appeared nonsensical to Laqueur. If the Library could successfully raise that kind of money, it wouldn't need an affiliation in the first place.

All this left the partnership in ruins. The agreement was officially terminated two years before it was due to expire. Those members of the Library's Executive Committee from the University resigned, and in time the money paid to the Library was returned. The Library was back where it had been in 1967 and its financial situation was worse than ever.

From 1970 Laqueur's academic career to some extent displaced his role as the Library's director. He became, in his own words, something of an absentee landlord. Through his presence at Tel Aviv University (TAU) for one term each year, the University's administration became aware of the Library and that it might be possible to acquire its holdings. Laqueur encouraged this view, for he saw no alternative. He spoke of the matter with Zvi Yavetz, the deputy dean of the Humanities Faculty, professor of Ancient History and head of the History Department – one of the most influential men at TAU. Yavetz quickly came to appreciate the significance of the Library and was in favour of acquiring it. In time Fred Lessing, a German-American businessman and philanthropist who was involved both with TAU and the Library, evolved a scheme to move the Library to Israel.

At the same time and through the offices of Laqueur, efforts were made to strengthen the Executive Committee (which had become depleted by the resignation of the Reading members) and to increase the German-Jewish presence on it. This led to a meeting in May 1971 between the Committee and members of the Council of Jews from Germany. These representatives were Dr Siegfried Moses (the Council's president, who was successor to Leo Baeck, its founder), Fred Lessing, Robert Weltsch and Arnold Paucker (the latter two from the Leo Baeck Institute in London, conveniently located in an office at 4 Devonshire Street).

At the meeting Moses expressed the willingness of the Council members present to 'accept responsibility' for financing the work of the Library. Quite what this meant was not clarified. The Council members expressed concern that the Library remain under Jewish control, stated that they wished to form a 'partnership' with the Committee, and suggested that, since the Library had survived for such a long time, there surely wasn't any great urgency in dealing with its problems. Kessler responded to these remarks and the discussion then turned to work which Kessler had been engaged in to bring about a merger with the London School of Economics. The Council members were opposed to this and argued that if Reading had been unsatisfactory why should the LSE be any better? Kessler replied that merging with the LSE would not involve the problems of financing a new building. It was agreed that Kessler should proceed to negotiate with the LSE, but that no final decisions should be taken concerning the future of the Library without another meeting.

In the event there was no formal partnership between the Council and the Committee. Instead, Moses, Weltsch and Lessing were elected onto the Committee. Paucker, Weltsch's deputy, was to be elected after Weltsch's death. This German-Jewish presence and particularly that of the energetic and determined Fred Lessing, had a profound impact on the thinking and actions of the Committee. There were effectively two factions, the Anglo-Jewish and the German-Jewish, and their outlooks clashed in several important ways (a private letter by one of the English faction to Kessler speaks of 'those dreadful Germans'). The Germans were constantly insisting on the need to maintain 'Jewish control' of the Library. Among people such as Lessing there was a strong feeling that if the Library were absorbed into the British academic world – even if its name were preserved – it would lose its essential identity. For the British contingent the primary concern was to preserve the collection in London. Whether its specific Jewish identity was preserved seemed to a certain extent a secondary consideration, one that the Library might simply not be able to afford. These two views were irreconcilable; a struggle for which would decide the fate of the Library was inevitable. In relation to the interest expressed by TAU, the Germans more or less supported the idea of a deal, while the British opposed it and preferred the thought of a merger with the LSE or some other British academic institution.

In February 1971 it was reported to the Executive Committee that the warden of St Antony's College, Oxford had made a proposal for taking over the Library. The warden was Professor Raymond Carr and the College, which was only about 20 years old, was anxious to build up its resources. Taking over the Library would have been a prestigious undertaking. Yet Laqueur was unable to take the offer seriously. The College had no specific Jewish connection, and wasn't really a natural home for the Library, and he believed it lacked the financial resources to bring a merger off. Nevertheless, the interest in the Library must have been heartening. At this point in 1971, no less than three major academic institutions were courting it and there was good reason to believe that something must come of one of the proposals.

In July 1971 Laqueur was in America, teaching his term at Brandeis. His presence in the United States also generated interest in the Library. He was not committed to the idea of a Tel Aviv take-over at this stage and would have been prepared to strike a deal with an American institution, if one showed willing. In July the *Chicago Daily News* published a lengthy article on the Library, summarising its history and discussing its prospects with Laqueur. By this time the activities of the Institute had been 'severely curtailed' and the paper reported that:

> ... the Wiener Library is not alone in feeling the pinch of escalating costs in Britain. Half a dozen other highly regarded private research institutions in London face similar difficulties. Universities are eager to acquire their materials and the major barrier so far has been the effort of the institutions to preserve their own identity and some independence of policy.[1]

The paper further reported Laqueur as saying that in his view most such institutions would, in one way or another, be absorbed by universities during the coming years. This article also appeared in the *Los Angeles Times,* and Laqueur hoped that it might generate some renewed interest among American universities.

Several informal approaches were made by Tel Aviv between 1970 and 1972. None of them received a positive yes or no, but Laqueur's talks with Yavetz progressed, and in July 1972 Yavetz wrote a formal letter to Kessler stating that:

While we have on several past occasions submitted our proposals orally and in writing, this may be the opportunity to do so more formally, in the name of the President of Tel Aviv University, the Rector and others concerned.[2]

Yavetz then outlined the University's willingness to support the Library, develop its holdings, establish research scholarships for British academics to come and use the Library, and to take on all those members of Library staff willing to move to Israel (although TAU was only prepared to guarantee them temporary jobs). Above all they were prepared to offer assurances that the Library would continue as a separate and distinct entity, and that its specific German-Jewish identity would be strenuously safeguarded. This was to be achieved by means of a specially constituted governing body:

> We suggest the establishment of a governing body consisting of the present board of the Wiener Library, the Council of Jews from Germany and Tel Aviv University to supervise the functioning of the Wiener Library at Tel Aviv University, to assist and advise it in its future development.[3]

Against this background, the academic profile and reputation of the Institute was maintained largely through projects that were coming to fruition after some years of research and preparation. In 1972 the Institute of Contemporary History oversaw the publication of *A Reader's Guide to Contemporary History*, an edited collection of bibliographical essays published by Weidenfeld and Nicolson. The editors were Laqueur and Bernard Krikler. The contributors were specialists in regional politics, and the book was organised into ten chapters covering each of the major regions of the world. Hardly the stuff of bestseller lists, the volume was nevertheless important in confirming the authoritative standing of the Institute in the academic community.

Concerning the Library's prime interest, during the 1970s a lively academic debate developed in Britain, which generated a good deal of scholarly research into various aspects of Nazi Germany. At the core of the debate was the distinction between an 'intentionalist' analysis of Nazi policy towards the Jews, which argued that Hitler was intent from the very beginning on a 'Final Solution' of the Jewish 'problem' and a 'functionalist' one. Intentionalists like Lucy Dawidowicz held that Hitler was therefore the prime mover of the Holocaust and that responsibility should be placed on him. Functionalists like Jeremy Noakes, Richard Overy, Geoffrey Pridham, Norman Stone and others argued that the Hitler regime was characterised by multiple centres of power, each featuring struggles between elites and those on the periphery. While Hitler ruled supreme over all, he often kept himself aloof from the details.

Responsibility for the Holocaust must therefore be a more complex issue than blaming the man in overall charge.

Many of the writers involved in this debate made use of the Library in their researches and some used its publications as vehicles for their ideas. But in general the Library concentrated more on other areas and, as the financial crisis deepened, it became ever more introspective.

The Library was also faced with the task of collecting materials published by right wing extremists which set out to deny the reality of the Holocaust. While sporadic efforts at this sort of revisionism had been made ever since 1945, the 1970s saw an upsurge which has continued unabated to this day. Major publications have included Richard Harwood's *Did Six Million Really Die?*, Arthur Butz's *Hoax of the Twentieth Century* and the works of Robert Faurisson, Ernst Zündel and others. With the publication of David Irving's *Hitler's War*, historical revisionism became more systematic and attempted to become academically respectable, spawning its own periodical literature, for example the glossily produced and well-financed *Journal of Historical Review*, launched in 1984. While the Library collected such publications, the *Bulletin*, with its altered priorities, was no longer available to bring such dangerous tendencies to the attention of a wider public.

On the fund-raising side, Fred Lessing busied himself in America and his efforts led to the establishment in New York of an organisation called the Friends of the Wiener Library. This group raised funds for the Library, taking advantage of favourable American tax laws. Lessing controlled these monies, giving him a certain edge on the Executive Committee, which he exploited to push forward the TAU scheme.

In 1973 the Library celebrated its 40th anniversary. This feat of endurance was marked by a good deal of well-wishing in the Jewish press, but very little by way of practical help. In private there was very little to celebrate. The financial position was becoming increasingly desperate. Matters were exacerbated when the BBC announced that it would be changing its long-standing relationship with the Library – to the latter's further financial detriment.

In the spring of 1974 the Executive met in an atmosphere of crisis. A short-hand account of this meeting has been preserved and it gives a vivid picture of the passions and despair felt by the various parties:

Weltsch: We are running out of funds. . . urgent situation. Our activities are reduced. Living from hand to mouth. Future of Library not assured. Urgency means to take measures at right time before it is too late. Very much impressed by fact that two gentlemen from Tel Aviv will no longer be able to act in our favour if we do not act now. Then one opportunity is definitely gone. If English Jewry can make offer matching Tel Aviv then Library should stay here. Must make decision now.

Lessing: Speaking also for Behr, I propose we should decide right now.

Kessler: Have we all the facts to take hard and fast decision?

Lessing: I think so.

Montefiore [Alan]: Might not change in directorship of LSE make difference?

Schapiro: LSE renew statement of interest. New director. One knows his interests but I cannot express any views.

Weltsch: Prof Dahrendorf friend of mine. His interests are in different field. European politics. Would not have much time to study this, even if he were interested. LSE planning a new building but no money for it. English government grants no longer valid. It would be a grave for our books. As German Jews at Tel Aviv their university teaches German background . . . very active point in their interest. Would keep up our purposes. Has dragged on for 18 months now. See no real possibility of changed condition. There is nothing which leads me to take responsibility to delay decision with risk that in one or two years we are at end of our resources. . .

Montefiore: Still think that if Diaspora solution could be found would be better for World Jewry as whole. William Frankel and Isaiah Berlin [were] ready to make appeal when Middle Eastern War broke out. Money diverted to Israel. Meeting of Anglo-Jewish academics last year. They thought they were not in a position to take up question of financing of Library. Second meeting of this body due next week. Don't expect much more to come out of it.[4]

By the summer of 1974 the crisis was such that several members of the English faction of the Executive Committee, including Alan Montefiore, published a long letter in the *Jewish Chronicle*. In it the authors spelled out the alternatives for the Library:

Many past and present members of the committee . . . have been especially anxious that such an irreplaceable library should remain as one of the central and richest resources of Western European scholarship, including as it does, indispensable material for the study of the tragic history of Western European Jewry.

The alternative to this would be to transfer the library eventually to Israel, where Tel Aviv University is undertaking to house it and to maintain its identity from 1980. . .

We did not dissent from the proposal made at a recent meeting of the executive committee that a generous offer from Tel Aviv should be, in principle, accepted. There was, however, unanimous agreement that this acceptance of Tel Aviv's offer should be subject to the condition that if by the end of 1974 a suitable endowment for the Wiener Library can be obtained in this country, it should, after all, continue in London on its present site.[5]

One effect of this letter was that a chartered accountant named Lewis Golden contacted Bernard Krikler with an offer to help raise funds for the Library. Although Krikler sent Golden a little material on the Library, somehow this contact was never followed up and Golden was soon taken up with other matters. It seems likely that Krikler did not take this offer very seriously, since Golden had never before contacted the Library and knew nothing at all about its work. This was Krikler's mistake, for Lewis Golden was a man who could have helped.

In November of 1974 the agreement with Tel Aviv University was struck. A late effort to endow the Library had failed, yielding only a single donation of £10. The factions on the Committee held true to the end. Only Alan Montefiore and Werner Behr were neutral. In time it was Behr who was swayed by the argument in favour of Tel Aviv and his vote that decided the matter.

The final decision to sign up with TAU caused further resignations from the Executive Committee, with most of the British faction feeling they could no longer serve on it. Kessler resigned as chairman, to be replaced by Werner Behr (who served until his death in 1976, when Fred Lessing took over), but felt such a degree of commitment to the Library that he decided to continue as a committee member.

Tel Aviv University undertook to give the Library an index-linked sum for five years, during which time existing research programmes could be brought to a conclusion. If the Library could secure the means to maintain its existence independently during that period, TAU would bow out.

Reaction to the news that the Library was to leave Britain was relatively muted at first. It was very widely reported, but for the most part without much comment or controversy. In Germany a livelier debate followed. Heinrich Guttmann, the president of the Franz-Oppenheimer Organisation, writing in the *Allgemeine Jüdische Wochenzeitung* called the decision 'incomprehensible' and argued in the strongest terms that the Library should be brought to Berlin. In Tel Aviv the Library would lead the existence of a 'Sleeping Beauty'. In Berlin, it would grant Germany the opportunity to honour the work of its creator and at the same time plant a memorial for the devastated German Jewish community.

This letter drew a sharp response from the journalist Erich Gottgetreu in Jerusalem, who argued that the collection properly belonged in Israel, since this was the centre of modern Jewish life and the place where the collection was most urgently needed to aid the work of studying the sociological, economic and political background of the Holocaust.

At its annual meeting in London the PEN Centre of German-Speaking Writers Abroad expressed its 'consternation' at the news and called on the Thank You Britain Fund, established mainly by German-Jewish refugees and administered by the British Academy, to enable the Wiener Library to carry on in London. The PEN Centre's president, H.G. Adler (a long-standing personal friend of Wiener's) wrote to *The Times* that 'It is difficult to imagine that it should be impossible to raise the necessary funds to keep the library in London where it belongs.'[6]

In the *Times Higher Education Supplement* an editorial complained that the Library should not be moved into a 'war zone' and slammed the Executive Committee for the 'scandalous neglect of their academic responsibilities' in letting things come to such a pass. This drew a furious response from Laqueur, who wrote: 'I am grateful to the writer of the article . . . for not having misspelt my name; it is the only correct fact in his report.' It was far from being the fault of the Executive Committee, who 'engaged in an uphill struggle to get financial support from official and unofficial sources', but 'encountered indifference'.[7]

Ironically, just a month after making the fate of the Library public, the *Jewish Chronicle* was able to publish an announcement that £25,000 had been granted to the Library by the Volkswagen Foundation. However this was given to fund specific research projects and could in no way form the basis of an effort to keep the Library in London.

Meanwhile the controversy simmered on. In March 1976 the German daily *Die Welt* wrote up the story under the headline '100,000 Books Depart'. This article was the first to propose that the contract with Tel Aviv involved secretive or underhand dealings it suggested that the German faction won the day by means of a 'skillful chess move' and that a 'veil of secrecy' had been spread over the details of the contract. There is little evidence that any of this was true, yet charges such as these continued to be levelled at the Library, much to the irritation of Laqueur and the Executive.[8]

In April 1976 a group of PEN Centre members took up the matter in the correspondence column of *AJR Information*, the organ of the Association of Jewish Refugees:

The secrecy surrounding this plan to whisk away from this country what is, perhaps, the most valuable contribution by the remnants of German Jewry to the cultural life of Great Britain is little short of a scandal. It shows such a lack of responsibility by the self-appointed representatives of former

German Jewry in this country to our cultural heritage and such a lack of feeling of gratitude towards this country . . . that it is difficult for us to find suitable words of protest particularly after the debacle of the ill-fated 'Thank You Britain Fund'.

The letter concludes with a demand that the AJR 'publish a full and frank report of the whole matter giving the whole truth and nothing but the truth about the future of the Wiener Library.'[9] Despite an editorial note that this issue would be taken up again, *AJR Information* carried no further articles on the controversy. The 'debacle' referred to a fund of around £100,000, collected by Werner Behr and put at the disposal of the British Academy. Many German-Jewish refugees felt that the money was channelled into inappropriate projects and presumably wanted some of it used for the Library's benefit.

But by the end of 1976 public interest in the problems of the Library had died down. Efforts continued to secure the Library in some form, but finding practical support was as impossible as ever. While it was accepted by Laqueur and the Executive that the contract with Tel Aviv was a necessary evil, it was also felt that the collection in London should be maintained. As a result it was decided that the core of the collection should be preserved on microfilm. Ironically, money for this was raised far more easily than for keeping the Library as a whole.

The funding came from three sources: the National Endowment for the Humanities in the United States, the Deutsche Forschungsgemeinschaft and the Volkswagen Foundation. No British body agreed to support the project. The largest portion came from the American body (which had been approached by Laqueur). Using the money was no straightforward matter, since each donor had rigid criteria to be met. The US money could not be used to microfilm any book that was held in a university library on the eastern seaboard. So the staff of the Library had to undertake considerable bibliographic research before filming could go ahead. The Forschungsgemeinschaft could, strictly speaking, not fund projects outside Germany. So they gave the money to an intermediary in Germany and the Library recovered the microfilming costs from this intermediary.

At the time, the project was one of the largest microfilming schemes undertaken in the United Kingdom. Deputy librarian Tony Wells wrote a report on it for the *British Library Newsletter* in 1982. He pointed out one of the great unexpected benefits of filming the collection, especially the newspaper cuttings, namely their conservation:

The poor quality of the original paper . . . had made the effects of continuous folding and unfolding particularly severe. Cuttings would frequently disintegrate in the hands of those preparing them for filming. Preparation was thus very wearisome. . . the worst shock was to discover how poor the ratio was between preparation time and filming time: about 6:1 in terms of man-hours.

And he was also able to highlight another unforeseen benefit:

In addition, the library now has space for bequests and deposits which it had to turn away in the past.[10]

Although this was of course looking on the bright side.

That the whole microfilming programme was carried through in just two years is an enormous tribute to the hard work of the Library's staff at the time.

The controversy over the Library flared up again violently in 1980, the year the move was to take place. It was triggered by an article in the *Sunday Times* in March, written by Gitta Sereny. It featured a number of views by people associated with the Library, either as users or through sitting on its Executive Committee. Among them Professor Max Beloff, formerly an Executive Committee member, who stated 'I didn't know this move was happening, and it could have been avoided.' He also made the point that putting the collection beyond the reach of most European scholars would greatly diminish its worth:

An institution such as this doesn't function in isolation: it has to be used in conjunction with other research facilities, which in fact don't exist in Israel.

Laqueur also featured in the article, telling Sereny that 'The people at Tel Aviv feel it is very important that there is a Wiener Library in London' and that plans for the future were being formulated:

The board is beginning a new drive to develop the collection in London. We intend to re-expand; the building to become a well-equipped modern research centre, with conference rooms and, we hope, even guest rooms for visiting scholars.

The piece finished with this summing up by Sereny:

Only a miracle can stop things now, says Laqueur. So, what a triumph if, at this last minute, government, academia, foundations, and individuals of all faiths and nationalities who have profited from this institution in the past, or hope to in the future, would combine in one great effort to compensate the University of Tel Aviv, who have been so generous, and to provide endowment for the Wiener Library to remain in London.[11]

It was, of course, not to be.

Meanwhile the article triggered a storm of correspondence about the Library. The angriest exchange was between Laqueur and D.C. Watt of the London School of Economics. Watt wrote a long letter to the *Times Literary Supplement*. He intended to put the whole debate concerning the Library in a historical context. He claimed that Dr Wiener had stipulated in his will that the Library should not leave London and further claimed that this was the reason for the ultimate failure of the affiliation with Reading University. He went on to point to the 'irony' that 'those who were unwilling to see the Library move to Reading now contemplate with equanimity its removal to Tel Aviv.' Watt went on to doubt the veracity of the claim that the Library had received no material support from the British historical profession. The implication of his letter was that in some way the director and Executive had brought the crisis about. Chief librarian Christa Wichmann recalled angry scenes at the Library with visitors demanding to know why the Library was going and making extraordinary verbal attacks on the management and staff of the Library.[12]

Laqueur replied in stinging terms, defending the Library and pointing out that 'what he says about its history is almost entirely wrong'. Laqueur continues, 'Professor Watt's invocation of the shade of Dr Wiener and his testament is touching but entirely fictitious.' In fact Wiener had made no mention of the Library in his will, although it was generally understood that he wanted it to remain in London if possible – he had, of course, tried to send it to Israel himself in the 1950s. Laqueur went on:

> Wiener of course did not want to transfer the library from London. Nor did the executive committee in 1974; every member would have preferred, other things being equal, its continued stay in London. Only the lack of financial support influenced their decision.
>
> We continued our efforts to save as much as possible even after the contract with Tel Aviv University was signed; and thanks only to several generous grants from abroad (we were turned down by every single British foundation to which we applied), all rare material – and much more in addition – has been microfilmed.[13]

In May of 1980 Laqueur wrote an article in the German daily *Die Welt*, summing up the controversy and laying the blame for it firmly at the feet of the British historians who were so outraged at the Library's going. While it was widely being claimed that the Library's Executive and director had been secretive and that no one knew of its plight, Laqueur pointed out that the issue had been raised repeatedly both in the press and at public and private meetings. He also took a mischievous pleasure in pointing out that of all the writers who had criticised the Library, only three were up to date with their membership fees.

He went on to make several points which place the controversy in an interesting perspective. At first, he wrote, the controversy had seemed merely to be the sort of academic squabble which is fairly commonplace:

But then suddenly one came to speak of certain fundamental considerations. A German correspondent in London summarised the controversy in one sentence: 'the British have a bad conscience in relation to Jewish institutions'. This means, in plain words, that the historically-determined Jewish character of the Wiener Library is a thorn in the side of some British historians, that they would gladly incorporate its holdings into an English library and simultaneously 'de-judaise' the institution. Such 'annexationist' efforts by scholars and librarians are not rare. However, in this case they touch on a raw nerve. For the Wiener Library is not just an ordinary specialist library, but has a specific tradition, and the claim that it does not have the right to follow this tradition, that it should give up its Jewish past is – to put it mildly – to be seen as tactless.

It is interesting that in this debate Jews and non-Jews by no means find themselves in two distinct camps. Certain Anglo-Jewish historians are of the opinion that a more or less worthy burial in England is preferable to a continuation of the Institute abroad, while some English people concede – albeit with regret – that the library has a perfect right to insist on its independence.[14]

Laqueur's position was clear: continued independent existence in Israel was preferable to incorporation into another library in Britain. Yet Laqueur was keen that the Library maintain some presence in London if that was at all possible. His conviction that all other avenues had been fruitlessly explored was contested at the time by David Kessler in *The Times* in April 1980. Kessler wrote:

During my chairmanship great efforts were made to overcome the Library's financial problems by finding a suitable home in this country in association with one or other university and I am not convinced that we exhausted all the possibilities. My successor and the director (whom I had appointed) thought otherwise and were determined to move the Library to Tel Aviv University. . .

Those of us on the Executive Committee who disagreed were outmanoeuvred and some resigned immediately. Two of us stayed in the hope that something could be salvaged and even at the last meeting I attended I proposed, without avail, that the books remain here and the microfilm be shipped to Israel.[15]

Professor Sir Max Beloff chipped in with a letter in *The Times* in which he made a veiled attack on the Executive Committee for having refused to ratify the merger with Reading. George Mosse replied that the merger foundered on a straightforward question of money: 'there was no plot'. And he adds that 'in its 40 years in London the Wiener Library has not been overwhelmed by public and private support'.[16]

But it was all too late to prevent the inevitable. By July 1980 the microfilms were in the Library and the books were in the packing cases. The shelves were largely empty. It was without doubt the Library's most trying moment and few believed that it could recover. Laqueur and Wichmann were convinced that it had a future of some sort, but even they could not have foreseen the extraordinary recovery the Library was to stage in the course of the next decade.

NOTES

1. David M. Nichol, 'Library Culls Horror of Hitler', *Chicago Daily News*, 24–25.7.1971.
2. Wiener Archive, Wiener Library.
3. Wiener Archive, Wiener Library
4. Notes on the Executive Meeting held on 18.2.1974, Wiener Archive, Wiener Library.
5. Letter to the *Jewish Chronicle*, 19.7.1974, signed by Julius Gould, David Kessler, Alan Montefiore and Leonard Schapiro, sent from the London School of Economics.
6. H.G. Adler, letter to *The Times*, 16.12.1975.
7. Editorial in *Times Higher Education Supplement*, 21.2.1975; Walter Laqueur, letter to the *THES*, 11.4.1975.
8. Alfred Starkmann, 'Hunderttausend Bücher reisen ab', *Die Welt*, No. 56, 6.3.1976.
9. Letter to *AJR Information*, April 1976, signed by F. Hellendall, Arno Reinfrank, Gabrielle Tergit, Egon Larsen, H.G. Alexander, Peter Fury, A. Apfel, and Helen Rosenau-Carmi.
10. Tony Wells, 'Wiener Library Microfilming Project', *British Library Newspaper Library Newsletter*, No 4, Summer 1982.
11. Gitta Sereny, 'Nazi Past Moves out of London', *The Sunday Times*, 9.3.1980.
12. D.C. Watt, letter to the *Times Literary Supplement*, 11.4.1980
13. Walter Laqueur, letter to the *Times Literary Supplement*, 18.4.1980.
14. Dann jedoch kam man plötzlich auf grundsätzliche Erwägungen zu sprechen. Ein deutscher Korrespondent in London faßte die Kontroverse in dem Satz zusammen: 'Die Engländer haben ein schlechtes Gewissen jüdischen Institutionen gegenüber.' Das heißt im Klartext, daß der historisch bedingte jüdische Charakter der Wiener Library einigen englischen Historikern ein Dorn im Auge ist, daß sie gern die Bestände einer englischen Bibliothek einverleiben würden unter gleichzeitiger 'Dejudaisierung' dieser Institution. Derartige 'annexionistische' Bestrebungen von Wissenschaftlern und Bibliothekaren sind nicht selten. In diesem Falle aber berühren sie einen empfindlichen Nerv. Denn die Wiener Library ist nun einmal nicht nur eine gewöhnliche Fach-Bibliothek, sie hat eine spezifische Tradition, und die Forderung, daß sie nicht das Recht habe, diese Tradition weiterzuführen, daß sie sich von ihrer jüdischen Vergangenheit loslösen und freimachen sollte, muß – gelinde gesagt – als Taktlosigkeit empfunden werden.

Es ist interessant, daß sich in dieser Debatte Juden und Nichtjuden keineswegs in zwei verschiedenen Lagern befinden. Einige englisch-jüdische Historiker sind der Meinung, daß ein mehr oder weniger würdiges Begräbnis in England einer Weiterführung des Institutes im Ausland vorzuziehen sei, während manche Engländer – wenn auch mit Bedauern – zugeben, daß die Wiener Library durchaus das Recht habe, auf ihre Eigenständigkeit zu bestehen. Walter Laqueur, 'Den Briten ein Dorn im Auge', *Die Welt*, 22.5.1980.

15. David Kessler, letter to *The Times*, 19.4.1980.
16. Prof. Sir Max Beloff, letter to *The Times*, 12.4.1980; Prof. George Mosse, letter to *The Times*, 16.4.1980.

CHAPTER THIRTEEN

A Renaissance

THE DETERMINATION expressed by Laqueur in the press and in private
that the Library should remain in London and find a new role for itself
was perfectly genuine. Furthermore it was shared by the Executive Committee. True David Kessler resigned from the Executive altogether in 1980,
but in a letter to Bernard Krikler he wrote:

> I notice that item 6 on the agenda for the AGM refers to the re-appointment
> of members over 70 years old. As I passed my 70th birthday several years
> ago, I think it is time that I made way for a younger person and I do not
> therefore wish my name to go forward for re-appointment.[1]

Certainly Kessler must have been bitterly disappointed at the way things had
turned out. Under the circumstances, his was a dignified and graceful withdrawal.

Laqueur and the Executive had as their priority the issue of fund-raising.
One of the consequences of the completion of the Tel Aviv University deal was
that no further money would be coming from Israel. Any hope of continuing
in London depended on securing new support and lots of it. To add to
their difficulties, the CBF, in its capacity as landlord to the Library, was
questioning the need to go on leasing 4 Devonshire Street. Demonstrating to
the CBF, and to everyone else, that a London Wiener Library was a viable
entity meant getting hold of money and donations of books as quickly as
possible.

The Executive proceeded by reviewing all the influential and wealthy people
with whom they had any contact and systematically getting in touch with them
to ask for help. This brought together a group of well-connected people eager
to help out. One of the first to sign up and one of the most enthusiastic and
helpful was David Pryce-Jones, a freelance writer and historian, who had been
actively involved in fund-raising for the London Library. Another recruit was
Beryl Scholl, brought in by Bernard Krikler.

Mrs Scholl, a member of the footwear clan, recommended making a grant application to the Chicago-based Scholl Foundation. An application was drafted and rapidly dispatched in April 1980 to the Foundation's executive director, blessed with the fiscally apt name James P. Economos. Economos wrote to Krikler that a decision would be reached in September and if favourable, the money would be transferred in December. This application was successful and gave the fund-raisers a great moral boost. In purely practical terms it also ensured that the Library could continue in business until at least the end of 1981.

Krikler thought of a plan to found a British version of the Friends of the Wiener Library which already existed in the United States. This would become the focus of fund-raising efforts and would meet, as far as possible, the Library's running costs. This plan was altered with the reappearance of Lewis Golden.

Golden had contacted Krikler again after he read a letter in *The Times* at the end of March 1980. The letter was signed by a group of academics (many of them had been associated with the Library in the past), who expressed their collective dismay at the Library's removal. Golden telephoned Krikler and this time he was taken more seriously. Golden asked for the Library's audited accounts for 1979 and the current budget. Having seen these he wrote to say he was willing to 'have a go'.

He was then introduced into the Library's circle. Laqueur wrote to Alan Montefiore about him, describing him as 'the man who saved the London Library' (Golden was serving as its treasurer, later he was its chairman), and remarking that:

> He is a very quiet man, with a distinguished war record (a parachutist at Arnhem). He has done enormous things for various organisations if his heart is in it. He is semi-retired from his business after he was told that he was seriously ill and acquired a large farm, which he made into a model farm. He was not very intimately connected with Jewish causes but Philip Mishon thinks we may go a long way if we have his full support.[2]

In fact Golden had just started a ten-year stint as president of Westminster Synagogue, having previously been its chairman and before that its treasurer. In the early post-war years he had been a regular speaker at Hyde Park's Speakers' Corner, at Ridley Road in the East End and elsewhere on the Association of Jewish Ex-Servicemen's platform against fascism and anti-Semitism.

Golden was soon receiving a stream of letters, asking his advice and keeping him informed of developments. However he had already made up his own mind about what the Library needed: the same as any other ailing body, a healthy endowment fund.

He put this view forward, giving as his opinion that the Library should aim for an endowment fund of £1 million, although he was sure privately that this was not enough (but he thought that saying so would be more than the Library's personnel and supporters could cope with at one go). He liked the idea of an endowment because, from the donor's viewpoint, it offered a once-and-for-all solution, while donations towards running costs, special projects and so forth were commonly seen as throwing money into a bottomless pit. He also recommended that no public appeal should be made until a significant amount had been raised. It was agreed that employees of the Library should remain discreetly in the background – if they went to meetings with the potentially generous, it might appear that they were merely intent on raising money for their own salaries.

The rest of 1980 was taken up with a campaign of writing letters and establishing contact with people, enlisting support, getting contributions learning about other possible donors.

Initially the money raised was kept in the Library's general account, but Golden soon insisted on opening a separate account, to ensure that endowment money was not used for general purposes.

At the same time Golden suggested that rather than follow Krikler's suggestion of a Friends of the Wiener Library scheme, there should be an official Wiener Library Endowment Appeal, fronted by the great and the good. This was taken up and ideas were sought concerning whom to contact. One put forward by Alan Montefiore was James Callaghan. Callaghan had been a supporter of the Library during the 1940s and had served on its board. Laqueur was less than keen: he had written to Callaghan in 1978, when Callaghan was Prime Minister and the Library was looking for money for the microfilming project. Callaghan had brushed this appeal aside in a very brusque manner, which left little room for a further approach. However others felt that his lack of interest in 1978 was probably due to his obviously heavy work-load at the time. An approach now might be more successful.

And so it proved. Montefiore wrote to Callaghan at the end of 1980 and received a very warm reply, expressing willingness to help in whatever way was thought best. Furthermore Callaghan swung into action, contacting Arnold Goodman and Harold Lever and helping to draw them into the project. Eventually Callaghan was invited to serve as president of The Wiener Library Endowment Appeal. A group of prominent individuals agreed to serve as vice-presidents. These were: Sir Isaiah Berlin, Sir Hugh Fraser, Lord Goodman, Sir Keith Joseph, Lord Lever, Sir Harold Wilson. The chairman was Alan Montefiore, the treasurer Lewis Golden, the secretary Bernard Krikler.

Golden and Krikler worked closely together and did not always find this easy. Golden was (and remains) a hard taskmaster, with a reputation for being difficult to please. (In almost the first mention Laqueur makes of Golden he writes: 'he already accuses me of not being active enough'[3] – not many people have ever levelled such an accusation against Prof Laqueur). Eventually things came to a head between Krikler and Golden and both resigned from the Appeal Committee. However Golden allowed himself to be talked back onto the Committee, while Krikler's withdrawal was permanent. The two men nevertheless managed a personal reconciliation, worked together on appeal-related matters and indeed became good friends.

By the end of 1980 the stage was set for a Wiener Library revival. The Appeal Committee met at the end of November. It consisted of Alan Montefiore, Lewis Golden, Rabbi David Goldstein, Frank Green, Ben Helfgott, Dr Harry Levitt, Theo Marx (chairman of the AJR), David Pryce-Jones, Mrs M. Gore, Beryl Scholl, Chaim Bermant and Rabbi Hugo Gryn. The ideas being kicked around at this time included approaches to Sir Michael Sobel, Arnold Weinstock, Mrs Gestetner; David Pryce-Jones had been to see Michael Sacher and was following this up, Laqueur had seen Lord Weidenfeld who was offering help and suggesting other possible donors; Montefiore had seen James Callaghan, who had suggested a social gathering hosted by himself and Mrs Muriel Montefiore – they being the only surviving members of the 1946 meeting at the Savoy, which had given birth to the Library's first Executive Committee.

A distinct fund-raising advantage was the fact that Laqueur had recently published *The Terrible Secret*, an important and much-discussed book, which provided tangible proof of the valuable work the Library supported and generated. Copies were sent to potential donors to increase their interest and this drew a good response.

By 1982 the Appeal was ready to go public. In mid-January Lord Weidenfeld hosted a lunch at his home, together with Sir Isaiah Berlin, at which Callaghan officially launched the Appeal. The *Jewish Chronicle* reported on this and claimed (rather optimistically) that 'almost half the sum has already been raised.' In fact by early 1984 the fund stood at £310,000, with pledges outstanding that would bring the total to £500,000. The *Chronicle* also reported that Fred Lessing, chairman of the Executive Committee, had 'pledged himself to donate $100,000 a year for the next five years'.[4]

This was also something of a misunderstanding. When the Appeal was launched, Lessing pledged to match donations, pound for pound, up to £500,000. This was an extraordinarily generous gesture, which effectively cut the Appeal's task in half. It was also a very attractive thing with which to approach potential donors. However when the Appeal finally achieved its £500,000 target and Golden contacted Lessing to ask him to make his donation, Lessing wrote that this had never been his intention. Despite some lively correspondence between the two men, the money was never paid over, although Lessing continued to channel monies from the American Friends of the Wiener Library and to give from his own pocket. Yet here as with Krikler, while Golden was perfectly willing to ruffle a few feathers in pursuit of what he believed to be right, he also used his considerable skill and charm to heal the rift and dissolve any lingering acrimony. In the years before Lessing's death, he and Golden became firm friends again.[5]

The Library found a great many willing and generous donors in the United States, and this was due primarily to the efforts of Lessing and Christopher Dreyfus. Dreyfus has been described by Golden as 'glamorous and mysterious', and also as rather a private man. His efforts on the Library's behalf have been unstinting: Golden calculated that between 1981 and 1986 he was instrumental in collecting no less than $230,000 for the Appeal.

In April 1982 a two-page advertisement was taken out in the *Jewish Chronicle*, paid for by the Golden Charitable Trust. The first page was given to an appeal from James Callaghan:

In the 1930s we failed to prevent the rise to power of the Nazis, with devastating consequences for millions of men, women and children.

Now it is our duty, Jew and non-Jew alike, to preserve in London, where it is readily accessible to researchers from all parts of the world, the unique Wiener Library record of this catastrophe.

I appeal to the Jewish community to give a lead while there is still time. An endowment fund of £1 million will enable the Wiener Library to remain a living memorial to those who died.

On the facing page appeared a listing of the Appeal's officers, a blurb about the history and achievements of the Library and a very blunt statement that:

There will not be another chance. Please help now, generously.[6]

Callaghan also gave an interview on BBC Radio 4 concerning the Library's work and needs and wrote a letter to *The Times*.

In May this appeal was followed up with an appeal in the *AJR Information* newsletter, the organ of the Jewish refugee community. The article likened the Library to the memory of the Jewish community and expressed the hope that 'Anglo-Jewry will meet the challenge, and the members of the AJR will play their part.' The AJR in fact proved itself to be a real friend to the Library, making a donation of £10,000 out of its own funds and helping to raise significant sums from its members.[7]

Fund-raising was one thing, but the Library needed books almost as urgently as it needed money. Fortunately an improbable yet highly significant opportunity presented itself early in the Library's revival. One day in 1983 the Library's bookkeeper Anne Goodwin drew Christa Wichmann's attention to the existence of a collection for sale at a shop in Hammersmith. The peculiarity of this collection was that it had been put together using the Wiener Library's published catalogues. Wichmann inspected the books and chatted to the bookseller, Mr Gray. He had assembled the collection because he believed that no collection like the Wiener Library's existed in the United States. His plan had been to gather a significant number of recently published books held by the Library and offer the collection for sale to an American university as a kind of replica Wiener Library in miniature. Unfortunately when the collection numbered 1,000 volumes and he offered it, he found that he had miscalculated. There was no interest in it at all. Nevertheless what Wichmann found was 1,000 essential volumes on the Wiener Library's subject matter. Since all the books were fairly recent, they all belonged to the group of the Library's former holdings which had not been preserved on microfilm. Mr Gray was asking £15,000 for the lot.

Wichmann returned to the Library and at an early opportunity met with Lewis Golden. Golden was quick to appreciate the significance of the opportunity and agreed to try to find the money. While Wichmann returned to Hammersmith to beat the price down, Golden spoke to David Pryce-Jones, who approached Paul Hamlyn, the publishing magnate and Claus Moser, who in turn approached Dr Abraham Marcus. Between them, Hamlyn and Marcus donated the necessary sum and the books were bought. The Hamlyn–Marcus collection formed the core of the revived London Wiener Library, providing readers with the best of modern scholarship on the subject and giving new heart to all who used, served or simply wished the Library well.

Over the next years other major collections were acquired. When Robert Weltsch, the director of the London Leo Baeck Institute and founder of the *Leo Baeck Yearbook*, retired to Jerusalem, he did not take his extensive and important personal library with him and this was eventually purchased by the Wiener Library. Similarly when Executive Committee member Eduard Rosenbaum died, he bequeathed his collection to the Library. Lutz Becker, a German film-maker and expert on German cultural history, deposited an important library of 2,000 books, collected by his father Hermann Becker, about Germany after 1945, the division of the country into two states and the social and political processes of the Cold War period. Lutz Becker later strengthened the Library's photo archive by depositing his collection of photos and negatives on permanent loan. The Library also received the private libraries of Michael Hecht, Joel Cang and Julius Hollos. These three donations greatly strengthened the Library's holdings of material relating to post-war

Central and Eastern European history. The library at the Ministry of Education donated an extraordinary collection of Nazi school textbooks, in which arithmetic is taught in terms of how many SS and SA men march past Hitler at a parade, and biology by a display of photos of 'low quality' races like Jews and Gypsies contrasted with 'high quality' Germans; 'healthy young people – Germany's future'.

Archive material also came. To cite just some examples, a considerable number of items from the estate of Professor Sir Otto Kahn-Freund, consisting of typewritten reports and memoranda relating to War Crimes trials and the pursuit of war criminals, as well as material relating to the Control Commission regarding the treatment of defeated Germany. In October 1983 a reunion of people involved in the work of the Jewish Relief Unit of the Jewish Committee for Relief Abroad was held in London and this led to an archive being set up at the Library to collect materials relating to the work of this body.

In 1983 the Library celebrated its golden jubilee and this offered a natural occasion for fund- and profile-raising. A major exhibition was staged entitled 'On the Track of Tyranny' (after the volume of essays published by the Library in the early 1960s). Organised by Christa Wichmann and Tony Wells, the exhibition was spread over four of the Library's rooms, with a display about the Library itself in the entrance hall. Room 1 detailed the rise of fascism as an international phenomenon; room 2 concerned Nazi Germany; room 3 dealt with the Second World War, including the Holocaust; room 4 described postwar developments and the mounting tension between East and West.

The formal opening was attended by Lord Annan, the German ambassador Dr Jurgen Ruhfus and Sir Claus Moser. Golden chaired the occasion, introducing each of the speakers. The exhibition ran from mid-April to mid-May; it was well attended and did much to establish the fact in the mind of the wider public that the Library was alive and kicking in London. A travelling version of the exhibition was also assembled and this was shown at several venues in Germany.

But the events staged by and for the Library did not always go smoothly. One which should have been a major coup and brought the Library money and support, was organised by Christopher Dreyfus. Dreyfus staged a reception in February 1984 in Hollywood at the commissary of 20th Century Fox at which the guest speaker was Henry Kissinger. He was introduced by the Republican Senator William Cohen, who spoke movingly of the Library's importance. The party was attended by a number of the Hollywood film-making elite. Yet organisational failures meant that this prestigious event raised a paltry $6,000 – almost all of which went to cover the costs of staging the event.

The confusion arising from there being two Wiener Libraries was also harmful to fund-raising. Many people took the attitude that if the 'real' Wiener

Library had moved to Israel, why should they support the London institution? On the other hand if the London Wiener Library was the 'real' one, why didn't it have all its original materials? Clearing up such issues was made doubly complicated by the fact that the officials at TAU had confidently expected the London Wiener Library to shut up shop after the transfer of the books. There was a certain amount of hostility arising from its stubborn refusal to sink into oblivion. Eventually this matter was resolved when Montefiore, Golden and Dreyfus went to Tel Aviv in August 1984. Agreement was reached that the two 'sides' would 'co-operate in all possible practical ways in all future activities connected with our Appeal.' This was made possible because the London Wiener Library agreed to pay over to the TAU Wiener Library 25 per cent of all monies raised by the Appeal until the goal of £1 million was reached. Thereafter the monies would be divided half and half. From Tel Aviv's point, this was an excellent deal, enhanced by Golden on his return making a personal gift to the university as a goodwill gesture. In fact the deal turned out to be so generous that the London Wiener Library later renegotiated it. In the event, £94,000 was paid by the London Wiener Library to the Tel Aviv Library in addition to £6,000 which had been paid by Lessing, a total of £100,000 which matched the money paid by Tel Aviv in the 1970s. Fred Lessing, the chairman of the Executive Committee, played a vital role in these negotiations. He was indeed well placed to mediate in the battle of the Wieners – being prominent on the board of TAU. Without his intervention, it is likely that the London Wiener Library would have had to close down, since the Tel Aviv Wiener Library was legally entitled to insist on this.

With the internecine squabbling sorted out, the Appeal prepared to relaunch itself in the autumn of 1984. Preparatory to this Joan Stiebel was recruited as appeal co-ordinator. Joan was brought in by Alan Montefiore and Ben Helfgott, who both knew of her from her days as joint secretary of the CBF, and her time as Otto Schiff's private secretary. Through this work she had built up an impressive list of contacts and a wealth of know-how. She immediately added a new group of fund-raisers to a sub-committee of the Appeal. This group made itself responsible for thinking up ideas for Appeal events, organising them and making sure that nothing like the Kissinger fiasco happened again. In general the Appeal Committee was an elastic entity – people came and went, introduced their friends and acquaintances and so on – and in this way the flow of ideas, energy and contacts was kept going. In short, Joan's presence made a marvellous impact. Meetings took place at the Wiener Library, usually at lunchtime, with Golden in the chair. His habit of ensuring that meetings began at 1pm sharp and ended precisely one hour later was a source of amusement to many.

The relaunch was eventually scheduled for October, to coincide with an open week at the Library beginning on the 21st. The launch was held at the Painters Hall on the 22nd and the main speaker was Lord Elwyn-Jones. Others in attendance included Sir Keith Joseph (an enthusiastic supporter of the Library) and Sir Claus Moser. The Executive Committee later reported that the Painters Hall reception had raised in excess of £60,000.

The Library's Open Week featured conducted tours of the Library, special exhibitions, a book sale, twice-daily screenings of films on video and a series of talks by celebrity speakers including Janina David, the author of *A Square of Sky*, Chaim Bermant and Dan Jacobson.

Not long after the relaunch, on 12 November, Lewis Golden assisted by the solicitor, Martin Paisner, instituted a new body, The Wiener Library Endowment Trust. He explained that this was being done to guarantee 'an essential separation of functions.' The Trust would have:

> . . . power to make investments and to distribute the income, the most usual beneficiary of that income being the library in London. So constituted the trust is independent and able to resist any pressures that might otherwise deflect either the capital or the income of the endowment fund from this vital purpose.[8]

With the Trust in place, the long-term financial security of the Library was one step closer to becoming a reality. The trustees were Lord Annan, Christopher Dreyfus, Rabbi Hugo Gryn, Lewis Golden and Alan Montefiore. The Wiener Library has the right to appoint two of the five trustees. Lewis Golden served as executive trustee from the Trust's foundation. This involved him in managing the Trust's investments, producing the annual accounts, calling meetings and (no doubt a pleasurable task) recovering taxes. At the end of 1994 he gave up producing the accounts, although he maintains an eagle eye on the accountant who has taken over.

Also around this time the decision was taken to launch a *Wiener Library Newsletter*, the purpose of which was to keep the Library's supporters and friends informed of appeal-related events and to disseminate news and stories relating to the Library, its staff, its supporters and its collections.

In 1985 the AJR again showed its commitment to the Library, when it published a renewed two-page appeal to its members in its *AJR Information*. Included was a donation and reply form inviting contributions. This included details of a scheme whereby donors could have a bookshelf or an entire bookcase dedicated to the memory of a loved one. This proved to be a popular scheme and within a year some 56 plaques (designed for the Library by the artist Roman Halter) adorned the Library's bookcases.

By the end of 1986 the Appeal fund stood at about £650,000 and the fund-raising zeal was as strong as ever. A series of small dinners was held, each featuring a celebrity guest speaker. This was a suggestion of Joan Stiebel's, intended to maintain the impetus created by the relaunch and to introduce more people to the Library and gain their support. These evenings were catered for by a contact and friend of Joan's, Gill Burr. She had worked for Joan at the CBF and was involved in setting up the 'Helpful Eight Committee', which raised funds for the CBF. Learning of Joan's involvement with the Library, she offered the choice of a cash donation to the Appeal or catering for all Appeal events. This was an offer too good to turn down and Gill has generously supplied food for dozens of Appeal events over the years.

In the summer of 1986 the Library staged a major exhibition to mark the 50th anniversary of the Berlin Olympics. Held in memory of Leonard Montefiore, it was organised by P. Yogi Mayer, a long-standing friend of the Library and himself a former athlete (Yogi Mayer had in fact worked briefly at the Library when it was moving into its Manchester Square premises. He had unpacked boxes of books and had felt the rough end of Louis Bondy's tongue because he couldn't resist stopping work and reading). A reception held to open the exhibition was attended by several representatives of the British Olympic Committee and was addressed by Walter Laqueur, Professor Erich Segal and Duff Hart-Davis. Rabbi Hugo Gryn made an appeal on behalf of the Library.

It was also during this year that Ernst Fraenkel, an enthusiastic supporter of the Appeal for several years, was invited to join the Executive Committee of the Wiener Library, at the same time as Ludwig Spiro from the AJR. Fraenkel, a retired businessman, was immediately invited to act as the Committee's treasurer. He had been drawn into the Library's circle by a coincidence and a misunderstanding. His son happened to be a student of Alan Montefiore's. Montefiore, mistakenly thinking that his pupil was William Frankel's son, thought that here was a potentially useful contact. He encouraged the young man to try to involve his illustrious father. Unaware that he was being mistaken for someone else, Ernst Fraenkel did indeed become involved. He was in any case well aware of the Library's existence, having met Wiener and visited the Manchester Square premises (His impressions of Wiener were not altogether favourable.) In the years since then, he has gone on to make a major contribution to the future security of the Library and to exert a decisive influence on its development.

In 1987 the support base of the Library was further strengthened with the formation of the Young Friends group. Intended as an informal grouping of interested people aged 20–40, it was set up by Wendy Pollecoff and Lewis Golden's son Jonathan, and for several years staged early evening events with a variety of guest speakers. Both Pollecoff and Golden graduated in time to the Library's Executive Committee.

The year 1987 saw further fund-raising triumphs: in January Ernst Fraenkel got things off to a flying start when he and his wife gave a dinner for their friends in the Library's reading room. Sir James Callaghan was the guest of honour and Walter Laqueur spoke. The occasion raised some £30,000 from the 28 guests and some who had been unable to attend.

In the summer Mrs Elizabeth Maxwell, wife of the newspaper tycoon, spoke at the Library during a reception at which a Russian film documenting the liberation of Auschwitz was screened. Alan Montefiore and Rabbi Hugo Gryn lent their support, speaking on a theme close to Alfred Wiener's heart, the need for constructive dialogue between the Jewish and Christian communities.

But the most impressive event took place in the autumn. A dinner was held on 18 November at the Banqueting House, Whitehall, attended by HRH The Duke of Edinburgh as guest of honour. The dinner committee consisted of some 19 people. Those most actively involved included Joan Stiebel, Patricia Mendelson, Denzil Jacobs and, of course, the indefatigable Lewis Golden, who served as committee chairman. Walter Laqueur's secretary Liz Boggis provided secretarial and administrative support (Golden has described her as 'an invaluable person'). James Callaghan, recently elevated to the peerage, involved himself actively. It was estimated that mounting the dinner would be a financial hazard best avoided and Lord Callaghan was asked 'to approach a particular person to foot the bill.' The approach failed but an anonymous donor, now known to have been Golden himself, came to the rescue.

Guests at the dinner included the German ambassador, Baron Rüdiger von Wechmar, the Chief Rabbi, Lord Jakobovits, Lord and Lady Wilson, Lord and Lady Callaghan, Lord and Lady Elwyn-Jones, the Hon Simon Marks, Sir Keith Joseph and a host of others. The loyal toast was proposed by Alan Montefiore; it was followed by grace spoken by Rabbi Hugo Gryn. After brandy and liqueurs Lord Callaghan proposed a toast to the Wiener Library and this was seconded by Lewis Golden who made an emotional appeal for funds and spoke of the need in peacetime of a record of the Nazi era and its horrors:

> There is such a record, in London. It's at the Wiener Library, in Devonshire Street. Those who don't know it should visit it; and they'll see for themselves both a ghastly chronicle of death and an inspiring testament to life.
>
> Man's days are as grass, and the long arm of death reaches out and touches us all, each one of us, in due time: death from natural causes; death by chance; death, honourable death, on the field of battle. And we learn to face that prospect with resignation; perhaps with equanimity; sometimes,

even, with serenity. But death by cold design! Death by cruel decree! Death at the hands of state murderers! Death because one is born a Jew, or is thought to be born a Jew! Death because one is a Russian, or a Pole, or a communist, or a homosexual, or a gypsy, or a freemason, or any of the myriads of victims selected by an evil state to be done away with! Death for men, women, children, babes in arms! Death before the firing squad, death in the gas chambers, death on the gallows! Death through starvation, or exhaustion, or untreated disease, or lethal injection, or brutal beating!

Enough! We all know it happened. And we all know it happened, not a thousand years ago, not in the dark ages, but in our time: in our century: in the century when man touched the face of the moon, and reached for the stars: in our wonderful, wonderful century. And we all know it happened, not ten thousand miles away, but almost on our own doorsteps, an hour or so away, by aircraft flight, from where we sit and dine tonight. And we all know it happened because it was ordained, arranged, executed, not by wild and savage barbaric hordes, but by men and women of a civilised and cultured people, bearing the name of a great and proud nation, a nation which, both before and since, has rendered signal service to all mankind: in science, in medicine, in literature and in music. In our time, and on our continent, we all know it happened: yet a crime so great that its very contemplation makes us doubt our sanity. And who among us, in the still of the night, has not cried out: show us, O Lord, show us: show us that we have been dreaming, that it isn't true. But our prayers are never answered, for alas it is true. And our children, and our children's children, and all who come after, will know the truth, and will keep it before their eyes, because there is the record, ever since 1933, documented almost from day to day: there is the record of the growth of evil, never equalled before or since: this record of our time.[9]

Lewis Golden later described this speech as 'a "no holds barred" appeal with no mercy shown for the feelings of anyone listening [and the audience included the German Ambassador], and it worked.'

The event was described by Joan Stiebel as the 'crowning effort of the Wiener Library Endowment Appeal.' It was widely reported in the press, the *Evening Standard* running an article titled 'Another Battle in the War of Words', which was built around an interview with Lord Callaghan. In the *Jewish Chronicle* it was front-page news.

The guests at the dinner pledged a total of £220,000. These pledges were enough to bring the Appeal to its target of £1 million. In fact the dinner raised £250,000 in total. It was of course a great achievement (Golden, laconic as ever, described the occasion as 'a good show'). But he and the Appeal Committee already knew that it was not enough. Reporting to the Executive Committee,

Golden gave his view that a second million would be needed. With this admission, it became clear that fund-raising would need to be a feature of the Library's existence for several years to come.

After 'the Dinner' activity slumped somewhat. The pause for breath and reflection was also called for by the fact that Lord Callaghan let it be known that he wished, before very long, to retire as the Appeal's president. Joan Stiebel too announced that she wanted to ease her work-load. (She had been enticed to join the Appeal with assurances that it would only occupy her for one day a week; within a couple of months she was working four or even five days a week.) Nevertheless money continued to come in from donations and bequests (following the death of Oscar Joseph the Appeal benefited to the tune of £38,000 from the Oscar Joseph Charitable Trust; another donation of £10,000 came in from Margot Pottlitzer's estate). Both Lord Callaghan and Joan agreed that the occasion of their retirement should be used for further fund-raising.

Meanwhile the Library's activities surged on. Spring 1988 saw the staging of an exhibition to commemorate the 50th anniversary of the Austrian Anschluss. The opening was attended by the president of the Board of Deputies and other dignitaries and the exhibition was well attended throughout.

Another major development was the launching of the Fraenkel Prize, awarded for an essay in a subject related to the Library's subject matter. The idea was first floated by Ernst Fraenkel at the Executive Committee meeting of May 1988. He thought it would be an excellent way of making the Library better known in educational and academic circles. It should be open to young historians under the age of 30; he was willing to guarantee a £5,000 prize for the first five years. This proposal was discussed and refined over the coming months and announcements placed in the press in time for the following meeting. The first year's prize was eventually won by Professor Margaret Stieg, of the University of Alabama, for her work on public libraries in Nazi Germany and the Fraenkel Prize has gone on to become a major annual event for historians and writers.

October 1988 brought news of the death, at the age of 97, of Mrs Leonard Montefiore. This was received with considerable sadness. She represented one of the very few remaining links with the Wiener Library of the 'LGM' era and had herself contributed generously to the work of the Library after the death of Leonard Montefiore.

In 1989 it was decided to recruit a Director of Studies to develop the Library's educational activities, to raise the Library's academic profile still further and to assist with fund-raising. The idea was proposed by Ernst Fraenkel and it is apparent that one of the things he had his eye on was the eventual retirement of Walter Laqueur and the need to recruit and groom a successor.

The appointment was made in October 1989, the choice falling on a young and ambitious academic called Dr David Cesarani. Cesarani had taken a first at Queen's College Cambridge, an MA at Columbia University in the United States, and a doctorate at St Antony's Oxford. While preparing his PhD he was appointed Montague Burton fellow at Leeds University and after completing his doctorate in 1986 he became Barnett Shine research fellow at Queen Mary College. Around this time he also became involved in public debates about Israel and Nazi war crimes, eventually serving as principal researcher for the All-Party Parliamentary War Crimes Group.

Cesarani hit the ground running, rapidly setting up a one-day conference on the *Protocols of the Elders of Zion* and organising an early-evening lecture series on 'Unfinished Business' left over from the Second World War. Speakers included Professor Norman Stone, Dr Richard Overy and Frederick Raphael.

On the fund-raising side Lord Callaghan retired as president of the Appeal, to be replaced by the Rt Hon Merlyn Rees. Merlyn Rees acknowledged that Lord Callaghan's was a hard act to follow, but gave warm-hearted assurances that he would be no less active than his predecessor. Lord Callaghan had agreed that a James Callaghan Fund should be established, to collect funds for The Wiener Library Endowment Appeal that focused on international affairs. In September 1989 Joan Stiebel also stepped down. In doing so she lent her name to a last fund-raising venture: The Joan Stiebel Educational Fund of The Wiener Library Endowment Trust – which brought in £44,000 almost at once and more in succeeding months. Joan's farewell party was attended by over 100 people; they were addressed by Lord Joseph, who paid her a number of generous and well-earned compliments. Alan Montefiore and Ben Helfgott, welcoming the guests, declared that recruiting Joan had been the best thing they had ever done for the Library.

The year 1989 was also marked by the retirement of Bernard Krikler. He had been with the Library for almost 20 years and had contributed to nearly every aspect of its development over this period. In a generous tribute to him, Walter Laqueur stated that the very survival of the Wiener Library was due largely to Krikler. Sadly, Krikler died just three years later, at the early age of 65.

The year was not without its exhibition. In October, to mark the 40th anniversary of the founding of the Federal Republic, the Library staged 'From Enemy to Ally: Germany 1945–1949', opened by the German ambassador Herr von Richthofen, and attended by Sir Isaiah Berlin.

Nineteen hundred and ninety saw further losses to the Library: in May Fred Lessing died. He had served as the chairman of the Executive Committee since David Kessler stepped down in the 1970s and had been a driving force behind the TAU deal. Although he was based in the United States and thus never developed an intimate relationship with the Library or its staff (few of whom he would ever have recognised), he was conscientious about chairing meetings and unfailingly did what he felt was best for the Library. He was replaced by Ernst Fraenkel. The Library's Memorial Hall was renamed The Fred Lessing Memorial Hall in tribute to the former chairman.

Also in spring 1990 Lewis Golden announced his intention to step down as treasurer of the Endowment Committee. At the meeting of the Committee in May, he addressed his colleagues:

> Membership of this appeal committee has been a remarkable experience for me. We've all worked together in a solemn, indeed a sacred task: the maintenance for all time of our unique and precious Wiener Library. We know that we have to secure that vital continuity of an infamous record. We owe it to the memory of the dead. We owe it also to the living, who must always be able to see for themselves what can happen in a civilised society: such evil, such terror, so exhaustively applied, as to pass all understanding: what can happen in a civilised society, and how it can happen.

Sombre stuff, but he also acknowledged, with considerable relish: 'what fun it has always been!' Although like Lord Callaghan a hard act to follow, the Committee unanimously approved the appointment of Denzil Jacobs as Golden's successor.[10]

A splendid fund-raising event was proposed and sponsored in the early part of 1991 by Anthony Weldon, a member of the Appeal Committee, in connection with an exhibition of paintings by Franz Hals at the Royal Academy in Piccadilly. The private view and sumptuous buffet was thoroughly appreciated by those who attended – and the swelling coffers of the Endowment Fund benefited substantially. Mr Weldon has organised several other highly successful fund-raising events, mostly linked with artistic performances of one sort or another.

In December 1991 Laqueur, now 75 years of age, announced his intention to retire at the end of the following year. Although he would continue to be associated with the Library in some capacity, his life as an academic and writer was his priority and he felt that 'the challenges of the problems facing the institution in the future could best be met by someone who could devote the bulk of his or her time to it.'

For Laqueur the 1980s had been an extraordinarily productive time. While continuing to administer the Library and keep up with the demands of his teaching commitments (most of the time his working life was multicontinental), his output as a writer was prodigious. In 1980 he published a novel, *The Missing Years*, followed in 1981 by another, *Farewell to Europe*.

Re-engaging with historical and political subjects he produced *Germany Today* issued in 1985. In 1986 he published *Breaking the Silence* (written with Richard Breitman). Nineteen hundred and eighty nine saw the publication of the classic *A History of Zionism* and *Der lange Weg zur Freiheit*. The following year saw *Stalin: the Glasnost Revelations*. The autobiographical *Thursday's Child Has Far to Go* appeared in 1992 and 1993 saw *The Black Hundred* (about right wing extremism in Russia).

Such achievements were not likely to go unrewarded. In February 1985 he had been awarded the annual prize of the German Inter Nationes organisation. The following January he received Germany's highest civilian honour, the Grand Cross of the Order of Merit, at a ceremony at the German Embassy in London. Ambassador von Wechmar spoke of his achievements and read from one of his works. In May 1987 he was awarded an Honorary Doctorate by the Hebrew Union College for his 'outstanding contribution to the study of modern history.' Numerous other American universities honoured him in a similar fashion. Since retiring Laqueur has continued to be associated with the Library as its academic consultant.

The decision to appoint Cesarani as Laqueur's replacement went through more or less on the nod, it being decided that advertising the post was unlikely to turn up anyone who hadn't already been rejected for the post of director of studies. Cesarani's record in educational and outreach work and as an organiser of academic meetings was impressive. On the fund-raising side, he concentrated on bringing in donations to make particular events possible and was succesful in this. In certain respects he resembled Laqueur at his appointment in 1964: youthful, energetic, aggressive and brimming with ideas of what he wanted the Library to become.

With the appointment of Cesarani to the directorship, the Library clearly entered a new phase of its existence. While some uncertainties about its future direction remained, its existence was now on a firmer financial footing than it had ever been before. The situation inherited by Cesarani, Fraenkel, Merlyn Rees and Denzil Jacobs was an immeasurably easier and more secure one than their predecessors (Laqueur, Lessing, Lord Callaghan and Lewis Golden) had faced in their day.

The James Callaghan Fund, planned when Lord Callaghan retired as president of the Appeal in 1989, was launched in style at the Great Hall of Lincoln's Inn in October 1993, in front of 300 guests, with the Rt Hon Peter Brooke as guest of honour. He had stepped in late in the arrangements to cover for John Major, who had agreed to be guest of honour but had to withdraw. The loyal toast was proposed by Sir Leslie Porter, the chairman of the dinner committee. Lord Callaghan spoke of the horrors of the Nazi past and the unique role and responsibility of the Jewish people:

The history of the Jewish people throws on you a special mission of leadership as a people whose contributions to culture, to art, music and painting have left a permanent mark on our civilisation.

You must always be in the lead to uphold, defend and strengthen human rights everywhere, for your own history is a permanent lesson of the horrors that can engulf a people when the basic quality of human life is trampled underfoot. . . I urge most strongly that you should contribute with the utmost generosity, so that the present generation will be able to learn what terrible events can befall the human race when evil triumphs and that, with that knowledge, they will dedicate themselves to upholding the basic human rights of all their fellows – whatever their race, creed or colour.[11]

Lewis Golden proposed a toast to the Callaghan Fund and spoke of Lord Callaghan's very active role as 'the perfect president':

. . . he lent us his name; and persuaded several peers of the realm and other distinguished persons to add their names as vice-presidents; and effected other vital introductions for us; and spoke for us at meetings; and hosted dinners for us; and wrote hundreds of letters for us; and arranged for His Royal Highness Prince Philip to be the guest of honour at our fund-raising dinner in 1987; and concerned himself, whenever asked to do so, with all the detailed arrangements for that important occasion . . . and in the last days, when we were searching for a worthy successor, he was even instrumental in arranging for Merlyn Rees to take over from him . . . The perfect president? A bit over the top, perhaps? In 1980 when Jim Callaghan assumed office as president, the endowment trust funds stood at zero. When he handed over in 1989 they stood at £1.7 million . . . £1.7 million and rising.[12]

Guests at the launch included the German Minister Plenipotentiary Dr Friedrich Kroneck and Mrs Kroneck, Lord Annan, Lady Diana Britten, Lady Callaghan, Lady Merlyn-Rees, Lord and Lady Rayne, Lord Rothschild, Lord and Lady Swaythling, Lord and Lady Young of Graffham and a host of others including Dr Wiener's two daughters Ruth Klemens and Mirjam Finkelstein and their husbands.

Ernst Fraenkel had generously sponsored the occasion. Golden had acted as deputy chairman of the dinner committee responsible for all the detailed arrangements, helped by Gill Burr, Patricia Mendelson and Joan Stiebel, with Liz Boggis shouldering much of the burden with her customary competence and aplomb.

A final link with the past was severed in 1993 when Christa Wichmann, chief librarian for 25 years, announced her retirement. She had been honoured by the German government in March 1993 with the Cross of the Order of Merit and praised by the Embassy Minister Dr Kroneck for 'a labour of love which you have always performed in an exemplary way to the enrichment of scholarship throughout the world.'[13]

By the end of 1994, the Endowment fund stood at almost £2.7 million and since then it has passed the £3 million mark. Lewis Golden regarded this as being roughly half what will be needed to allow the Library full financial independence for all time. Achieving this will require several more years of work, but there seems no reason why the goal may not ultimately be reached.

For anyone concerned with or about the Library, perhaps the most satisfying aspect of its renaissance in the 1980s and 90s has been the fact that its cause has finally been taken up by the Jewish community in Britain. True, much of the money raised for the Endowment has come from abroad and from refugees living in the United Kingdom but for the first time in its 60-year history, really significant amounts have been donated by Anglo-Jewry.

There is if anything a danger that the pendulum may one day swing too far the other way. Were the bulk of the staff and committee members ever to have no German-Jewish background, the Library would risk losing touch with its roots. This would be tragic, since it could then no longer properly serve as a memorial to German Jewry. It would cease to be what today it unquestionably remains: Dr Wiener's Library.

NOTES

1. David Kessler, letter to Bernard Krikler, 3 April 1980.
2. Letter from Walter Laqueur to Alan Montefiore, 5.8.1980, Wiener Archive, Wiener Library; Phillip Mishon served as national chairman of the Association of Jewish Ex-Servicemen from 1966–68.
3. Letter from Walter Laqueur to Alan Montefiore, 4.8.1980, Wiener Archive, Wiener Library.
4. *Jewish Chronicle*, 22.1.1982.
5. This information comes from a conversation between the author and Lewis Golden.
6. *Jewish Chronicle*, 2.4.1982.
7. *AJR Information*, May 1982.
8. *Wiener Library Newsletter*, Vol. I, No. 2, Oct. 1985.
9. Speech made by Lewis Golden in seconding the toast to the Wiener Library on 18. 11.1987, at the Banqueting House, Whitehall.
10. Minutes of the Appeal Committee meeting, 3.5.1990.
11. Quoted in the *Wiener Library Newsletter*, No. 19, Winter 1992/3.
12. A toast proposed by Lewis Golden at the dinner held at the Great Hall of Lincoln's Inn, 15.10.1992.
13. Quoted in *Wiener Library Newsletter*, No. 20, Summer 1993.

Conclusion

I T IS FITTING, at the end of this reconstruction of the Library's existence, to return to what is fundamental: the Library's collection and its work.

By the end of 1994 the Library's holdings stand at around 50,000 books and 2,500 periodicals, of which about 250 are currently being subscribed to, and featuring such rarities as a near-complete set of all the camp periodicals produced by internees in British internment camps during the war. There are original unpublished documents, including extensive memoirs by survivors, Jewish family trees, documentation on the Kurt Waldheim controversy and a collection on the persecution of Gypsies. A collection of 1,000 video tapes containing some 4,000 programmes recorded from British, German and French television stations is being added to weekly. The photographic collection comprises many thousands of images of Nazi persecution in all its phases; it is supported by an illustrated books section of the Library containing tens of thousands of pictures. A special collection contains diverse items, from examples of the yellow star to ghetto and camp currency, Nazi board games centred on hounding Jews and many original posters. The Eric Colebeck stamp collection contains thousands of examples of stamps issued to commemorate events in concentration camps. It is thought to be one of the world's greatest collections of its kind. And there are any number of other collections and rarities, important for scholarship and the work of teaching the Holocaust to a younger generation.

The academic activities of the Library have revived remarkably in recent years. Each year sees a series of themed early-evening seminars. Two series have focused on reassessments of 'Great Reputations' and involved speakers including academics, writers and MPs; one series laid bare 'The German Muse' and included papers on the female collaborators of Bertolt Brecht and 'Wagner's Jewish circle'. Another series concentrated on issues arising from the election of a fascist councillor in Millwall and featured Keith Vaz, MP and Herman Ouseley, chair of the Council for Racial Equality.

Half-day seminars have covered areas as diverse as the Dreyfus Affair, resistance in the Third Reich, and the Warsaw Ghetto Uprising and conferences have proved a major attraction. Topics have included the Nazi seizure of power, Genocide and rescue in Hungary 1944 (speakers included Professor Yehuda Bauer, Professor Richard Breitman and Professor Dina Porat) and Family history: survivors, refugees and their children (an event so popular that it had to be repeated in order to satisfy demand).

Since 1993 the Library has hosted an annual Bernard Krikler Memorial Lecture, in honour of the former deputy director. Speakers have included Professor Dan Jacobson (a personal friend of Krikler's), Professor Kenneth Minogue and Al Alvarez.

Such events testify to the lively life of the mind being pursued and fostered at 4 Devonshire Street. Every year sees the Library's reputation grow and greater numbers of users join. For this reason and to maintain the Library's position among its sister institutions, it is planned to make the catalogue available on computer. This will eventually bring all the disparate collections within the scope of a single finding aid. Ultimately electronic mysteries such as networking with other libraries and storing materials on CD-ROM will become options to look at. In any case, an automated catalogue, while creating a short-term nuisance as catalogue records are transferred, will significantly improve the service users can expect when they visit the Library.

Another planned development is the revival in some form of the *Wiener Library Bulletin* as a forum for news about developments at the Library and academic papers on historical subjects related to the Library's subject. If this project succeeds the Library will once again have a voice in the international debate on Holocaust studies and the activities of the extreme right.

In conclusion it is true to say that while the Wiener Library faces many challenges and difficulties in the years ahead, it has risen phoenix-like from the nadir of 1980 to become a remarkably vigorous and vibrant institution, dedicated to the joint task of remembrance of an appalling past and the building of a better future.

Bibliography of Wiener Library Publications

The following list of publications of the Wiener Library cannot claim to be complete. It is based on a survey conducted by the Library staff in 1969 and has been updated.

AMSTERDAM 1933–40

Books and pamphlets

Wirtschaftsboykott, Amsterdam, 1934 (Materialen zur Zeitgeschichte, Heft I).
Der Kirchenstreit in Deutschland. Bibel und Rasse, Amsterdam 1934.
Dokumentensammlung über die Entrechtung, Ächtung und Vernichtung der Juden in Deutschland seit der Regierung Adolf Hitler. Abgeschlossen am 15 Oktober 1936, Amsterdam, 1936.
Photographische Dokumentensammlung über die Entrechtung, Ächtung und Vernichtung der Juden in Deutschland seit der Regierung Adolf Hitler, Amsterdam, 1936.
Die nationalsozialistische und antisemitische Literatur Deutschlands seit der Machtergreifung Hitlers (np, nd – it cannot be firmly established whether this publication ever appeared).

Periodicals

Die jüdische Informationszentrale, No I, July 1934 – No 8, April 1935. Some issues also in English and French.

Mimeographed Reports

A huge number of these reports were produced and distributed. It is unlikely that a complete set was taken from Amsterdam to London in 1939. Each report contains a number of items. The titles given here are taken from the lead item of each report.

Der Berner Prozess um die Protokolle der Weisen von Zion: Bulletin, No 1 (29 April 1935) – No 22 (13 May 1935).

Mai-Bericht über die Lage in Deutschland, Amsterdam, May 1940.

Röhm, von Schleicher, die Juden und die 'Times', Amsterdam, Sept. 1934.

Rothschild siegt bei Waterloo, Amsterdam, Sept. 1934.

Polen und seine Minderheiten, Amsterdam, Sept. 1934.

Internationale Meinung, Amsterdam, Sept. 1934.

Der Vernichtungsfeldzug gegen das deutsche Judentum, Amsterdam, Sept. 1940.

Zum Berner Prozess über die Protokolle der Weisen von Zion, Amsterdam, Sept. 1934.

Union antijudaique universelle, Amsterdam, Sept. 1934.

Zum Tode von Baron Edmond de Rothschild, Amsterdam, Sept. 1934.

Aus Alfred Rosenbergs 'Weltkampf', Amsterdam, Sept. 1934.

Propaganda im Ärzteblatt, Amsterdam, Sept. 1934.

Das dritte Reich im Spiegel der Weltpresse, Amsterdam, Sept. 1934.

Der Berner Prozess um die Protokolle der Weisen von Zion, Amsterdam, Oct. 1934.

Widerruf, Entschuldigung und Richtungswechsel der national sozialistischen 'Deutschen Zeitung' in New York, Amsterdam, Nov. 1934.

Bericht über Sigilla Veri. Das grosse internationale Lexikon der Antisemiten. mit einer photographischen Beilage, Amsterdam, Nov. 1934.

Das erste jüdisch-christliche Symposium, Amsterdam, Nov. 1934.

Katholischen Stimmen zur Rassentheorie und Judenpolitik, Amsterdam, Nov. 1934.

Julius Streicher im 'Kalendar der deutschen Jugend, 1935', Amsterdam, Dec. 1934.

Angriffe gegen ärztliche Wissenschaft und Judentum, Amsterdam, Dec. 1934.

Was erwartet die Juden im Saargebiet?, Amsterdam, Jan. 1935.

Julius Streicher, Amsterdam, Jan. 1935.

Stimmen zur Lage der Juden an der Saar, Amsterdam, Jan. 1935.

Antijüdische Auslands-Propaganda, Amsterdam, Jan. 1935.

Aus dem Bereich der Wirtschaft. Religion und Rasse, Amsterdam, Jan. 1935.

Gedanken über die weitere Behandlung der Juden in Deutschland, Amsterdam, Jan. 1935.

Die Fronten und Bünde in der Schweiz, Amsterdam, Jan. 1935.

Neuer Boykottfeldzug in Frankfurt am Main, Amsterdam, Feb. 1935.

Nationalsozialistische Agrarpolitik, Amsterdam, Feb. 1935.

Agitation gegen Judentum und Hochfinanz, Amsterdam, Feb. 1935.

Die medizinische Revolution, Amsterdam, Mar. 1935.

Zur Lage in Deutschland. Ende Februar 1935, Amsterdam, Feb. 1935.

Aus 'Der Schulungsbrief . . .' Berlin, Dezember 1934, Amsterdam, Mar. 1935.

Julius Streicher in Köln, Amsterdam, Mar. 1935.

Reichssteuerbrief, Amsterdam, Mar. 1935.

Zur antisemitischen Bewegung in Irak. Zwei Berichte aus Bagdad – Ende 1934, Amsterdam, Mar. 1935.

Ägypten, Amsterdam, Mar. 1935.

Juden in leitenden Stellungen der Sowjet-Republik, Amsterdam, Mar. 1935.

Zur Lage der Juden in Brasilien, Amsterdam, Mar. 1935.

Veränderte Geschichtsauffassung, Amsterdam, Mar. 1935.

Sharper Isolation of Jews in Germany, Amsterdam, Apr. 1935.

Die gefahrdrohende Lage der deutschen Juden, Amsterdam, Apr. 1935.

Nach dem Urteil in Bern. Pressestimmen aus aller Welt, Amsterdam, May 1935.

Nach dem Berner Prozess. Feststellungen und Beobachtungen, Amsterdam, May 1935.

Aus kleinen deutschen Blättern, Amsterdam, May 1935.

Die Boykottlücke Palästina, Amsterdam, June 1935.

Sur manière dont on trait les juifs en Allemagne, Amsterdam, June 1935.

The Position of the Jews in Germany (Middle of June 1935), Amsterdam, June 1935.

The Treatment of Jewish Emigrants Returning to Germany, Amsterdam, June 1935.

Die Aufreizung zu Judenverfolgungen in Deutschland, Amsterdam, June 1935.

Zu den Ausschreitungen gegen die Juden in Deutschland, Amsterdam, July 1935.

Wie lange noch? Die Aktion gegen die Juden, Amsterdam, July 1935.

Der unblutige Pogrom, Amsterdam, July 1935.

Ein Schweizer schreibt aus dem Dritten Reich, Amsterdam, July 1935.

Apolda im Dritten Reich voran, Amsterdam, July 1935.

Vor gesetzgeberischen Massnahmen, Amsterdam, Aug. 1935.

Was geht in Deutschland vor? Amsterdam, Aug. 1935.

Aus der Schacht Rede. Was die deutsche Presse nicht meldet, Amsterdam, Aug. 1935.

Wirkungen der Nürnberger Judengesetze, Amsterdam, Sept. 1935.

Die Lage der Juden in Deutschland, Amsterdam, Sept. 1935.

Zur wirtschaftlichen Vernichtung des deutschen Judentums, Amsterdam, Oct. 1935.

Opfer des Krieges und des Antisemitismus, Amsterdam, Oct. 1935.

Die Nürnberger Judengesetze und die Haager Konvention von 1902, Amsterdam, Oct. 1935.

Nach den Nürnberger Reichstagbeschlüssen, Amsterdam, Oct. 1935.

Deutschland und die Olympischen Spielen. Tatsachen über die Behandlung der jüdischen Sportler, Amsterdam, Oct. 1935.

The Situation in South Africa, Amsterdam, Oct. 1935.

Bolschewismus und Judentum. Amerikanischer Widerspruch gegen national- sozialistische Behauptungen, Amsterdam, Oct. 1935.

Bericht über die Verbreitung und Wirkung des Kol Nidre Rufes, Amsterdam, Nov. 1935.

Letter written by a German Jew to a friend in Denmark, Amsterdam, Nov. 1935.

Letter concerning the Order by Goebbels to Remove the Names of Jews from New War Memorials, Amsterdam, Dec. 1935.

Olympia-Material Nr 2, Amsterdam, Dec. 1935.

La situation des juifs en Espagne, Amsterdam, Dec. 1935.

Soll das deutsche Judentum wirtschaftlich völlig zugrunde gerichtet werden? Amsterdam, Nov. 1935.

Das Echo des Weltgewissens, Amsterdam, Nov. 1935.

Ein Freund des Dritten Reiches verurteilt die Judenverfolgungen, Amsterdam, Dec. 1935.

Die Judenverfolgung in Deutschland als Problem des Weltpolitik, Amsterdam, Jan. 1936.

Hitlers Rede in Schwerin und ihr Echo, Amsterdam, Jan. 1936.

Zur Lage der Juden in Deutschland. Januar 1936, Amsterdam, Jan. 1936.

Die Lage der Juden in Rumänien, Amsterdam, Jan. 1936.

La situation des juifs en Roumanie, Amsterdam, Jan. 1936.

Einzelheiten zur Lage der Juden in Deutschland. Januar 1936, Amsterdam, Jan. 1936.

The Position of the Jews in Germany, Amsterdam, Feb. 1936.

Die Juden in Deutschland, Amsterdam, Feb. 1936.

The Refugees from Germany, Amsterdam, Mar. 1936.

The Position of the Jews in Egypt. The Aims of the Antisemitic World Propaganda, Amsterdam, Mar. 1936.

The Fate of the German Returning Emigrants, Amsterdam, Mar. 1936.

Die antisemitische Propaganda in Elsass und Lothringen und ihre Abhängigkeit von den Deutschen, Amsterdam, Apr. 1936.

Die beiden Schreiben des verhafteten Pfarrers Middendorf, Amsterdam, May 1936.

Zur Lage der österreichischen Juden, Amsterdam, May 1936.

The Position of the Jews in Germany, May 1936, Amsterdam, May 1936.

Notes on the Position in Egypt, Amsterdam, May 1936.

The Position of the Jews in Sweden, Amsterdam, June 1936.

The Basel Trial Relating to the Protocols of the Elders of Zion, Amsterdam, June 1936.

Zur nationalsozialistischen Propaganda in Palästina, Amsterdam, July 1936.

Die Juden in Italien, Amsterdam, Oct. 1936.

Zur Broschüre: 'Verzeichnis jüdischer Verfasser juristischer Schriften, Amsterdam,

Oct. 1936.

Behind the Scenes of the Four-Year Plan, Amsterdam, Nov. 1936.

'We Are Taking up the Offensive', Amsterdam, Nov. 1936.

The Economic Campaign of Annihilation against German Jewry, Amsterdam, Nov. 1936.

Gestapo and the Jewish Organisations, Amsterdam, Nov. 1936.

The Spiritual Torture, Amsterdam, Nov. 1936.

Nach dem Urteilsspruch in Chur, Amsterdam, Dec. 1936.

Erschütternde Dokumente über die deutschen Judenverfolgungen, Amsterdam, Dec. 1936.

Illegale Arbeit der NSDAP in Spanien, Amsterdam, Dec. 1936.

Die Auslandsarbeit der NSDAP, Amsterdam, Dec. 1936.

The Position of the Jews in Germany, January 1937, Amsterdam, Jan. 1937.

The General Situation in Germany, Amsterdam, Jan. 1937.

The Economic Campaign of Annihilation, Amsterdam, Jan. 1937.

The Fight against Jewish Emigrants, Amsterdam, Jan. 1937.

The Gestapo at Work, Amsterdam, Jan. 1937.

Report on the Position of the Jews in Colombia, Amsterdam, Apr. 1937.

Italienische Autoren über die Judenfrage, Amsterdam, Apr. 1937.

The Jews in the Prussian Province of Pomerania before 1933 and at the Beginning of 1937, Amsterdam, Apr. 1937.

On Anti-Jewish Actions in Upper Silesia, Amsterdam, Apr. 1937.

Das Palästina-Problem. Die Meinung seiner Eminenz des rumänischen Patriarchen Dr Miron Cristea, Amsterdam, Aug. 1937.

Economic Destruction of the Jews within the German Economy, Amsterdam, Dec. 1937.

The Passport Question, Amsterdam, Dec. 1937.

Memorandum on Recent Developments in the Jewish Situation in Mexico, Amsterdam, Jan. 1938.

Neue Passbestimmungen für deutsche Juden, Amsterdam, Jan. 1938.

Rumänien und seine Juden, Amsterdam, Jan. 1938.

Die erste jüdische Zeitung aus Rumänien nach dem Regierungsantritt Goga's, Amsterdam, Jan. 1938.

Um die Juden. Combat de générosité, Amsterdam, Feb. 1938.

Jüdischer Klassiker der deutschen Rechtswissenschaft, Amsterdam, Feb. 1938. [about H. Sinzheimer]

Memoranda from the Palestine and Polish League of Nations Unions relating to the Jewish Question in Eastern Europe, Amsterdam, Mar. 1938.

Um die Zulassung österreichischer Flüchtlinge. Eine Erklärung des holländischen Justizministers, Amsterdam, Mar. 1938.

Situation of the Jews in Austria, Amsterdam, Apr. 1938.

Anti-Semitic Disorders in Vienna, Amsterdam, Apr. 1938.

National Socialist Propaganda Net in Middle Europe Laid Bare, Amsterdam, Apr. 1938.

Um die Zulassung von Österreichern in Holland. Eine Antwort des Ministerpräsidenten Colijn, Amsterdam, Apr. 1938.

The Poisonous Mushroom (Der Giftpilz), Amsterdam, Apr. 1938.

Die deutsche Staatskontrolle über das Vermögen der Juden, Amsterdam, May 1938.

Die sozialen Grundlagen und Zielsetzungen des polnischen Antisemitismus, Amsterdam, May 1938.

Territoriale Autonomieforderungen der Ukraine und die Juden in Pélen, Amsterdam, May 1938.

Ein Schweizer erlebt Deutschland, Amsterdam, June 1938.

The Jews in Vienna under the Terror, Amsterdam, June 1938.

The Jews in Vienna. Individual Cases, Amsterdam, June 1938.

Die Lage der Juden in Deutschland, Amsterdam,, Ende Juni 1938, Amsterdam, July 1938.

Italy and the Race Question, Amsterdam, Aug. 1938.

The New Anti-Jewish Enactments in Italy, Amsterdam, Sept. 1938.

The Race Doctrine in Italy. German–Italian Discrepancies, Amsterdam, Sept. 1938.

Die Aushungerung jüdischer Ärzte in Deutschland, Amsterdam, Sept. 1938.

Minorities in Poland, Amsterdam, Oct. 1938.

Keine jüdischen Rechtsanwälte mehr in Deutschland, Amsterdam, Oct. 1938.

Die deutschen Pogrome. November 1938, Amsterdam, Nov. 1938.

Ärztliche Versorgung der Juden, Amsterdam, Nov. 1938.

The Position of German Jewry, end of October 1938, Amsterdam, Nov. 1938.

Die Hilfstätigkeit der schwedischen jüdischen Gemeinden für jüdische Flüchtlinge, Amsterdam, Nov. [or Dec.] 1938.

The German Pogroms. November 1938. Reports from Vienna, Amsterdam, Dec. 1938.

Lists of Rabbis in Germany, Amsterdam, Dec. 1938.

Das polnische Regierungsprogramm für die jüdische Auswanderung,, Amsterdam, Dec. 1938.

Wichtige Mitteilungen, Amsterdam, Dec. 1938.

Letter relating to H. Rauschning, 'Die Revolution des Nihilismus', Amsterdam, Dec. 1938.

The German Pogroms. November 1938, Amsterdam, Dec. 1938.

The German Pogrom. November 1938, Amsterdam, Jan 1939.

The Expropriation of German Jewry, Amsterdam, Jan. 1939.

Das Niemandsland in Polen wird aufgelöst, Amsterdam, Feb. 1939.

Les refugiés allemands en route pour la Chine, Amsterdam, Feb. 1939.

German Foreign Propaganda, Amsterdam, Feb. 1939.

Zur Frage der Niederlassungsmöglichkeiten für deutsch-jüdische Ärzte, Amsterdam, Feb. 1939.

Die Gesetzgebung des neuen Polen und die Juden, Amsterdam, Mar. 1939.

Die Behandlung der Judenfrage durch die polnischen Regierungskreise, Amsterdam, Mar. 1939.

Ein Vorschlag für die Einführung der Zwangsarbeit für die Juden Polens zwecks kolonisatorischer Umschulung, Amsterdam, Mar. 1939.

22,000 jüdische Flüchtlinge in Holland. Aus der Arbeit des holländischen Flüchtlingscomités, Amsterdam, Mar. 1939.

Gruppeninteressen und Menschlichkeit. Um die Zulassung jüdische Ärzte nach Schweden, Amsterdam, Mar. 1939.

Brief aus Shanghai, Amsterdam, June 1939.

Der Cuba Skandal, Amsterdam, June 1939.

The Protocols of the Elders of Zion. More Publications on the Berne Trial, Amsterdam, June 1939.

Die Ausschaltung des italienischen Judentums, Amsterdam, June 1939.

Excerpts from a Talk Given by His Excellency Archbishop John Gregory Murray of the St Paul Diocese, Minneapolis, January 31 1939, Amsterdam, July 1939.

The Refugee Problem, Amsterdam, July 1939.

Six Years of Hitler, Amsterdam, Aug. 1939.

Die Auswandererabgabe der deutschen Juden, Amsterdam, Aug. 1939.

Confidential Report on Nazi Officials in Nuremberg Enriching Themselves with Jewish Property, Amsterdam, Aug. 1939.

Hilfsaktionen für die polnischen Juden, Amsterdam, Oct. 1939.

Prof Schorr angeblich in Rowo. Die schwierige Lage in Wilna und Warschau, Amsterdam, Oct. 1939.

Die Deutschen in Warschau. Das Martyrium der jüdischen Bevölkerung, Amsterdam, Oct. 1939.

Das Hilfswerk für die polnischen Juden, Amsterdam, Nov. 1939.

Die jüdische Zwangsansiedlung in der Wojewodschaft Lublin, Amsterdam, Nov. 1939.

Litauische Regierung gegen antisemitische Ausschreitungen, Amsterdam, Nov. 1939.

Die polnischen Juden im 'Niemandsland', Amsterdam, Nov. 1939.

Die Lage der Juden in Polen, Amsterdam, Dec. 1939.

Die Lage der Juden in Polen. Neue deutsche Verordnungen, Amsterdam, Dec. 1939.

Neue Bestimmungen für die Einwanderung nach Shanghai, Amsterdam, Dec. 1939.

Der Arbeitszwang für die jüdische Bevölkerung im Generalgouvernement, Amsterdam, Dec. 1939.
New Ordinances Relating to Jews in Poland, Amsterdam, Jan. 1940.
Arbeitszwang der Juden für zwei Jahre, Amsterdam, Jan. 1940.
Die Lage der Juden in Deutschland (Mitte Januar 1940), Amsterdam, Jan. 1940.
Die Deportation der deutschen Juden, Amsterdam, Feb. 1940.
Zur Lage der Juden in Polen, Amsterdam, Mar. 1940.
Zur Lage der Juden in Polen (März 1940), Amsterdam, Mar. 1940.
Der Auswanderungsdruck. SOS Rufe deutscher Juden, Amsterdam, Mar. 1940.
Is Any Enlightenment on the Position of the jews in Germany Required?, np, nd.
Einzelheiten zur Lage der Juden in Deutschland, np, nd.
Kollektivbeleidigung und Minoritätenschutz in Nowegen, np, nd.
Zur Lage der Juden in Griechenland, np, nd.

LONDON 1939–45

Periodicals

The Nazis at War: Materials on Germany designed to aid the study of men, affairs and trends, No 1 (24 Oct. 1939) – No 71 (17 Apr. 1945).
Materials on Germany, No 1(15 Oct 1939) – No 4 (30 Oct. 1939).
Jewish News, No 1 (7 Jan. 1942) – No 46 (24 Sept. 1945).

Books and pamphlets

This is also not a complete listing.

A List of Rabbis in Germany up to October 1938, London, nd.
Nazi Literary Propaganda, London Feb. 1940.
A. Wiener, *Three Weeks in Holland. January – February 1940,* London 1940.
Inside Germany. An Account of the Situation, August 1940, London 1940.
German Jewry 1941, London 1941.
Germany and Japan. Contempt Coupled with Fear, London Dec. 1941.
Laval Against France, London Apr. 1942.
The Persecution of Hungarian Jews. Six Years of German Pressure, London 1944.
The Jews in the War, London May 1944.
The Position of the Jewish refugees in England, London Jan. 1945.
The Political Soldier, London Mar. 1945.

In addition, a number of bibliographies and other book lists were produced during this period.

LONDON 1945-90

Periodicals

The Wiener Library Bulletin, Vol. 1, No. 1 (Nov. 1946) – Vol. 19, No. 3 (1965); N.S. No 1 (Autumn 1965) – No 53/4 (Spring 1981); Special Issue to mark 50 years of the Wiener Library (1983).

H. Kehr (ed.): *Index to the Wiener Library Bulletin 1946–1968*, Nendeln/ Leichtenstein 1979.

Auszüge aus der deutschen und österreichischen Presse Vol 1, No 1 (1947) – Vol. 15, No. 13 (1963).

A Survey of the International, Especially German, Press (English version of above).

Quarterly Select List of Accessions, unnumbered, first issued in 1967, in progress, issued quarterly.

Journal of Contemporary History, Vol. 1, No. 1 (Jan. 1966), in progress.

Wiener Library Newsletter, No. 1 (Autumn 1985), in progress.

Books and pamphlets

Jewish Survivors' Reports. Documents of Nazi Guilt.

1) M. Leichtenstein, *Eighteen Months in the Oswiecim Extermination Camp*, London, May 1945.

2) I. Taubes, *The Persecution of Jews in Holland, 1940–1944. Westerbork and Bergen-Belsen*, London, June 1945.

3) M.E. Mannheimer, *Theresienstadt and from Theresienstadt to Auschwitz*, London, July 1945.

4) *From Germany to the Riga Ghetto and the Kaiserwald and Salaspilz Extermination Camps. Three Letters by Deportees*, London, Aug. 1945.

5) P. Littauer, *My Experience during the Persecution of the Jews in Berlin and Brussels 1939 – 1944*, London, Oct. 1945.

6) J. Jacobson, *Terezin. The Daily Life 1943–1945*, London, Mar. 1946 [includes appendix by David Cohen].

The Jews of Berlin. Two Reports, London, Aug. and Oct. 1945.
Jews in Europe Today

1) *Two Reports by Jewish Relief Workers in Germany*, London, Nov. 1945.

2) M. Warburg, *Personal Experience of Camp Inmates at DP Centre of Föhrenwald, Bavaria*, London, Feb. 1946.

Europe 1945

1) *Germany under Allied Occupation, April 1 to October 1 (as Mirrored in the German Press)*, London, nd.

2) *Germany under Allied Occupation, October 1 to December 31 (as Mirrored in*

the German Press), London, 1946.

3) L.W. Bondy, *Report on a Recent Journey to Germany*, London, nd.

Jewish Population in the US Zone of Occupation of Germany, London, Mar. 1946.

Restitution. European Legislation to Redress the Consequences of Nazi Rule, London, 1946.

A. Wiener, *A Visit to Holland, March 1946*, London, Apr. 1946.

Organised Antisemitism in Great Britain 1942–1946, London, May 1946.

The British Press and Its Reactions to Recent Events in Palestine, London, July 1946.

Statistical Details of the Deportation and Present Number of Jews in Italy, London, Sept. 1946.

New Jewish Communities in Germany, London, Oct. 1946.

German Political Parties and the Jews, London, Oct. 1946.

Nach dem Ende des Palästina-Mandats. Die Britische Politik im Spiegel der Britische Presse, London,, Aug. 1948.

Terror in Cairo. Report of a Swiss Eye-witness, London, Aug. 1948.

The New Government of South Africa as Viewed from Britain, London, Sept. 1948.

Ten Years after the German Pogrom of November 9-10 1938. A Survey of the Recent Reactions, London, Nov. 1948.

E.G. Reichmann, *Germany's New Nazis. Impressions from a Recent Journey through Germany's Danger Zones*, London, Aug. 1951.

I.S. Neumann (ed.), *European War Crimes Trials. A Bibliography. Additional Material Furnished by the Wiener Library*, London, & New York 1951.

Jewry and Germany. Reconciliation of Interests. The Approach to Reparations, A Survey of Developments 1949–1952, London, Mar. 1952.

Survey of Leaders, Articles and Letters to the Editor in British Newspapers and Periodicals dealing with German Neo-Nazism and Nationalism, London, 1952.

The Naumann Plot. Evidence from the Impounded Documents, London, July 1953.

Wiener Library (ed.), *Memoirs of Nazi Germany. Autobiographies, Letters, Reminiscences of Prominent Personalities Published after the War*, London, 1955.

Ausnahme-Gesetz gegen Juden in den von Nazi-Deutschland besetzten Gebieten Europas, London, 1956.

Wiener Library (ed.), *Postwar Publications on German Jewry. Books and Articles 1945-1955*, London, 1956.

L. Kochan, *Pogrom. 10 November 1938*, London, 1957.

The Wiener Library Catalogue Series

1) I. Wolff (ed.), *Persecution and Resistance under the Nazis*, London, 1949.

[reprinted in 1953; 2nd edition, revised and enlarged 1960].

2) I. Wolff (ed.), *From Weimar to Hitler. Germany 1918–1933*, London, 1964.

3) I. Wolff (ed.), *German Jewry. Its History, Life and Culture*, London, 1958.

4) I. Wolff and H. Kehr (eds), *After Hitler. Germany 1945–1963*, London, 1963.

5) H. Kehr (ed.), *Prejudice – Racist, Religious, Nationalist*, London, 1971.

6) H. Kehr (ed.), *German Jewry Part II. Additions and Amendments to Catalogue No 3 1959–1972*, London, 1972.

7) I. Wolff and H. Kehr (eds), *Persecution and Resistance under the Nazis. Part I: Reprint of Catalogue No 1, Part II: New Material and Amendments*, London, 1978.

M. Beloff (ed.), *On the Track of Tyranny. Essays Presented by the Wiener Library to Leonard G. Montefiore, OBE, on the Occasion of his Seventieth Birthday*, London, 1960.

L. Stein and C.C. Aronsfeld (eds.), *Leonard G. Montefiore, 1889–1961. In Memoriam*, London, 1964.

Z.A.B. Zeman, *Nazi Propaganda*, London, 1964.

Papers Read at the Conference 'The Study of Contemporary History in Europe', London, 1966.

M. Mindlin and C. Bermant (eds.), *Explorations, An Annual on Jewish Themes*, London, 1967.

D.C. Watt (ed.), *Contemporary History in Europe*, London, 1969.

B. Krikler, *Anglo-Jewish Attitudes to the Rise of Nazism*, London, nd.

W. Laqueur (ed.), *A Dictionary of Politics*, London, 1971.

W. Laqueur and B. Krikler (eds), *A Reader's Guide to Contemporary History*, London, 1972.

W. Laqueur (ed.), *Fascism: A Reader's Guide*, London, 1976.

C.S. Wichmann, *Stationen der Tyrannei. Die Wiener Library London, 1933–1985*, London, 1985.

K. Sabatzky, *Meine Erinnerungen an den Nationalsozialismus*, London, nd.

Index